DOCTOR L

DOCTOR LARK

The benefits of a medical education

Bill Larkworthy

MOSAÏQUEPRESS

Published by

MOSAÏQUE PRESS

Registered office:
70 Priory Road
Kenilworth, Warwickshire
CV8 1LQ
www.mosaïquepress.co.uk

Printed in the UK.

ISBN 978-1-906852-06-1

To Maria,
my source of strength in hard times
and love and happiness at all times.

Ah, fill the cup, what boots it to repeat
How time is slipping underneath our feet
Unborn tomorrow, and dead yesterday,
Why fret about them if today be sweet!

– *THE RUBAIYAT OF OMAR KHAYYAM*
EDWARD FITZGERALD (TRANS.)

Contents

Cover photo: Maria Larkworthy.

Introduction

ONE BITTERLY COLD WINTER FORTY-FIVE years ago, I found myself marooned on a nuclear bomber station on the wind-swept plains of Northern Germany, a junior doctor in the Royal Air Force.

Christmas celebrations were in full swing and, as the lowest ranking medical officer, I had been handed the short straw and was on call for the festive season. This didn't prevent me from partaking of a large turkey dinner, nor from dozing contentedly afterwards. And sure as a glass of port follows a good meal, the inevitable happened. I was summoned by an urgent call.

"Come quickly, sir, there's been a suicide, there's blood everywhere."

I dashed and skidded over the icy paths to sick quarters and forced my way through a knot of airmen who crowded the entrance, chattering excitedly. A trail of blood led me to the victim who was in the operating theatre being cleaned by a couple of orderlies; surprisingly, in view of the generous quantity of blood splashed about, no source of bleeding could immediately be found.

Clearly the 'suicide', a mop-headed corporal named O'Malley, could neither see nor walk a straight line and though practically legless, grinned lopsidedly around the room, not unhappy to be the centre of attention.

We asked one of his mates what had happened. It seemed O'Malley had been drinking solidly in the Corporals' Club since Christmas Eve, became maudlin on Christmas Day, pulled out a penknife on Christmas afternoon, declared he was going to end it all and set to work cutting off his thumb. Sure enough, eventually we found a ragged incision on the back of his left thumb. Drunks can bleed profusely but even so, this was barely credible.

"What on earth have you been up to, corporal?" I demanded.

His brow furrowed as he attempted to concentrate and get a fix on my position with wobbly, bleary, bloodshot eyes. He paused, hiccupped, took a deep breath and in an Irish brogue slurred, "I was depressed, sor, I wanted to kill myself."

In my supercilious, know-it-all young flight lieutenant doctor's voice I exclaimed, "But corporal, you don't commit suicide by cutting off your thumb!"

After a moment's reflection he replied, "Ah well you see, sor, I don't have the benefits of a medical education."

THAT WAS A LONG TIME AGO, BUT THE STORY has stuck in my mind and led me at times to reflect on the benefits I've had from my medical education. For someone like me from modest origins, the benefits have been many: a fascinating career, a passport to all walks of life, to immense job satisfaction, to friendship and to an adequate income. Not least, because I qualified in 1957, I have witnessed, and participated in, the miraculous developments of the past half-century in medical science and life in general.

'Doctoring', as I thought of it when I was young, has taken me to many far-flung parts of the globe that I might not otherwise have visited. Many of them – Malaysia, Cyprus, Germany, the Persian Gulf – I recall with a fondness bordering on tearful nostalgia while just as many others – Aden, Bangkok, Moose Jaw – have thankfully faded in my memory like a snapshot left too long in the sun.

Much of that travel was courtesy of the RAF, both by way of overseas postings and the journeys necessitated by the work I was sent there to do. Sometimes it was comfortable, like the mammoth tour of RAF bases between London and Hong Kong by de Havilland Comet. Sometimes it was... less comfortable. Observing *terra firma* above your head from the seat of a Mirage fighter jet while flying upside-down is, in my experience, a sure way to nausea.

At least that was a seat and a means of emergency egress, should the need arise. I was singularly unimpressed when I learned that my space in a Canberra bomber – actually a face-to-the-tarmac *couchette* in the nose of the beast – did not come with the luxury of a parachute. "Well Bill," said my ever-helpful flight crew, "where you are, it will be impossible to get out." On such occasions, I had to remind myself that I had actually volunteered to go along for the ride.

My medical education also introduced me to a cast of characters and plots richer than those of any costume drama or soap. I met the military equivalent of WAGs, the spouses who had to be repatriated because they couldn't deal with a 'hardship' posting in the sun and warmth of Malta, and at the other end of the scale, Gurkha soldiers who knew real hardship and laughed in its face. They were fighting communists, the insurgents *du jour*, in the jungle of Malaysia. Even in hospital, sick or wounded, these troopers remained highly disciplined: they would snap to attention under the sheets when I approached if they were too ill to get out of bed.

Across my path have strayed various eccentrics, charlatans, buffoons and braggarts; 'doctors' who weren't what they seemed and unsung heroes who most definitely were; a colleague driven to enlist the services of the Russian Mafia and one of Saddam's 'human shields' who lived to drink another bottle of Dom Perignon. There was even a genuine celebrity, the explorer and writer Sir Wilfred Thesiger, who late in his life was a regular visitor to Dubai. One time I fixed his feet with a scalpel. "Perfect," he told me, "now I'll be able to take that walk in the desert with Charles." Yes, *that* Charles.

Medicine carried me into the most glorious, beautiful desert of the Middle East and across the thresholds of palaces of breathtaking opulence in the 'magical' kingdom of Saudi Arabia, to a pinnacle of sorts when I could rightly claim to be 'physician to HM the King'. He was a pleasant and dignified man who was grateful when the treatment I prescribed was a success, quite unlike the megalomaniac, drug-addled hospital director who had me thrown into prison — the lowest point in my career. That's when you find out who your friends are, and I've been fortunate to have collected some good ones, especially in Riyadh.

True, there are some things a medical education didn't teach me, like how to fix a leaking car radiator with the contents of a spice shop (think yellow), an antidote to boredom on the Canadian prairies, or how to distinguish between a taxi and a police car on the sinful streets of Patpong... but that's a story in itself. It did teach me indirectly how to operate a modern fast jet's ejection seat – a skill, not surprisingly, that I have never had call to demonstrate.

Doctors collect stories as they follow their careers; it's in the nature of the job. Some are touching, some horrifying, some sad and many quite funny, certainly in retrospect. I was amazed, as I compiled this memoir, at what came flooding into my mind, one memory triggering another and stories appearing seemingly out of nowhere. Tales I thought I had forgotten came forward, sometimes with the startling clarity of an ageing brain and sometimes, I admit, with embellishments of half-remembered events — well, anyway, this is my life, this is how it looked to me — and it's how I made the most of my medical education.

Bill Larkworthy
Provence, France

AUTHOR'S NOTE

I HAVE TRIED TO BE ACCURATE but I wrote with no records and no notes – any inaccuracies or errors of interpretation are mine and accidental.

Some names have been changed to protect the privacy of individuals.

BL

Part One

'Per ardua ad astra'*

Myself when young did eagerly frequent
Doctor and Saint, and heard great Argument...
With them the Seed of Wisdom did I sow,
And with my own hand labour'd it to Grow...

– THE RUBAIYAT OF OMAR KHAYYAM
EDWARD FITZGERALD (TRANS.)

* 'Through adversity to the stars' – motto of the Royal Air Force

The author and his older brother, Leslie, about 1936.

One

I WAS SIX WHEN THE SECOND WORLD WAR broke out, or to be more precise, spread itself over our home in Plymouth like a chill fog off the Channel. I remember the moment as clearly as yesterday. Just after eleven in the morning of 3 September 1939, my family of four silently gathered around the wireless. It was a wooden box with a fretwork face and round knobs that you weren't supposed to touch; we called it a wireless at the time to acknowledge the miracle of music and voices travelling through the ether, as if by magic, and not down wires like a telephone, which for some reason made more sense to my young mind.

Through the fizz and crackle of static the British Prime Minister, Neville Chamberlain, droned on in measured, unemotional tones: "This morning the British ambassador in Berlin handed the German government a final note stating that, unless we heard from them by eleven o'clock that they were prepared at once to withdraw their troops from Poland, a state of war would exist between us. I have to tell you that no such undertaking has been received, and that consequently this country is at war with Germany."

I didn't understand what was going on but became fearful, complained of a pain in my stomach and my mother gave me half a teaspoonful of bicarbonate of soda dissolved in water – her sovereign remedy for all symptoms abdominal. Later I asked my brother what it was all about. Leslie was two years older but he didn't know either.

For us it was both a good time and a bad time. Good, because a nation at war becomes united. There is a sense of facing danger together, of having a common enemy, of 'mustn't grumble', of getting on with others and everybody striving to do their best for the common cause. These qualities became infused into my six-year-old spirit and as the war progressed Nazi and Japanese aggression deepened my patriotism.

A bad time: well, Jerry could drop a bomb on you.

Everybody believed that German planes would be overhead any day. At school we had endless gas mask and bomb shelter drills but it wasn't until the early summer of 1940 that enemy Messerschmitts, Heinkels and Junkers appeared in numbers in the skies over England.

Most of the air raids were at night. Our house in Seymour Avenue had a cellar and we sheltered there among tins, preserves, old magazines and boxes. If the air-raid sirens started wailing in daylight hours and we were at

The author's parents, Jack and Esther Emma Larkworthy, on their wedding day in Plymouth, 1928.

The author, his brother and mother at home in 'Sunday best', about 1936.

school, we were quickly ushered into the shelters which had been thrown up in the school yard. When the 'all clear' sounded, we would march back to our classrooms singing at the tops of our voices, *There'll always be an England* or *Rule Britannia* – great for morale but when we heard that a shelter in another school in Plymouth had taken a direct hit which killed all fifty children in it, that morale took a serious dip.

In the next two years, Plymouth suffered the most concentrated bombing of any British city. During the Blitz, the city lost altogether 1,174 lives. I vividly recall on many occasions emerging from our air raid shelter and seeing the sky a deep red from horizon to horizon as Plymouth burned. In one week in 1941, the centre of the city was flattened but the tower of Charles Church was left standing, unscathed, an omen we regarded as showing that the Lord was on our side. Not that we needed reassurance; we had known that from the start.

Like other boys in the city, Leslie and I would collect shrapnel. At the end of air raids, we would beg to be allowed to go for a walk in the nearby streets where we would pick up jagged pieces of metal, some still hot. We became proficient at recognising the noise of German aircraft engines and were able to distinguish their throbbing sound from the continuous note of British aircraft and the joyous singing of the Rolls-Royce Merlin of the

Spitfire. It was a matter of some considerable youthful pride to be able to reassure grown-ups and say confidently, "That's one of ours."

We were less confident one summer afternoon when we had a close encounter with a Messerschmitt Bf 109. My brother and I were in the country, about five miles from Plymouth wandering along a hot and dusty road, when suddenly there was a roar and the German aircraft flashed before our eyes. 'The Hun' was hedge-hopping to escape the RAF. It must have been only a millisecond before he disappeared but in that time the yellow nose cone, yellow wing tips, black and white cross on the fuselage and swastika on the tail all registered. The pilot was gazing down at Leslie and me through hexagonal goggles with a malicious grin on his face. We were sure he would come back to machine-gun us and dived into a ditch where, with Leslie's protective arm around my shoulder, we crouched for half an hour; thrilled, frightened and excited.

To do her part, my mother joined the Women's Voluntary Service but with my father it was a different story. He was a registered conscientious objector and as such was an outcast, particularly in a city subjected to so much brutal bombing; a city with proud military and naval traditions. It's impossible to know how much he suffered at the hands of others. He must have appeared before a tribunal which declared his job – he was an engine driver on the Southern Railway – a reserved occupation and did not imprison him or direct him to other work. While relatives enlisted in the armed forces, he continued to drive trains. Some carried munitions and all were fair game for marauding German aircraft.

My father was a man of strong moral conviction and a stubborn nature. Later the family claimed that I had inherited his stubbornness but I prefer to think of it as dogged determination. His beliefs had no religious basis. He was no coward: he single-handedly extinguished a blazing incendiary bomb and when congratulated, shrugged and walked away. Within the family he was an outsider. I don't recall specific embarrassments but in my tender years I was segregated from much of what was going on.

Although my father had no professed religious beliefs, the rest of the family was strictly Church of England and practised the lowest Anglicanism. This would have a profound effect on my life and even today, seventy years later, I have pangs of guilt if I catch myself having a good time – well, sometimes anyway.

On Sundays Leslie and I went to church, at least once; games at home were forbidden; in the summer we weren't allowed to go swimming; we could listen only to the BBC six o'clock news on the wireless and reading was limited to 'improving' books. Playing cards (the Devil's Book) were of course outlawed. I wonder now how we survived.

Our local church was St Judes. The vicar, the Reverend H G McMaking, led a seriously low-brow congregation. Week after week the theme of his sermons was 'Eat, drink and be merry, for tomorrow we die!' I can see him now as he stood in the pulpit, a tall, well-fed man of God with rosy cheeks and a remarkably thick fringe of white hair surrounding a natural tonsure, thundering that message again and again. Sometimes his credibility was enhanced as, with his white priest's robes swirling and fist (two fists for added emphasis) raised on high, he was illuminated by a solitary divine ray of sun beaming through a stained glass window. Then he would lean confidentially over the edge of the pulpit and with a gentle smile, drop his voice – and I knew he was talking personally to little open-mouthed, eight-year-old me – "And what? And what if? And what if when you leave this church as you cross the road YOU ARE KNOCKED DOWN BY A BUS AND KILLED?" I sat quaking... he thundered again, "Will you be ready? Will you be prepared to meet YOUR GOD?" Me, prepared? What's prepared?

In a few years I reached the age for confirmation and I, with a couple of other boys of my age, attended the vicarage once a week for 'preparation'. Perhaps this was what he was talking about.

But the only clear recollection I now have of all the weeks of tuition of the Rev H G McMaking was that he discussed masturbation with us, telling us what a dreadful sin of the flesh it was and how it could lead to a weak constitution, lassitude, sterility, visual defects, mental deficiency, deafness, madness and early death.

The problem was that none of us knew what he was talking about. We discussed it among ourselves when we left the vicarage and elected one of our number, me, to ask next time.

"Please, sir," I said at the beginning of the session, "we don't understand, what's this master thing you talked about last week?"

His eyes lit, he beamed, he said, "Well boys, it's like this." And short of an actual hands-on demonstration, he gave an account easily understood by any pre-pubertal boy. "Ho hum," I thought, "this sounds fun." I couldn't wait to get home and try it out. Nothing happened, my hormonal juices hadn't yet kicked in... but some months later they did; to my utter, incredulous amazement.

A FEW YEARS LATER I JOINED THE YOUTH club run by the church. My motives were simple: my testosterone had reached boiling point and there were girls there. Admittedly many were pretty plain (they were the religious ones) but there were a few who were the stuff of adolescent male dreams.

At that time a certain American evangelical preacher, Billy Graham, was touring the land and converting sinners by the drove. We had our very own in-house evangelist in the form of a local dentist, David Barley, a young man with tight, curly ginger hair and an ever-present welcoming Christian smile. At each meeting he would put on a lively fire-and-brimstone act and scare the living daylights out of his fearful audience over their sins, some real but most imagined. Mr Barley's wife played the piano for him. Pamela was her name; she was pretty, petite and a divine inspiration of an entirely different order. How they missed the way we lads would gaze in raptures of feverish imagination at the turn of her ankles, the curve of her derriere on the piano stool and the swaying of her perfect chest as her fingers danced over the keys, I cannot guess.

Before club evenings, at which we played table tennis or billiards while studying the girls, Mr Barley would assemble us spotty adolescents and give us hell for half an hour. Then, following a few fervent prayers and several hallelujahs, we would kneel and pray in silence with our eyes closed. After five minutes he would call for those who had 'seen the light' to come forward to be blessed. I would peek between my fingers and each week, to my astonishment, saw everybody go up to him one by one, have him rest his hands on their heads and mutter a blessing. This happened week-in, week-out and week-in, week-out I didn't go up; obviously I couldn't... I hadn't Seen the Light.

At last the ultra-religious dentist stopped me one evening as I was leaving. "Bill," he said, "we have been discussing your case and we want to know why you haven't yet seen the light?"

"Well, I'm very sorry but I just haven't seen any light," I replied.

He told me what a glorious opportunity I was missing and I promised to try harder – I didn't go back.

The next time I saw him he was hot gospelling in Union Street (a notoriously sinful part of Plymouth), I was emerging from the Odeon cinema, it was a Sunday and I had been indulging in first class sinning. I had taken myself alone to the cinema where I puffed away on a tuppenny packet of Wills Wild Woodbine cigarettes. As I emerged, he was standing on the opposite side of the road, on a soap box, the pretty Pamela standing next to him with tambourine at the ready and a small crowd around him. Our eyes met, he stared; I smiled, waved to them and walked nonchalantly away.

But divine retribution was waiting around the corner. Soon I was to be overtaken by a calamity of immeasurable proportions. My hair began to fall out in handfuls. By the age of fifteen I had a parting an inch wide. People were noticing, friends looked and smirked. I was acutely embarrassed and full of self-pity... life was over for me; something had to be done.

I saw an advertisement in a paper which guaranteed to cure baldness with a course of tablets; the problem was the cost, two guineas for the course. I worked at odd jobs, I scraped together the money.

The tablets were brown in colour there were enough for three months at one a day. The advertising blurb said impressively that they contained 7-dehydrocholesterol and the promoter guaranteed his probity by declaring that he was an ex-RAF squadron leader Spitfire pilot. Simple me... many years later I came across those very same tablets when doing my midwifery training; they were given routinely to pregnant women, cost virtually nothing and were simply vitamin D tablets. And later still I was to learn that the rank of squadron leader is not synonymous with honesty.

My hair continued to fall out in clumps, I came to accept it and as I looked at the many bald members of my family, more than a few on the female side, it was clear that fate had dealt me a low card. But there were a few advantages. By the time I reached my twenties I was as bald as I am now, five decades later; a bald head, a bow tie and I could pass for a senior registrar while I was still a medical student.

REGARDLESS OF THEIR DIFFERENCES my parents were totally in agreement that for their sons a good education was of the utmost importance. Fortunately early in the war my brother and I passed what was then known as the 'scholarship', later to become the 11 Plus, and we entered a good local grammar school, Sutton High.

Leslie was brilliant at school; I was no better than average. He picked up prizes galore; he was even selected to appear in a children's quiz on the BBC because he was so bright.

Childrens' Hour was broadcast every afternoon at five and was the first BBC programme to introduce what were destined to become extraordinarily popular quiz shows. The director was 'Uncle Mac' (Plymouth born Derek McCulloch) assisted by Violet Carson (later Ena Sharples of Coronation Street) and the competition was between schoolchildren in the different BBC regions.

Leslie did well until the final question posed by the avuncular Uncle Mac. "What do the letters MCC stand for?" Pause. Eventually Leslie hesitantly replied, "Middlesex Cricket Club." Wrong: the 'M' was for Marylebone – but how could a wee lad from post-war Plymouth be expected to know that, when Test and County cricket had not been played for six years, and frankly less than one in ten adults would have known the answer either. Leslie was to go on to achieve great academic success – he ended his career as a professor of chemistry with his own personal chair in the University of Surrey.

Somehow I managed at the age of fifteen to get a good School Certificate, the equivalent of today's General Certificate of Education, and thoughts turned to the future. Nothing was further from my mind than a career in medicine. There were no doctors in the family.

I decided on a career in the Royal Navy; Dartmouth College and a midshipman's uniform appealed. I passed the written exam with ease, did reasonably well before the selection board but to my surprise failed the medical because I had a cyst adjacent to a testicle. This had to be dealt with. While waiting for the surgery, I applied as an alternative to join the Army. I took and passed the written examination for the Royal Military College Sandhurst; the officer cadet uniform was also appealing. In order to make sure that I would not again fail the medical, I was admitted to hospital to have the cyst removed. This was my epiphany; a new world opened before my eyes. What interest, what fascination and what a way of life this doctoring has to be. Even the antiseptic smell of the hospital caused a frisson in my solar plexus. The team spirit and dedication were evident everywhere – the doctors were clever and kind, the wards well-organised, the nurses compassionate and disciplined and all practised their art against a backdrop of scientific knowledge with admiring, grateful and respectful patients – but most attractive of all, it was the doctors who were at the top of the hierarchy.

I became totally absorbed in the idea of medicine as a career, discovered exactly what I had to do to get into medical school and wrote to four London teaching hospitals for prospectuses.

In the meantime I was summoned to an Army establishment on Salisbury Plain for what was called the WOSB, the War Office Selection Board examination, which consisted of several interviews and various exercises involving ropes, planks, barrels and ladders. The object was to lead a group of fellow candidates through imaginary minefields or other military obstacles. Again I did reasonably well and this time passed the medical. The final interview was with a pleasant, ancient, kindly general with white hair, red tabs on his collar and a white walrus moustache.

His very first question was, "If the Army does not accept you, what will you do?" to which I immediately replied, "I'll study medicine, sir."

"And how would you set about doing that?"

I confessed that already I had prospectuses from Guys, St Thomas', St Bartholomew's and University College Hospitals.

"Well," he smiled, "it appears to me that you really have your sights set on becoming a doctor. I suggest you do just that and then you can join the Royal Army Medical Corps."

So I followed his advice and went to medical school but when the time came, the Army and Royal Navy were only offering short service commissions of five years so I chose to take a three-year commission in the Medical Branch of the Royal Air Force – uniform not quite as impressive but still not bad.

In May 1945 the war against Germany was over and three months later the Japanese surrendered. A further two months on, at the insistence of the Labour members of the National Wartime Government, a general election was called. An ungrateful nation kicked out Winston Churchill, replacing him with Clement Attlee, and a Labour government was voted in with an overwhelming majority.

For Britain (and for me) a new era dawned, that of the Welfare State. Utopian promises were made and included state funding for higher education and grants for students. Student loans and tuition fees did not exist in those days. Tony Blair introduced them forty years later and these days many medical students when they qualify embark on their careers with debts in excess of £30,000.

I applied to the medical schools in London and was accepted after the first interview at University College on condition that my Higher School Certificate 'A' levels were adequate. Because botany and zoology were not taught at Sutton High and I needed those subjects, I moved to Plymouth Technical College (now a university) and in a year passed those at 'A' level. I was awarded a Local Authority Scholarship and in 1952 entered medical school.

Two

THE FIRST EIGHTEEN MONTHS at University College was a slog through anatomy, physiology, histology (microscopic structure), pharmacology and biochemistry – all basic to moving on to clinical medicine. Anatomy was a particularly difficult subject which held little pleasure for me but, recognising its seminal relationship to the practice of medicine, I had to grit my teeth and get down to it.

Human anatomy consists of the most excruciating memory exercises; of memorising complicated structural relationships, insertions of muscles in bones, innervations of muscles, the courses of arteries, veins and nerves, the skull and skeletal anatomy, the anatomy of joints and the viscera; heart, lungs, kidneys, liver, intestine and not least the brain and nervous system.

To my surprise, I didn't find that dissecting what was once a living body helped me to learn human anatomy.

There were sixty students in my entry and we were allocated a body in groups of six. We assembled in the dissecting room, a large, white-tiled, well-lit hall reeking of preservatives. Awaiting us were a dozen cadavers covered in white sheets on regularly arranged dissecting tables.

We gathered around our allocated tables, each group with an Anatomy demonstrator. The dean gave a short homily on our duty at all times to respect our subjects and we were off, the sheets lifted and the corpses revealed to our bulging, fearful, young eyes.

The bodies had been embalmed and immersed in formalin for months. It was difficult to think of these inanimate objects as holding a spark of life. All the tissues were stiff and inelastic; the skin was a muddy brown colour. The dissection of what looked like aged, dried, boiled mutton – as muscles appeared to me – bore no relationship to the neat illustrations in textbooks in which the arteries were red, the veins blue, the nerves yellow and the muscles a deep salmon pink. In the cadaver the viscera, heart, lungs, liver and intestines were all a greyish brown colour with a rubbery hard consistency.

We had been told not to ask about the origins of the body we dissected but one of my group somehow discovered that she was an Irish woman who had died a couple of years previously in what was in effect a Poor Law hospital in the East End of London. To our chagrin, when we got to dissect the pelvis, we discovered our subject had undergone surgery many years before and all the female bits were missing.

For the dissection of the brain, extras were distributed; we were each given one of our very own. I didn't speculate on the source of mine.

One morning the dean appeared in the dissecting room accompanied by a uniformed senior police officer. A very serious problem had been brought to his attention by this inspector from Tottenham Court Road police station. The day before, an agitated old lady had presented herself at the desk of the duty sergeant and produced from her shopping bag a human ear. She had discovered it at the top of the escalator at Warren Street tube station, which happened to be nearby.

A quick count on our cadavers showed that all ears were present and correct. We pointed out, with perhaps a little more enthusiasm than such a misdemeanour warranted, that the Middlesex Hospital was also nearby and that its students were known to be a wild bunch. Later, we made enquiries through friends at the Middlesex. There were no missing ears there either… maybe the ear hadn't come from a dissecting room?

Human physiology, the study of function, was as complicated as anatomy. Pharmacology on the other hand was fun; we experimented on each other and on one occasion studied the effects of smoking a cigarette on a fellow student who had never smoked, measuring pulse, blood pressure and observing how a normal person could turn an interesting shade of green.

Biochemistry was also amusing and we soon learned that the quickest way to identify a test substance was to taste it; unwittingly following the time-honoured medical practice of uroscopy – minutely observing the colour and clarity of a patient's urine and tasting it. Sweet urine contained sugar and diabetes mellitus could be diagnosed confidently – mellitus from the Latin *mellite*, honeyed. Fortunately these days we have chemically impregnated sticks for testing urine for sugar and other substances.

After eighteen months, we sat our second MB (Bachelor of Medicine) examination; 'A' levels took care of the first MB, and the third MB would be the final qualifying examination. I struggled through second MB and, mildly surprised, passed.

In May 1954, I crossed Gower Street from University College to University College Hospital, donned a white coat, bought a stethoscope and entered the wards.

LONDON IN 1954 WAS A DIFFERENT world. Post-war austerity lingered. Trolley buses with overhead cables glided silently through the streets, steered by recently arrived drivers and conductors from the Caribbean without whom London Transport would have come to a halt. Beer, the life-blood of most medical students, was the equivalent in today's money of four pence a pint and petrol less than two shillings a gallon... a pound would buy forty-five litres. The air was smoky and foggy, the buildings grimy. Jack the Ripper-type fogs occurred most autumn evenings. When the smoke of several million coal fires mixed with the dense fogs to create 'pea-soupers', traffic stopped, everybody coughed and not only the wards but the corridors of London's hospitals were filled with bemasked chesty patients attached to oxygen cylinders.

My clinical training began with six months 'clerking' on the medical wards, the first three months on the Professorial Unit. Four patients were allocated to each student, and I remember mine as clearly as one remembers one's first car.

The first was a drayman with Whitbreads Brewery, Henry Albert Wright. He was in his mid-fifties, a big jolly man with a florid complexion, a handlebar moustache and an explosive laugh which startled the ward. For years he had driven a cart, a brewer's dray holding three dozen barrels of beer and drawn by two shire horses, in the area immediately around the hospital. Each morning he would collect his laden cart and the horses from stables next to St Pancras station and deliver three or four barrels of beer to ten pubs; at each he would pause for a quickie which consisted of at least three pints of beer. At the end of the day he would return to the stables, his cart loaded with empty barrels, make sure his horses were fed and watered, settle them down for the night and then go off with his mates for a proper drink of at least ten pints. He didn't seem to need food and that worsened his problem, which was cirrhosis of the liver caused by his vast consumption of alcohol.

For introducing medical students to the art of examining patients, he was almost perfect. He displayed, or rather the medical registrar displayed for us, typical physical signs associated with advanced alcoholic liver disease. For starters he was mildly jaundiced, his skin was slightly yellow, the whites of his eyes were more obviously yellow. He had swollen parotid glands; these are the salivary glands at the back of the lower jaws, below the ears, the ones which become swollen in mumps. The skin of his chest and back showed numerous spider-like dilated blood vessels; the palms of his hands showed contractions of the tissue beneath the skin (Dupuytren's Contractures, named after a French physician, Baron Dupuytren, who first described the condition and was by all accounts very bad-tempered); his abdomen was bloated with fluid and we could feel a large knobbly liver three inches below his right ribs. His lower legs were swollen with fluid which had gravitated to them.

Henry died of a massive haemorrhage three weeks after I clerked him. I attended his post-mortem examination. It was uncanny, uncomfortable, distasteful and frightening (leave alone the horrible stench) to see him opened from chin to pubis. The pathologist demonstrated the advanced cirrhosis of his liver, the large knobbly organ we had palpated when he was alive, and also displayed the immediate cause of Henry's death, oesophageal varices – enlarged veins at the lower end of his gullet. They looked just like the varicose veins one sometimes sees on the legs of very fat ladies. Henry's varices had ruptured; he had bled to death in an hour.

In contrast, my second patient was a small, skinny, bald-headed sixty-year-old Cockney called Bert. He had a syphilitic aortic aneurysm. Syphilis can affect any organ and system of the body. In times past it was treated with mercury salts which inevitably produced the witticism, 'One night with Venus, a lifetime with Mercury.' The great Canadian icon of clinical medicine, Sir William Osler*, said, "The physician who knows syphilis knows medicine." While that is no longer true these days, another of his aphorisms – "Look wise, say nothing and grunt, speech was given to conceal thought" – is eternal.

In Bert's case, the syphilis bacteria had settled in the first part of his aorta (the body's largest artery) just as it left his heart, a part of the aorta

---

* Osler (1849 – 1919) was Regius Professor of Medicine at Oxford from 1905 until his death.

whimsically known as the Girdle of Venus. The infection had so weakened the muscles of the wall of the aorta that under the pressure of the blood, as it squirted out when his heart contracted, the wall ballooned outwards and a pulsating lump, about the size of a pigeon's egg, could be seen forcing its way between the ribs in the front of his upper chest. In that era we had penicillin which would cure syphilis but Bert's case was too late for treatment. We were told that eventually the aneurysm would rupture and a dramatic spouting of blood would rapidly see off poor Bert. We students goggled in awe at Bert's lump, expecting it to burst at any moment.

My third patient was a pale wisp of a woman in her forties who had a severe iron deficiency anaemia and difficulty in swallowing. This was known as the Plummer Vinson syndrome (named after the physicians who had described it), a syndrome being a collection of signs or symptoms which consistently occur together to produce a recognisable clinical diagnosis. She exhibited a sign characteristic of iron deficiency anaemia, that of koilonychia – a word to roll around your mouth. Koilonychia indicates a spoon shaped depression in the finger nails. Her prognosis (her outlook) was excellent. The anaemia was easily treated with iron and the dysphagia (difficulty in swallowing) due to a fibrous web at the lower end of her gullet, could be permanently relieved by passing a rod down her oesophagus, like a sword swallower, and dilating its lower end.

The fourth patient, again a tiny woman, was in her twenties. She had striking brown pigmentation of her face and body. On her hands the palmar creases and knuckles were almost black; she had dark patches in her mouth and the scar from an appendicectomy had turned black. Her chest x-ray showed a remarkably thin heart and her blood pressure was low. An x-ray of her abdomen revealed that her adrenal glands were calcified, a sure sign of tuberculosis. She had Addison's disease (described by Dr Thomas Addison in 1849) caused by failure of her adrenals, the glands which sit on top of the kidneys and produce cortisone and other hormones. Adrenal failure due to tuberculosis was not uncommon fifty years ago; tuberculosis is making a comeback these days and is often associated with HIV infections which bankrupt the body's immune defences. Fortunately for our patient, cortisone had been introduced five years earlier and she made a good response to treatment.

In my clinical studies, I soon learned the rule that the successful practice of medicine depends on diagnosis, diagnosis and diagnosis. Without the correct diagnosis, proper management leading to a cure is unlikely. Diagnosis depends on three things: taking a detailed case history, performing a good physical examination and carrying out investigations in the laboratory, in the x-ray department, by various scans, radio-isotope studies, biopsy examinations, endoscopic examinations and function studies – but no matter what miraculous advances occur in investigating patients, the starting point will always be the doctor taking the history and examining the patient.

Occasionally a single physical sign can give an instant diagnosis, a 'spot diagnosis'. Some five years later while doing a locum in general practice, I saw a young man with vague symptoms. On examination I found a brilliant cobalt blue line along his gum margins. Instant diagnosis: lead poisoning. Asked what his job was, he replied, "Burning old car batteries." The fumes of burning batteries contain lots of lead.

I was a pretty average student at school, strived hard to get my 'A' levels in botany and zoology in a year and struggled with the second MB – but it was clinical medicine that hit the spot. I came alive: this was *it*. The Sherlock Holmes approach – Sir Arthur Conan Doyle was an Edinburgh doctor – was fascinating; discovering clues from the history and examination, confirming suspicions by investigations and then treating according to a proper diagnosis was immensely satisfying and exciting. What other job could be so great?

SIX MONTHS SURGERY FOLLOWED THE medical clerkships. We were now called 'dressers' which added a certain cachet. We were introduced to the mystique of operating theatres, of surgical rituals, of the effects of trauma, and had a spell in the Casualty department – so busy you scarcely had time to turn around before the next case appeared.

When I was a student at University College Hospital, professorial ward rounds always began at the front entrance of the old hospital, the redbrick cruciform building in Gower Street, now dwarfed by the huge brand new UCH in Euston Road.

At the appointed hour a beadle in a maroon gold-piped uniform with a shining top-hat threw open the glass front doors and through them would march the professor followed by lecturers, senior registrar, registrars and housemen – then we dozen or so students would tag along behind. We would first ascend a short flight of steps flanked on the left by a bust of Sir John Blundell Maple Bart MP and on the right by a bust of Sir Robert Liston.

Sir John Blundell Maple Bart MP was the wealthy owner of a huge furniture shop in Tottenham Court Road, just around the corner from the hospital: Maples. He was extremely successful and donated £200,000 (a great deal of dough in those days) for the hospital to be reconstructed in 1881. I was told as a student that his patronage stemmed from the life-saving care he received at UCH after he had been run down by a hansom cab in Tottenham Court Road. That could be urban myth; I've not been able to confirm that story.

The other bust was of the most colourful surgeon in the history of UCH – maybe indeed of British history – Sir Robert Liston. A Scotsman, born a son of the manse, Sir Robert trained in Edinburgh and became surgeon to the Royal Infirmary there. But his personality was abrasive and outspoken; he was so quarrelsome that his fellow surgeons banned him from working in the Edinburgh Royal Infirmary. Sir Robert took to heart the observation of that great lexicographer, Dr Johnson, that the "noblest sight a Scotchman ever sees is the high road that leads him to England" and moved south. In 1835, he was appointed the first Professor of Surgery at University College Hospital.

According to doctor and author Richard Gordon (*Doctor in the House* etc) he rapidly established a reputation as the "fastest knife in the West End". In pre-anaesthetic days, the quicker the surgeon, the better his results. Sir Robert's results were the best in London: only one in ten of his patients died of hospital gangrene; at Guy's it was one in four. Not surprisingly, he had a good private practice.

Sir Robert was tall, well over six feet; he was strong and fit. I remember a story of how he chased and collared a reluctant patient. The man was next in line for surgery but fled in terror when he heard horrifying screams coming from the operating theatre. The poor patient hopped off as quickly as he could (Sir Robert was going to chop off his bad leg). The operating theatre was at the very top of the hospital and the patient made it as far as the gents' loo in the basement (it's still there with white tiles and shining brass fittings). Sir Robert found him crouched and cowering; he picked him up and slung him over his shoulder; and after sprinting up a dozen flights of stairs he threw him on the table, had him strapped down and took his leg off in his standard time of two and a half minutes.

Those were brave days indeed – in my time as a student the operating table Sir Robert used was displayed in the medical school pathology museum. To gaze at it scared the daylights out of me. Made of wood, it had half a dozen slots for leather straps down each side to secure the patient's body and more around the curved top for firmly securing the patient's head. There were detachable extensions for the legs; they could be removed in a flash, just like patients' legs.

Sir Robert, like all trendy surgeons, operated in wellington boots and a long green frock-coat stiff with dried blood and pus. We were still waiting for Lord Lister (I later worked for his grandson, William, in Plymouth) to introduce his carbolic spray and Semmelweiss in Vienna to make himself very unpopular by showing that it was the medical students and doctors themselves who carried infection from patient to patient. No surgeon would dream of putting on a clean coat or scrubbing his nails; that was for pansy types... like physicians.

One of his most famous patients was a man with an enormous scrotal tumour; it was so big he had to accommodate his scrotum in a wheelbarrow when he wanted to move about. Sir Robert removed it in four minutes flat; it weighed forty-five pounds... just try and imagine that!

In another memorable operating session, he amputated a man's leg in under the standard two and a half minutes, but such excessive speed has its price. When he chopped off the leg (which fell into the usual receptacle – a box of sawdust) with the ultimate slice, to the surprise of his dresser holding the limb, three of the dresser's fingers accompanied the leg and plopped into the box. Then he accidentally sliced through the coat of a distinguished surgeon leaning over to get a better look.

The surgeon, an elderly visitor who was there to observe the Master's technique, had a heart attack and dropped dead on seeing the knife flash so close by him. Both the patient and the dresser died of hospital gangrene a few days later. Not infrequently operations at that time carried one hundred per cent mortality; but three hundred per cent was surely a record for one surgical session.

On another occasion, he was so speedy he took the man's testicles with the final exuberant slice; that patient was spared a eunuchoidal existence as he also died of hospital gangrene a few days later.

Sir Robert Liston's most famous surgery took place at University College

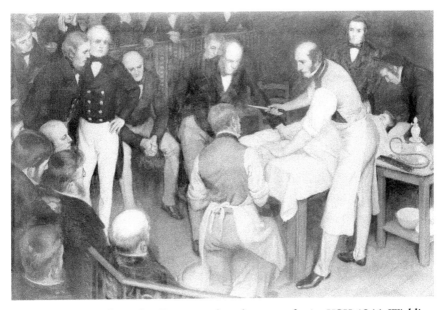

First operation performed in Europe under ether anaesthesia, UCH 1846. Wielding the knife is Sir Robert Liston. Standing at the left is Lord Lister who first used a carbolic acid spray for antisepsis. (Photo: Wellcome Library, London.)

Hospital on 21 December 1846. It was the first operation in Europe carried out under general anaesthesia. Ether was used. The patient was a butler called Robert Churchill and he needed to have a mid-thigh amputation for a malignant tumour of his leg.

A large and eager audience squeezed and jostled on tiers in the circular operating theatre. Dr William Squire was the anaesthetist. He determined to put on a show before the patient was brought in, so he asked if any of the assembled medical students would volunteer to be anaesthetised.

Sir Charles Brown, who was present, described what happened in his memoirs, *Sixty Years as a Doctor*:

> A young man called Shelbrake, of powerful build and a good boxer at once came forward and lay down on the table. After he had inhaled ether for half a minute he suddenly sprang up and felled the anaesthetist with a single blow and scattered the students before him like sheep before a dog. He soon regained his senses and the patient was then brought in.

Even today's TV doctors don't give such entertainment value.

Sir Robert then took over the show. "Today, gentlemen, we are going to try a Yankee dodge for making a man insensible," he announced to the assembled throng.

Dr Squire, by now chastened but recovered, introduced a red rubber tube into Mr Churchill's mouth and within a few minutes Churchill was unconscious. "Take your watches out, gentlemen!" commanded Sir Robert – his usual cry: he always liked to be timed – as he advanced on his patient.

He did the job in thirty-two seconds (no screams or wriggling). A few minutes later Robert Churchill came round and asked, "When are you going to start?" The gallery erupted in cheers and laughter. But when Churchill raised his leg and saw the stump he burst into tears.

AFTER SURGERY THERE WAS Obstetrics, where each student was required to deliver twenty babies. My first delivery was of a rather elderly lady, in her first pregnancy in her late thirties (elderly for those days). All went well. I was proud of myself. The swaddled infant was placed in a cradle, an open metal box suspended by metal hooks on a stand with the head pitched a few degrees down. I asked the new mother if she would like to hold her baby – she would. As I picked the baby out of the cradle, I hit its head against the metal hook with a clunk. "Sorry," I said, "it's my first baby."

"It's my first one too!" she cried as she examined the child's head for signs of damage.

Other specialities followed: anaesthetics, eye diseases, ear, nose and throat diseases, paediatrics, skin diseases and venereology. But none appealed to me as much as my first love – general medicine.

Three years flew by; final examinations, which occupied ten days, seemed never-ending. At last all was over and, in May 1957, I qualified with the degrees of Bachelor of Medicine and Bachelor of Surgery of the University of London – I was a doctor.

Three

ALTHOUGH QUALIFIED, I WAS NOT YET free to practise on the public at large. I was provisionally registered with the General Medical Council and had to serve a year's apprenticeship (internship), six months as a house surgeon and six months as a house physician to become fully registered. So I returned home to Plymouth and became house surgeon to a consultant surgeon, a Mr George Larks; that Bill Larkworthy was working for George Larks caused mirth among the hospital staff.

Mr Larks' character combined the forthright, plain speaking qualities of a Yorkshireman with the confidence and extroversion that I have since found to be a trait of surgeons. He was short; I looked down from the great height of five-foot-ten onto his glistening straight black hair sleeked down and reeking of Brylcreem. He had a narrow toothbrush moustache and walked with a bounce. He always wore a grey double-breasted suit; I think it was the same one every day during the six months I was his houseman. It made him look even more like a prosperous butcher at a meeting of the Rotary Club than a locally eminent surgeon. What he lacked in stature he more than made up in volume and panache; he had an opinion on every subject under the sun and everything he did had a flourish attached.

On one occasion the flourish was my downfall. During a ward round, with all his entourage dancing attendance, he needed to do a rectal examination. Sister held out the rectal tray containing the necessary bits, staff nurse turned the patient onto his left side, pulled down his pyjama pants and pushed up his legs. George donned a glove, dipped his index finger in the Vaseline pot and removed it with a flourish... too much Vaseline and too much flourish... a gobbet of Vaseline flew through the air and landed plum in the middle of his face, on the bridge of his thick horn-rimmed spectacles. I laughed; he glared; sister reddened; staff nurse tittered;

the waiting patient with his back to us turned his head and looked around, his eyes widening as he saw his surgeon advancing towards his rear end, right index finger extended in the air and his spectacles draped with petroleum jelly.

George Larks prided himself on being a general surgeon – could do anything; from cracking a nut and draining a clot on the brain, to doing an emergency Caesarean section, to amputating a gangrenous leg. He had qualified and done his surgical training in Leeds before moving to Plymouth. During the war he had been one of two general surgeons operating in Plymouth and had worked day and night during the Blitz. On one occasion a bomb had landed about fifty yards from the theatre in which he was operating; the electricity was cut but George soldiered on the best he could by hand-held torchlight.

Even without such inconveniences, the work was hard and the pay atrocious – in my first year I was paid £450 of which a third was deducted for food and accommodation. One day I mentioned the meagre salary to George. He flushed. "Larkworthy," he roared, "When I was a houseman we weren't paid at all, not a penny. If it hadn't been for coroner's post mortems I would have starved."

I was entitled to a weekend off a month but I had to get his permission. Always, but always, he said, "Larkworthy, you young fellows are so fortunate these days. When I did my house jobs I was lucky to get one weekend in six months."

Sad to relate, the last time I saw George Larks ten years later he was struggling to get out of his car. He had severe arthritis of both hips and could only stagger around with two walking sticks. It would be another six years before Sir John Charnley, in Manchester, developed his brilliantly effective artificial hip surgery of which I eventually became a beneficiary – a story in itself, but more on that later.

There are 168 hours in a week; I usually worked over eighty and once 130. When I began my stint, I saw the sunrise through the operating theatre windows on four successive mornings. I was working night and day and had doubts that I could stand the pace. When 'on take' for emergencies, there were not enough minutes in the hour, leave alone hours in the day.

I soon discovered from other house doctors that there was a supplement to be had for our pitiful salary; completing Part I of cremation certificates attracted a fee of two guineas (£2.10). During my six months as a house surgeon, of my patients who died, ten were cremated. Of course black humour dictated that this income should be known as 'ash cash'. Whatever its provenance, the local pub landlord accepted it.

George Larks loved to operate and it seemed that the longer the surgery, the greater his satisfaction. To me, standing for up to five hours on the opposite side of the operating table holding retractors, applying artery forceps to stop bleeding or swabbing to keep the field clear was just tedious. And once you have done half a dozen gastrectomies or removed a dozen breasts, surgery becomes pretty repetitive. This is not true of course, but that's how it seemed to me at the time.

The boss would chatter away during operations; he had a great passion for *The Rubaiyat of Omar Khayyam* and could recite all seventy-five verses. Imagine in a broad Yorkshire twang:

Awake! for Morning in the Bowl of Night
Has flung the Stone that put the Stars To Flight;
And Lo! the Hunter of the East has caught
The Sultan's Turret in a Noose of Light.

Stirring stuff, but another seventy-four verses reminding us of the fragility of life's thread was just too much and 'The Flower that once has blown forever dies' only emphasised that we were engaged in trying to stop 'the Moving Finger moving on' in life and death surgical situations. Fortunately old Omar favoured the liberal use of wine to soften the inevitable.

Six months as a house surgeon was followed by six months on the general medical wards, equally demanding but thankfully no endless hours in the operating theatres – and an unexpected introduction to flying and the Royal Air Force. What happened was this – a young man of twenty-two was admitted as an emergency suffering from a subarachnoid haemorrhage, a bleeding from the weakened wall of a small congenital dilatation of an artery at the base of his brain. Commonly known as a berry aneurysm, it was also commonly known that a further bleed could be fatal.

Our patient was comatose; he needed surgery but neurosurgical units were few and far between in the mid-fifties, the nearest being in Bristol. The safest approach would be to fly him by helicopter. My consultant agreed that I should contact the RAF Search and Rescue headquarters located at Mountbatten, a peninsula jutting into Plymouth Sound. Within half an hour of my explaining the situation, the RAF bosses had approved the mission provided that a doctor accompanied the patient. Once again my consultant concurred and, armed with oxygen and various bits of equipment, the patient and I boarded the helicopter which had landed in the hospital grounds. It was a Westland Whirlwind in the usual brilliant yellow livery of RAF Search and Rescue craft. I was not prepared for the horrendous noise that rattled every bone in my body. It didn't affect my comatose patient whose vital signs – to my relief – remained normal. We flew low at about a hundred miles an hour, meaning I could enjoy the view when not attending to my patient and I could also enjoy the thought I was escaping my on-call duties for a few hours.

That story had a happy ending in more ways than one. The patient was operated on that evening. He survived the haemorrhage and the surgery and made a complete recovery. The efficiency and willingness of the RAF to help – the embodiment of the service's motto, *Per ardua ad astra* (Through adversity to the stars) – impressed me and played no small part in the choice of my subsequent career.

Looking back to those times, we seemed pretty helpless in managing so many medical conditions. Compared with today's medical *armamentarium* we had fewer antibiotics, no powerful steroids, no effective anti-ulcer treatment, no effective asthma remedies and we couldn't investigate and treat patients with all the marvellous procedures which have come along in the past fifty years.

But it was the early days of the National Health Service, Aneurin Bevan's brainchild introduced in 1948. It was a world in which doctors and nurses were still respected. Sister ruled the ward with a rod of iron supervising not just the nursing care of her patients but making sure that the ward was spotless. We didn't have that particularly nasty antibiotic resistant staphylococcus MRSA floating around our hospitals and outbreaks of *Clostridium difficile* weren't to appear for another twenty years. We didn't suffer the evil effects of mass binge drinking and we didn't need to station police in casualty departments to control aggression against medical and nursing staff. In those days patients came to hospital to be treated by doctors and looked after by nurses; they were not statistics or targets. The administrative staff of my hospital in 1957 consisted of the hospital secretary with half a dozen assistants, working out of three offices. These days administrators outnumber the medical staff, determine priorities, set targets and have no understanding of, or possibly even care about, sick people's needs. It used to make me angry to think about what we've lost; now it just makes me sad.

AT THE END OF MY SIX months as a house physician, I became fully registered with the General Medical Council and could be let loose on society. However, I was invited to continue on the medical wards as a senior house officer. I enjoyed general medicine so I accepted the post. My pay, responsibilities and authority went up. I had to look after the junior doctors and to deputise for the consultants in the outpatient department. This post would last a year but then I would have to face the inevitable, that my National Service commitment, which had been deferred since 1952 so that I could study medicine, could be put off no longer. The moving finger does indeed move on.

In September 1959, I joined the Royal Air Force medical branch on a three-year commission but within a couple of years I extended my commission to five years when the RAF introduced a whopping great bonus of £3,000 for the addition of two years service.

It happened that I had a few free weeks before I entered the RAF – the obvious filler was general practitioner (GP) locums in Plymouth. The first locum, in the middle of the city, was for a Welsh doctor who had a busy practice; upwards of forty patients at each surgery.

Dr Jones took his holiday at home during my locum; I ate with the family in the evenings and was required to recount the day's events over dinner. One evening, as I struggled with one of Mrs Jones's truly awful curries – bland, plenty of raisins and for some reason, chunks of apple – I was startled to be told that the following day I would be giving anaesthetics for a nearby dentist. I had had training in dental anaesthesia as an undergraduate but always felt it was more of a smash-and-grab affair involving asphyxia rather than the controlled anaesthesia of the operating theatre.

The dentist operated in a Victorian terraced house. It was huge, no less than six operating chairs in separate rooms. There were patients everywhere, sitting in corridors clutching their swollen faces awaiting his mercy and others, having already suffered his mercy, spitting into bloody bowls. I made my presence known; he looked at me, clearly observing that I was dripping wet behind the ears, grunted a greeting and directed me to the first patient who was already in the chair. He was huge, he was blue, he was bloated and his belly rose out of the chair like a surfacing whale.

"Can I check his blood pressure?" I squeaked.

"Nonsense!" said the dentist.

Timorously I applied the mask and turned on the nitrous oxide (laughing gas); the man mountain turned a darker shade of blue and began to struggle. The dentist grabbed the mask from my hand, turned the flow to maximum, held the mask firmly in place and when the patient deflated and subsided in the chair, he whipped out all his teeth at an amazing speed. Rotten teeth were flying everywhere. A few hit the steel dish held by his nurse with a ping like an air rifle pellet, but she missed most; they landed scattered in bloody blobs on the floor.

Dazed, I followed him from room to room. In most cases I managed to anaesthetise the patients to his satisfaction. I must have gassed more than a dozen. At the end of the operating session, some two hours later, he muttered thanks for my services, leaned forward and popped a pound note in the top pocket of my jacket.

That evening, over dinner (watery cottage pie) with the family, I recounted my story. Dr Jones nodded, was in no way surprised, and gave a little shrug when I ventured that this was hardly a risk-free exercise. Saying that I thought that the fee for my services was meagre I reached into my top pocket for the pound note, pulled it out and, with a mirthless laugh, flourished it between my index and middle fingers. Dr Jones raised his eyes from his cottage pie, leaned across the table, plucked it from my fingers and as he pocketed it murmured, "Practice expenses."

From there I went to another locum in a delightful Devon village full of thatched cottages some eight miles from Plymouth. It was a dispensing practice and was run by a friend, Dr Teddy Reynard. The practice pharmacy held a large stock of pills, potions and gallons of liquid medicines of various brilliant hues in old fashioned pharmacy containers. Before I started, I had to solemnly declare that I would not disclose to the patients that Dr Reynard's aspirins were coloured pink... often during consultations patients would demand Dr Reynard's pink tablets for a variety of ailments, swearing they worked miracles. Dr Reynard had a partner in the next village; he was Dr Fox... no kidding.

One morning a local character attended the surgery. Betty lived on a ramshackle council estate on the outskirts of the village. She was no living doll, had the hairiest of legs, no mean moustache and six children (each, according to village gossip, by different fathers). Betty complained of abdominal discomfort and when I examined her I found a rounded lump rising out of her pelvis. "Why Betty," I exclaimed, "you're pregnant."

"Drat," she said. "Must have happened when I were pickin' watercress down in the meadow." Seeing my confusion, Betty explained, "I slipped and fell in the water, a nice handsome gentleman passing by pulled me out and I had to thank him somehow."

That wasn't to be the last I heard of Betty. Four years later, by a curious coincidence in Northern Germany, I heard the bizarre details of the outcome of that pregnancy.

A COUPLE OF WEEKS AFTER I finished that locum, I entered the Royal Air Force. Sixteen of us reported at a training depot near Blackpool, a motley group of young doctors, reluctantly becoming commissioned officers for Her Majesty. We were kitted out in standard RAF officers' uniforms which more or less fitted after the camp tailor had worked on them. A white-haired warrant officer tried to teach us how to salute and march properly and various sergeants introduced us to the vital task of correctly filling in RAF forms, the most important of which were those for taking leave and for claiming travel expenses.

To distinguish us as members of the medical branch, we wore *caducei*. The *caduceus* consists of a staff with two serpents entwining it in a double helix surmounted by a pair of wings and a crown. Our *caducei* were small, made of gilt, inserted into our uniform lapels and worn by every member of the medical branch from the lowliest junior technician to the mighty Air Marshal Director General. The *caduceus* was a symbol of the healing arts... or was it?

It appears that the *caduceus* was the staff of Mercury (Hermes if you are Greek) the messenger of the gods and in his own right god of commerce, death, deception and theft; cynics would say appropriate enough for the medical profession. How had it come about that the *caduceus* had been confused with the rod of Aesculapius, god of medicine, with its single snake? For this we can blame the Americans who had erroneously adopted the *caduceus* as the insignia of the US Army Medical Corps in 1902.

Not only was the *caduceus* the wrong symbol, the small gilt insignia soon tarnished and required regular polishing – a real fiddle especially trying to avoid dousing the uniform material with metal polish.

Soon after I joined I had my second experience of flying. It was a short trip but no less memorable because of that. We were taken as a group to Denham in Buckinghamshire to the factory of Martin-Baker, the company whose expertise and careful manufacture of ejection seats have saved the lives of thousands of military pilots throughout the world.

We assembled in a lecture theatre and a senior technician explained that in modern high performance military aircraft there is no question of bailing out in the traditional manner. Things happen so quickly and at such a speed that the only way to save the pilot is by forcibly expelling him well clear of the aircraft. To do this the pilot sits on an explosive charge, always armed before takeoff. If the pilot needs to 'punch out', in one swift movement he pulls a protective blind down in front of his face; instantly the cockpit canopy flies off and the charge explodes, hurling the seat, with the pilot still strapped to it, well clear of the aircraft. Pilot and seat then drift gently to earth under the canopy of a parachute deployed automatically from the seat.

Outside we gathered around a simulator which consisted of a standard ejection seat mounted at the bottom of what looked like miniature railway lines ascending vertically for maybe a hundred feet. After the technician explained that the commonest injuries caused by the shock wave of the explosion were crush fractures of the vertebrae and even damage to the base of the skull, I inwardly gave thanks that as a doctor I would never be exposed to such risks.

"Right," said our lecturer. He pulled a brass cylinder from his pocket, inserted it somewhere under the simulator seat, fiddled about a bit, turned to us, smiled and said, "Now the seat's armed, who wants to have a go?" I looked around to see which of my new colleagues was foolhardy enough – to my horror they had all taken a step backwards leaving me gazing at him with a foolish grin.

"Great!" he said with an air of surprise, "We don't often get a volunteer but today we have one. Sit here in the seat, doc – I'll strap you in. It's gonna be very tight but we don't want you to break your back – do we, doc?"

He made me tuck in my elbows and guided my hands to the blind pull. "Wait for it," he said somewhat anxiously, "let me get well clear and when I shout GO and you're ready, pull the blind down – sharpish, mind you."

I looked around at my delighted colleagues, eagerly anticipating the show and glad not to be in the hot seat. They grinned, he shouted "GO" and I pulled.

I don't remember the explosion, I scarcely remember being kicked up the backside by a mule but I vividly remember to this instant my feeling of utter astonishment as I looked down at my open-mouthed buddies gazing up at me. It must have taken less than a second for me to ascend those rails. The chair was wound down, I was unstrapped, got shakily to my feet, flexed and extended my spine; it worked, it was pain-free but my brain was numb and stayed that way until the next day.

AFTER INITIAL TRAINING, MY FIRST FIVE years in the air force were fairly uneventful. An early posting was to a boy entrant training depot in the Midlands.

Life as their general practitioner was not exciting; frequently on call but seldom called: young boy entrants don't suffer many illnesses. Came the summer, we were sent en masse to Dartmoor for field training. The base was in a former prisoner of war camp in south Devon, near Newton Ferrers. There were six hundred junior recruits and they were sent in batches of a hundred on expeditions and to camps in remote locations on the moor. My biggest challenge was blisters on the feet of those who had been sent on route marches – popping them and painting them brilliant blue with an antiseptic, gentian violet, seemed to do the trick.

One morning I rolled up to supervise sick parade, and as it was Saturday, I was not in uniform. Just before lunchtime, the adjutant summoned me to station headquarters. "Flight Lieutenant Larkworthy," said the adjutant, a skinny embittered man of forty who had reached the ceiling of his career, "you have upset the station commander. The Group Captain is annoyed with you."

"Really? What did I do?" I asked.

"By appearing in civilian clothes."

"But it's Saturday," I responded.

"Larkworthy, you have a flippant attitude; you should understand that we are all here to work seven days a week to look after and train our young charges, who are, after all, the future of the Royal Air Force. You will wear uniform at all times."

Irritated, I left his office. With admirable restraint I had refrained from pointing out that I was quite used to being on duty seven days a week, and hanging about bored to my back teeth, on call in the event that one of our precious young charges got sick or fell down and bruised his knee.

I returned to sick quarters to find that an order had been sent from the Group Captain; I was forthwith to carry out a hygiene inspection of the whole station, a sizeable undertaking. It was Saturday lunchtime; evidently the station commander was having a go at me.

It happened that one of my staff was a health inspector in civilian life doing his National Service and not liking it a bit. I took him along and together we carried out the inspection.

In the huge camp kitchen he nudged my arm. "Look at those plates," he said, pointing towards piles of metal plates stacked high. They were coated with tinplate and had seen long service. "Those plates are scratched, many are rusted and there's a real risk of them being a source of infection."

He was right; we finished the inspection. We couldn't find any other problems, didn't need to. My guns were loaded for a broadside. I returned to my office and wrote my report: Plates unsafe; no alternative but to condemn the lot. I took it to the adjutant who passed it to the Group Captain who then discovered that he had six hundred sixteen year olds with the healthiest of appetites on his hands and couldn't feed them..

According to Queen's Regulations for the Royal Air Force, a station commander could overrule the advice of a medical officer but had to take full responsibility if anything went wrong. He was in a quandary, could not reject my findings and dared not use the condemned plates. It was nearly midnight when six hundred disgruntled, desperately hungry boys were finally fed; he had borrowed plates from a naval base ten miles away.

Having re-read Queen's Regulations and emboldened by our authority, I decided that my expert colleague and I should inspect the camps dispersed over Dartmoor. We set off in an RAF Land Rover, bumped over the moor, nearly got stuck in one of its notorious bogs, but at the very first camp we struck gold. I was able to condemn the camp's Otway pit.

The British military in the field all over the world, from the hot plains of the Indian Raj to the deserts of North Africa, has used Otway pits for centuries to dispose of solid human waste by a process which depends on anaerobic (without oxygen) fermentation. The pit is large, the dimensions of a medium-sized room, completely covered to exclude all but the air above the surface crust. Large holes in the top allow the users sitting in a row to deposit their offerings; a crust soon forms and is vital to the pit's proper function. Beneath the crust anaerobic bacteria, which do not use oxygen, break down the material and no fetid odours are generated.

Many large empty tins had been thrown into the first pit we inspected, the surface crust was broken and air had been introduced. Aerobic bacteria were at work, fermentation was taking place and a rich odour of rotten eggs pervaded the surrounding air.

I ordered the pit to be filled in and a new one dug, a mammoth job especially on granite-based Dartmoor. Next on the lavatorial scene were the liquid disposal arrangements. Having boned up on all the technical aspects, I was able to point out that for the urinals the soakage pit was too small and the runaway incorrectly angled; I ordered that the system be reconstructed.

We then drove to a camp at a site called Powder Mills, in the middle of Dartmoor, not far from the celebrated prison which had been built during the Napoleonic Wars to house French prisoners. Powder Mills was where closely supervised French prisoners were employed in making gunpowder and dropping molten lead from the top of a tower into water to make shot. A pleasant broad Dartmoor stream meandered through the site.

The camp was in good order but the boys complained that nearly all their food had an unpleasant taste. With the Irish corporal cook, I inspected the kitchens and could find no cause. I asked about disposal of kitchen waste. The solid stuff was collected by a local farmer for his pigs; the liquid, the corporal proudly announced, was disposed of down a hole he had found in the ground conveniently nearby. "To be sure, when we pour the dirty water down this hole it never comes back." Problem was that the hole was upstream of where the kitchen staff collected water for cooking and although the water was sterilised before use it had a taste that lingered – correct disposal, problem solved, a couple of hundred boys much happier.

I was surprised a couple of days later when the station commander himself appeared unannounced in my office. He did at least knock on the door as he burst into my consulting room, sat down, plonked his service cap with its peak bedecked with scrambled egg on my desk in front of me; ran a hand through his wavy silver hair, brushed his equally silvery moustache with a forefinger, glared and said, "What's going on, doc? I had enough of you with those damned plates but was it really necessary to have that Otway pit re-dug? Strikes me you are being over-zealous."

"Not at all, sir" I replied as, with what I hope came across as scarcely concealed pleasure, I was able to draw his attention to instructions in the RAF Field Manual, a copy of which lay conveniently on my desk. With a passable imitation of Uriah Heap and to emphasise that my motives were simply to ensure the best of health of our precious boy entrants at all times, I said, "After all, sir, they are the future of the Royal Air Force."

Four

AFTER JUST A FEW MONTHS WITH the boy entrants, I was moved on. Maybe I was proving to be a thorn in the side of the commanding officer; whatever, I was happy to go and missed our precious charges not one whit. I was posted to RAF Lyneham, a vast Transport Command base in Wiltshire.

Nowadays Lyneham is in the news mainly as the bit of England's green and pleasant land to which the bodies of the young and brave are flown from distant battlegrounds. In my time, in the sixties, RAF Lyneham was the centre for casualty evacuation (CASEVAC) training, in which I became involved.

My first duty as a CASEVAC medical officer was to fly to Malta to pick up and escort back to Lyneham a planeload of 'casualties'. The aircraft was a Bristol Britannia, a four-engined turbo-prop nicknamed The Whispering Giant. It was the most comfortable aircraft I have ever experienced and totally wasted on this mission. The casualties consisted of a collection of neurotic naval wives and a motley assortment of naval ratings and airmen mostly with bed-wetting problems. The ladies were being sent home because they could no longer cope with the hardships of living on Malta… then, as now, regarded as a holiday destination. The airmen and sailors had become disenchanted with service life and had heard that bed-wetting was an easy way to get discharged; homosexuality and communist tendencies were other good ploys but bed-wetting was the easiest to demonstrate.

Our return flight to Blighty was without incident except for an altercation involving some hair-pulling between two navy wives; I hadn't thought that playground supervision would be among my CASEVAC duties.

If the Britannia was comfortable, the de Havilland Comet – the first jet airliner – was luxury. It carried us to all the RAF bases between Lyneham and

Hong Kong where I was not required to deal with casualties but to check the hygiene, potential hazards and inspect the medical facilities at each base.

The tour began with el Adem in Libya, overnight in Sharjah in the Persian Gulf and a refuelling stop in Aden; a two-night stopover in Gan, one of the islands in the Maldives; two more nights in Singapore and then three in Hong Kong before flying the same route home.

El Adem was a blisteringly hot, dusty outpost in the desert; it would be years before oil wealth and Colonel Gaddafi changed its face. Sharjah, a similarly blessed place in the sun, was for many years a staging post for flights to India and beyond for the British Overseas Airways Corporation, one of the forerunners of British Airways. We were lodged in the Officers' Mess in front of which a couple of exhausted oleander bushes struggled to survive, alongside daffodils and tulips – daffodils and tulips? They certainly needed watering, not to encourage growth but to wash the dust off their plastic petals. I imagine I would have been dismayed if I had known then that twenty-five years later, I would work in Sharjah for a year before moving to Dubai. By then of course the dust was largely under control... itself covered with buildings and tarmac.

Next day we flew to Aden, yet another blighted, hot, dusty, sandy, and totally arid spot. Aden was the headquarters of British military operations in the Middle East with a large RAF presence. It would close five years after my brief visit. The British were driven out by the wave of Arab nationalism which followed the Suez debacle. Four years of armed struggle against Arab factions using guerrilla and terrorist tactics ended in a no-win situation. The cash-strapped British government of the time wisely accepted that it wasn't going to come out on top and announced strategic withdrawal. The retreat was followed by a snub when Aden, which had become part of the Democratic Republic of Yemen, declined an invitation to join the British Commonwealth.

But for us Aden was just a refuelling stop on the way to Gan another four hours further east. Gan was marvellous; an island embraced by a deep blue sky reflected in the equally deep blue waters of the Indian Ocean; girded by brilliant, almost painfully white coral sands with palm trees dipping their fronds into the gentle waves; the sea making a gentle hiss as it broke over the coral reef some thirty yards offshore. I'm not making this up: Gan, one of the most southerly islands of the huge chain of the Maldives, is everybody's idea of a tropical paradise.

Gan was taken over by the RAF in 1957 as a staging and refuelling post for military aircraft in the Indian Ocean. It closed in 1976 when British forces withdrew from the Far East because Prime Minister Harold Wilson had devalued sterling and the country was once again going broke. As usual, when cutting the armed forces' budget (always the first to be chopped in an economic crisis, ahead of more vote-winning services) the government claimed that 'rationalisation' would in fact increase military striking power. I still can't see how that works.

When I set foot on Gan in 1961, there were a thousand men and one woman manning the RAF base. The one woman was pleasant, plump, fifty and a nursing sister. Fishing, diving, snorkelling and sailing were the main diversions but there was the usual branch of the armed forces cinema chain, the Astra; no walls, open-sided but with a tin roof, it could accommodate about three hundred, but when the tropical rains arrived during films – and they often did – the sound track became inaudible, the screening was abandoned and the good-natured, booing crowd adjourned to the island's favourite activity – drinking beer.

I was invited to the Sergeants' Mess for a drink or two and witnessed there what would come to be regarded in a few decades as a very ecologically friendly act. Although the base had been opened for only four years, the sergeants had constructed over the water's edge a jetty on which tables and chairs were set so that members could drink a cold beer or two while watching the sun set in all its glory over the rim of the Indian Ocean. What was so commendable was the way they had dealt with the lack of building materials on the island. They used crushed beer cans for the framework. To provide enough material for the job in hand required dedication, devotion and determination: they had to empty thousands upon thousands of cans. Their next project was to build a pier and evidently those brave lads were working hard on the raw materials that evening. Willingly I added my contribution.

Next day, accompanied by the station medical officer, I carried out a leisurely hygiene inspection. The kitchens, accommodation, messing and living quarters all satisfied Her Majesty's Regulations but I noticed an abundance of maggots in the breakfast cereals, the flour and the bread. The doctor assured me these were benign and not the vectors of disease. Once a man had been on the island for a few weeks, he scarcely noticed them or if he was a particularly fastidious sort, he would spoon them out of his cereal or knock them out of his bread. "A source of protein," he added. "The meat we get from Singapore is half bad by the time it gets here."

I asked about the mens' health. "It's good," he said. "They lead outdoor lives, take malaria prophylaxis seriously and there is nothing major, only the occasional minor injury. If there is a problem I can't deal with, I can send the patient to the RAF Hospital at Changi in Singapore in three or four hours."

"Mind you," he said with a grin, "six months ago my predecessor had to deal with a small outbreak of gonorrhoea."

My jaw dropped. "How on earth could that happen?"

"Easy, we had a planeload of wives, navy and air force, spend a night here en route to Singapore. Inside a week the men were queueing at Station Sick Quarters, some swearing they had caught a mosquito borne infection."

Singapore was hot, humid, busy, thriving and excitingly Chinese. These were the days when Singapore slings in the Long Bar at Raffles Hotel were served individually, not from a huge plastic bucket; when the transvestites strutted the original Bugis Street, not the sanitised one; when chilli crab could be eaten on the beach at a place called Bedok Corner. The hawkers cracked live crabs with a hammer and tossed them into the cooking pot; they were delicious. With white starched bibs tied around our necks, we ate with our fingers; the cold Anchor beer frosted the glasses; the palms swayed gently in a sultry breeze blowing off the South China Sea: not even the scraggy pye-dogs cocking their legs against the tin tables could detract from the perfect atmosphere. I vowed to return some day, and when I did, eight years later, I couldn't locate Bedok Corner. Eventually I found a taxi driver who said he'd take me there... it was now one kilometre from the sea, on reclaimed land.

The last leg of our outward journey was to Hong Kong. Landing at the old airport at Kai Tak was tricky and on our final approach I swear we flew down the main street, the Comet overshadowed by tall buildings on each side.

If Singapore was busy, Hong Kong was frenetic; thousands of Chinese scurrying everywhere; hawking and spitting beneath a plethora of signs which declared the habit 'evil and unhygienic'. Even then buildings were rising to dizzying heights, crowded onto the limited land area, with construction workers leaping around bamboo scaffolding like manic rhesus monkeys. Garlic-laden cooking smells pervaded every street, even in the early morning.

After a brief inspection of the RAF station at Kai Tak, I joined the aircrew who were familiar with the diversions on offer in downtown Hong Kong. The place was buzzing with life and frantic bar girls swearing eternal devotion if you bought them a glass of ersatz champagne for ten dollars. On every street corner, in every bar speakers blared the same song, the current number one pop song, *Yellow River*, but sung by Chinese bar girls it came over as *Yellow Liver*.

THE RETURN TO THE RAIN AND MISTS of RAF Lyneham in Wiltshire took five days; when I arrived I found a posting notice to Germany.

The base was in northern Germany, on the Dutch border and thirty miles from Liege in Belgium. During my three-year stint in general practice there I was promoted to squadron leader and, having learned that the RAF would encourage specialist training, took a permanent commission. I had to wait to enter specialist training and meanwhile set about enjoying the various aspects of life as flight surgeon to the aircrew, doctor to the families living on the base and an innocent abroad discovering the many diversions of living in Germany.

To help with the families, I had a nursing sister. She was supplied by an organisation called SSAFA (Soldiers, Sailors, Airmens and Families Association). Halfway through my tour, there was a change of sister. The new sister was jolly, middle-aged and competent. One morning, over coffee and biscuits, I discovered that she had only recently joined SSAFA and for the previous five years had been working in that very Devon village in which I had encountered Betty, that selfsame Betty who had suffered two mishaps while picking watercress – falling in the water and falling pregnant.

"Betty!" she exploded, convulsing with laughter. "How on earth do you know Betty?"

She nodded knowingly as I explained and told me that she had made it her personal challenge to prevent Betty getting pregnant yet again. To this end, many times a week and more frequently on weekends, she would rush into Betty's house, dash upstairs and turf out any gentleman she found, be he yokel, farmer or clergyman, but she admitted she had failed when Betty's generous nature overcame her in the watercress meadow.

Curious, I asked about the outcome of the pregnancy I had encountered years before. Sister chuckled. "It was a boy. Betty called him Rock because she thought Rock Hudson was lovely."

Rock made a dramatic entry into the world, she told me. "One afternoon, when – from long experience – Betty knew that 'things' had started and were moving along quickly, she sent her eldest to fetch me while she climbed the stairs in her council house. She had reached only as far as the landing when Rock suddenly popped out in her bloomers, rapidly followed by the cord and the afterbirth.

"I tell you, doctor, when I got there I found a real mess on that cramped landing. It was the devil's own job sorting out the mother, the baby, the placenta tangled with the cord and all enveloped in her big white bloomers drenched in bloodstained amniotic fluid.

"But," she added triumphantly, "Betty never got pregnant again on my watch."

Almost exactly four years to the day that Rock made his precipitate entrance into the world, and on one of those memorable evenings which everybody remembers – 22 November 1963 to be exact – the Officers' Mess was holding a formal dining-in night. We assembled in the anteroom, decked out in our RAF dress uniforms, and welcomed the large US Air Force contingent which shared the station.

The base had nuclear weapons; two loaded Canberra bombers and their crews stood by on instant alert to deal with the imminent and ever-present Russian threat. The Americans were constantly linked to the Pentagon and guards with side arms maintained an eagle-eyed vigilance over the British bombers and crews so that a unilateral nuclear war could not be launched.

Halfway through the dinner came the news of President John F Kennedy's assassination. As one the Americans rose, stood to attention with their right hands on their hearts and after a minute's silent tribute quietly filed out of the dining room. We completed our meal and assembled in the bar in sombre mood for a drink before calling an end to the evening.

But the night was far from over for me. A crash had happened in thick fog some fifteen miles from the base. It involved a car being driven by an RAF squadron leader with his family. The officer had been killed when he drove under the tailgate of a parked lorry; the injuries to his family were serious.

Accompanied by a senior administrative officer, a medical orderly and an

RAF policeman, we sped in the station ambulance to the scene. The German *polizei* had cleared the area and sent the wife and two children to hospital in Aachen. The body of the officer had been collected by a local undertaker.

By now it was midnight; with difficulty we located the funeral parlour in a terraced house in a nearby village just across the border in Belgium. No lights to be seen, we rapped on the door and eventually an upstairs window opened and an old crone poked her head out. She demanded to know what we wanted. She sent out her son, *le directeur des pompes funèbres*. My admin officer, in a halting mixture of German, French and English, told him that we had come for the remains of the RAF officer. The director bluntly refused, saying that he was sure that if we took *"le corps"* he would never see payment for the considerable services he had already performed.

After prolonged wrangling and a hand-written promise, he agreed to the release. He said the body was lodged in the village graveyard and his assistant, who slept in the workshop, would take us there. We all went to find the assistant and as we entered a large room full of coffins, *monsieur le directeur* yelled, "Jacques!"

From a coffin at the back of the room rose a gnome-like, wizened, stubble-faced creature dressed in a workman's uniform of a blue blouse and blue trousers. The director rapidly told the gnome what was wanted, the gnome nodded, scratched his bald pate, donned a black beret and motioned us to follow him. We stumbled through the darkened village streets but not too close to our gnome who ponged to high heaven. He evidently followed the custom of the local working man by having a wash on odd months and a shave on even months.

We reached a graveyard on the outskirts. It was large, the moon was full, clouds were scudding across the sky, cats squabbled and howled and there were numerous flickering candles in small red containers dotted around. Jacques led the way to the far side of the eerie graveyard, through a dry stone wall to a slate hut with a rickety, rotten door. The gnome took out a large key, inserted it in the lock, turned it and pushed the door open... it gave an almighty creak and the RAF policeman standing at my side spoke for us all when he said, "I just knew it would do that, sir."

On a slab of granite in the middle lay a coffin. Our gnome indicated we should view the contents. Inside was a white body bag. We unzipped it, revealing the body... but there was no head. We looked puzzled, the gnome smirked and unzipped the bag to its full extent — there was the head between the ankles.

A couple of days later, any lingering gloom after that gruesome experience was dispelled by the offer of a flight to Malta in a Canberra bomber. I was promised a good view of southern Europe: I would lie prone in the nose, the bomb aimer's position. Flying at high altitude required that I be fitted out with helmet, oxygen mask and a flying suit. That done, I reported to the squadron dispersal where I met my pilot, Gordon, a tall squadron leader with a deep voice and a prominent Adam's apple, and his side-kick, short and smiling Ken, the navigator.

As we climbed aboard, I noticed that both Gordon and Ken were equipped with parachutes and naturally enquired, "Where's mine?" They looked at each other and Ken said, with a ghost of a smile, "Well, Bill, where you are, it will be impossible to get out..." It was too late to reconsider so I scrambled into my prone position, connected the oxygen, checked its flow by watching the doll's eye blink at me as I breathed and marvelled at how close my nose seemed to be to the ground. It seemed even closer as we gathered speed to take off.

Flying at 35,000 feet, I did indeed have a spectacular view. In no time we were approaching the south coast of France. There was a heated discussion between the pilot and navigator and I heard Gordon say, "Why don't you ask Bill?"

"Why don't you?" responded Ken.

"Because you're the bleedin' navigator, mate, and you should know."

A moment's silence, then Ken said, " Er um, Bill, could you tell us as we cross the coast whether Marseilles is to our left or right?"

"Of course," I replied wondering what sort of navigation I was witnessing. "It's on our left," I announced as I viewed the Mediterranean shoreline.

"Thank goodness for that," said an apparently greatly relieved Ken.

When we reached Malta we flew around and around Valetta Harbour playing some form of Russian roulette as we dodged in and out between ships' masts, a heart-stopping game. "Okay down there Bill?" Gordon solicitously asked.

"Yes, thanks," I said with all the confidence I could muster, but it probably came out with a squeak.

It didn't take long for me to tumble to the fact that those two wise guys

The author (right) and his pilot beside the nose of their Canberra bomber. The bomb aimer's downward facing dome is just visible at right.

were winding me up. In the few hours we were in Malta, first one then the other confided in me. "Keep it under your hat, Bill," said Gordon. "I've been flying with Ken as my navigator for a couple of years but frankly he's not what he used to be, makes too many mistakes these days, God only knows where we'll end up."

Then as we strolled along the Gut, a street in Malta known to every Jolly Jack Tar in the Royal Navy, Ken said casually to me, "You know, Bill, Gordon worries me; he's getting very forgetful these days, but I guess he's still pretty safe and will probably get us home."

We did get home, but to a base of frenzied activity: the AOC's inspection was imminent. All RAF stations are subjected to annual inspections by one of the top brass, the Air Officer Commanding. In the weeks leading up to the great day, extensive tidying up occurs; squadrons have practice parades, boots are polished, trousers creased, stones painted white and an all-pervasive air of nervous anticipation grows.

On the Big Day, I was taking an antenatal clinic. One of my ladies, Mrs Anthony, complained of intermittent abdominal pain, I examined her and found she was in labour. Evidently it was progressing well. I told her she must immediately go to the RAF hospital some fifteen miles away and offered the ambulance but she told me her husband, Sergeant Anthony, would take her and off she went.

A few minutes later the breathless, distraught sergeant appeared. His car had broken down on the main road leading in to the base and the urgency of his wife's situation was rapidly becoming apparent.

I grabbed the midwifery bag and rushed to her. She was lying on her back on the grass at the side of the road surrounded by animated German camp labourers and batwomen. One glance revealed a black, hairy scalp presenting. Delivery was imminent. I told Sergeant Anthony to go to the guard post at the camp entrance and get police and screens. The husband returned – the police were fully occupied lined up waiting for the imminent arrival of the Air Officer Commanding with his entourage.

Nothing for it; and with scarcely any help from me, a baby boy appeared. I tied and divided the cord and held up the infant at the very instant the entourage of six cars passed. The AOC, dripping in gold braid, peered from his staff car as it drove past, slowly he turned his head to gaze at me kneeling on the grass behind a supine woman, holding up a baby in my outstretched arms as if offering it to him. The onlookers were crowding in on me to get a good look at the baby and had spontaneously broken into clapping.

Curiously, apart from the AOC's mystified expression, my most vivid memory of that moment is of a blackbird singing beautifully on a branch of the tree overhanging the natal scene.

At her post-natal examination, Mrs Anthony told me that she and her husband had decided to call the baby Mark. "I've heard the name Mark Anthony somewhere before and it's quite famous you know, doctor."

Five

To BEGIN SPECIALIST TRAINING, I WAS posted from Germany to Royal Air Force Hospital Nocton Hall in England. The hospital was situated seven miles south of Lincoln in the grounds of the ancient manor of Nocton. The area had been settled since Roman times; Lincoln, known then as *Lindum colonia*, was an important outpost of the Roman Empire. The manor house, Nocton Hall, was mentioned in the Domesday Book and had been given by William the Conqueror in 1068 to one of his generals, Norman D'Arcy, whose family held onto it for nearly three hundred years.

In its long history, the hall's most notable visitor was King Henry VIII who, in 1541, spent a night there with his fifth wife and bride of one year, Queen Catherine Howard. She was soon to suffer the same accusations and fate as his second wife, Anne Boleyn. A year after the royal visit to Nocton and at the age of twenty-two, Catherine was beheaded for incest and adultery.

The next royal connection was also with a queen of England, Lady Jane Grey, famous for having the shortest reign of all English queens. Nocton Hall and its estate had been bequeathed to her by her grandfather, the Duke of Suffolk. Through a little court intrigue – a popular if risky game of the time – Lady Jane Grey succeeded Henry VIII's son, the sickly boy-king Edward VI, although she was not in direct line for the throne. Her reign lasted nine days. She was forced to abdicate by Mary Tudor (Bloody Mary), the rightful queen, and imprisoned in the Tower of London with her husband. In 1548, to tidy royal affairs, Bloody Mary had the seventeen-year-old Lady Jane along with her husband (and, for good measure, her father) beheaded; since then Nocton Hall has been haunted.

In my time, an ethereal Grey Lady would appear at formal mess dining-in nights but had the decency to delay her entrance until some time after the port had made its way around the table for the third time.

Nocton Hall saw its final royal visitor in July 1969 when Princess Alexandra opened a new maternity unit. Local lore has it that when the hall was inspected to make sure its 'comforts' were up to scratch for such a distinguished visitor, it was decided that its venerable water closets would not be suitable to be graced by the royal derrière and a new suite in pink porcelain was installed. A sergeant in the Women's Royal Air Force, a moustachioed battle axe for whom the term woman seemed rather arbitrary, was entrusted with the key to the brand new suite. Came the day, came the call of nature. When the princess expressed a need, of course the sergeant could not be found. Her Royal Highness had to be content with the ancient crazed white porcelain and the pink suite, too grand for the hoi polloi, was removed the following day.

Nocton Hall's connection with military medical services began in the First World War when it was used by the Americans as a convalescent hospital for officers. In the Second World War, the US Army built a hospital, the Seventh General Army Hospital, in the grounds. The Royal Air Force took it over in 1945 and for forty years it served the many RAF bases in Lincolnshire and the local civilian population. In 1983, the Ministry of Defence closed the hospital as part of the reorganisation (i.e. budget cuts) of the armed forces medical services, but it was again loaned to the US Military during the first Gulf War to become what was called a contingency hospital. Some thirteen hundred medical staff were appointed but in all only thirty-five casualties were received.

Lincolnshire is ideal air base country. It is flat with the city of Lincoln and its six-hundred-year-old cathedral standing boldly on a hill in the middle, visible for miles. Bitter winds from the North Sea sweep across the county. It is so flat and wet it resembles the Netherlands; in medieval times, the southern part of the county became known as 'Parts of Holland'. Much of the county, called the Fenlands, is low and marshy and kept above water by a network of drains. It is fertile, growing root crops, potatoes and sugar beet – in my time the land surrounding the hospital was owned by Smith's, a company famed for potato crisps. The hospital was also in the middle of rich game bird shoots; pheasants foolish enough to pass into Nocton Hall's restricted air space were literally fair game for an assortment of shoulder-mounted ordnance and stood a good chance of being brought down by buckshot and gracing the mess dining table.

By definition service personnel are healthy specimens. They are young, they volunteered, they are looking for an active life and must pass a medical examination before joining the service. One would think that, in terms of clinical material, service hospitals would not have a lot to offer. Not so with Nocton Hall. With forty per cent of the beds occupied by civilians, the load of cases and variety of illnesses provided adequate medical experience. Although much of the work was run of the mill treating patients with ulcers, pneumonias or heart attacks, unusual cases came along to add spice.

One such was a local butcher who was admitted with high fever, severe headaches and nose bleeds. His eyes were startling, very red yet at the same time the whites could be seen to have turned yellow. The diagnostic clue in the history was that five nights before, he had attended a celebration in Lincoln. Unwisely, he had driven home through the fens, rolled his car into a ditch and woken at dawn to find himself lying in a drain. We made an early diagnosis of leptospirosis and our butcher responded quickly to antibiotics.

Leptospirosis is also known as Weil's disease (Adolf Weil described it in Hamburg in 1870) and is caused by a spiral-shaped bacteria, a *spirochaete* which resembles in shape the syphilis bacteria but has a hook at one end: *leptos* is Greek for hook. Usually rats are the reservoir for the leptospires and pass the bug in their urine. The water in the rat-infested drain was the source of the infection for the butcher.

I encountered Weil's disease three years later in Gurkhas in Malaysia and after another twenty years when I visited a colleague in the Seychelles. The sources were always rats. The friend I was visiting, Graham Pinn, an ex-RAF physician, was the consultant in medicine to the Victoria Hospital on the main island of Mahé. It appeared that disease-carrying rodents were making the potent local moonshine even more deadly. Graham told me that the locals distilled their hooch in the hills, away from prying eyes, but their distilleries were overrun by rats – moreover, not only did the moonshine contaminated by rats' urine transmit the leptospires, the impurities in it were toxic to the heart and brain. The locals who swigged the moonshine didn't seem to mind – they needed something to relieve the endless boredom of their tropical paradise. Although they could see what was happening to their drinking mates, the prospect of ending their days as emaciated, shambling, breathless, yellow idiots didn't stop them swigging the poisonous cocktail. Because these wrecks of humanity always appeared in tattered straw hats, ragged shorts and carried their clinking bottles in striped plastic bags, Graham called their condition the Triple 'S' syndrome – you could spot two or three examples of the syndrome, night or day, staggering their clanking erratic way along the streets of the capital, Victoria.

Back at Nocton, another unusual case I remember was a farmworker called George. He had been referred by one of the Nocton village doctors. He was aged fifty, a true son of the soil who spent his life digging the muddy fields around the hospital. George was accompanied by his wife, an anxious little country lady in her Sunday best. They brought a gift of a pheasant and she mentioned as she handed it to me that it was ready for eating as it had been hanging for three weeks; from the ripe smell and the occasional maggot dropping to the floor, I had no reason to doubt her.

George was baffled by his bizarre complaint. "It's my right thumb," he said. "It twitches." But this was no ordinary twitch. Within a few seconds not only his thumb but his index finger would be involved; then his hand and the muscles of his arm would follow and sometimes his leg would jerk uncontrollably and he would fall over. "But I'll tell you what," he confided, "if I'm in the field, I plant my fork good and deep as soon as I feel the twitch coming on, and squeeze it with my other hand – tight, mind – and then I don't fall on me face in the mud."

What George was suffering from was a form of epilepsy, Jacksonian epilepsy, named after the English physician John Hughlings Jackson who first described it. John Hughlings Jackson was the son of a Yorkshire farmer and brewer, born in 1835, just fifty miles north of Nocton Hall hospital where George gave me such a graphic account of his Jacksonian convulsions. In 1870 he published a paper in which he ascribed specific functions to specific areas of the outer layer of the brain, the cortex. He also described the form of focal epilepsy which became known as Jacksonian epilepsy. In 1876, by a remarkable quirk of fate, his beloved wife Elizabeth died suddenly following a Jacksonian seizure.

George's epilepsy occurred, like that of Mrs Jackson, because of damage to the part of the brain which controlled movement. George's Jacksonian epilepsy affecting his right side meant he had something on the left side of his brain and he did; he had a benign tumour, a *meningioma* which had grown to the size of a chestnut from the fibrous sheath surrounding his brain. It was removed and George was cured.

Not infrequently interesting cases turned up in young airmen. One such was a lad of twenty-two who had achalasia of the oesophagus, a disorder in which the swallowing mechanism is damaged by degeneration of the tiny nerves in the muscle of the gullet.

The normal swallowing mechanism is a marvel. Once food or drink enters the gullet, it is propelled to the stomach by coordinated contractions. You can swallow standing on your head, if that's your fancy – in fact we had an air commodore surgical consultant who would demonstrate this physiological fact at dining-in nights. We all knew he'd had one over the eight when he jumped on the table, stood on his head and drank a pint of beer without spilling a drop.

Our airman had noticed difficulty with swallowing for about a year. Whatever he took seemed to stick at the level of the lower end of his breastbone. But he recounted with glee that after a few months he had learned a trick. "When I've finished my breakfast, I stand up, grasp the edge of the table and with my mouth closed I squeeze down inside my chest hard and suddenly everything empties, and do you know, sir, if I want to, I can take another helping of sausage, bacon and eggs and when I get a bit peckish late in the morning I just squeeze again."

With achalasia, the oesophagus becomes enormously dilated and capable of holding a vast volume. He told me how he had once lost a girlfriend. "I was out with this girl, she was a real looker, we had a nice fish and chip supper in a pub and during the evening I drank a few pints of Guinness. I'd taken her home and we were sitting in my car. I leaned across to kiss her good night and suddenly she was flooded with a frothing mixture of fish and chips and Guinness. So was the car. I'd forgotten to do my trick."

Achalasia can be temporarily helped by dilating the lower end of the oesophagus with dilators and there is an operation which gives relief; but there's no way of revitalising the nervous mechanism which controls swallowing.

DURING MY SPELL AS A JUNIOR SPECIALIST at Nocton Hall, I did a couple of locum jobs in general practice. They could not have contrasted more. One was in a Yorkshire mining town, the other in the middle of the Lincolnshire fens.

The mining town was depressed and depressing; depressing because general mine closures had turned the place into a ghost town, literally depressed because there were huge dents in the surrounding countryside where mine shafts not maintained for years had collapsed. The town was halfway between two other mining towns called Wombwell and Penistone; names to conjure with.

I stayed at the house of the widowed mother of the doctor I was temporarily replacing. She was a formidable, handsome Yorkshire lady, blunt of speech, tall, grey-haired, imposing of stature with a magnificent bosom capable of supporting a loaded tea tray.

Chatting one evening, I mentioned to her that I had worked as a house surgeon for a consultant, a Yorkshireman called George Larks, and "wasn't that a funny coincidence with our surnames?"

She shot bolt upright. "George Larks!" she exclaimed, "I knew Georgie when I was a nursing sister and he was a house surgeon at the Leeds Royal Infirmary." She went on. "I remember Georgie's mother used to clean floors in the hospital to support him."

It seemed my erstwhile boss hadn't exactly relied on the fees from doing post mortems to keep body and soul together after all.

To those of us from the South of England, the broad Yorkshire accent could be almost impenetrable and many local expressions alien. It took a while to realise that the ladies of the town ended every sentence with "luv" and that when one of the local ladies said she was "On my Honda", she wasn't referring to her motorcycle but to her menstrual cycle. The female genitalia were curiously named – me clacker, me tuppence or me sixpence, although why one clacker should be tuppence and another clacker sixpence baffled me.

Again I was defeated when I paid a home visit to an old chap with heart failure. He was propped up in bed, lips blue and obviously short of breath. I asked him what the problem was; he replied, "Ahm jiggered."

"But do you have any specific symptoms, like perhaps some pain in the chest?"

"Nay lad," he wheezed, "Ahm buggered."

"Yes, but... " I began.

"Listen lad," he retorted obviously thinking he was dealing with a low grade mental defective, or even worse, a Londoner, "Ahm jiggered and Ahm buggered. Ahm reet jiggered and Ahm reet buggered an tha's all there's to it. Now give me some of yer bloody medicine and get me out of this bloody bed."

I sent him to the local hospital where they treated his heart failure and got him out of bed. When I last saw him, his only complaint was of the niggardly compensation the government was giving him for his emphysema after his lungs had been ruined by a lifetime down the pit working at the coal face.

The locum in Lincolnshire was in a village called Martin a few miles from Woodhall Spa. The area was desolate, the country flat. Martin looked like the sort of deserted town one sees in cowboy films with tumbleweed drifting down the main street.

Woodhall Spa is a town with a golf course and a few hundred cottages in which the occupants sit by their fires (even in summer) watching television and waiting for the grim reaper. Any smallholder worth his salt in Lincolnshire would aim to retire to a bungalow in Woodhall. The doctor in Martin had been there for years; his wife said years and years and years. After the doctor had briefed me, she took me aside and I listened for a full half hour to the problems of pernicious boredom, the awful weather, the dull neighbours and the isolation of Martin. After a few days I found that I sympathised with the lady; but there were a few lighter moments.

Surgeries were held in what were once the stables. Usually only a handful of patients turned up but one evening there was a long queue, and it turned out they weren't patients, it was a deputation. Their leader said, "It's Tom in the council houses, been up to his tricks again, needs lockin' up again."

"What do you mean?" I asked.

"Well, he has turns and when he has turns he gets violent. We want you to go and see him and sort him out."

"Tell me more," I gulped.

"Well, like last week after a bad turn he threw his boot through the television and next day he took a hammer to the children's rabbits... killed 'em all. Mind you, doctor," he added, "you'd best be careful. Last year he had our doctor on the floor in the post office and tried to strangle him."

Nervously I asked a few more questions, the most important being, "Where is Tom usually locked up?" It turned out to be the Lincoln County Asylum.

As soon as the deputation left, some giving me sympathetic looks, others shaking my hand, I phoned the asylum and eventually spoke to the mental welfare officer, a jolly sort. He chuckled and said, "That Tom's up to his tricks again, eh? Don't worry doctor, I'll sort him out." And he did; I didn't need to see Tom and what's more I got four and a half guineas for doing nothing except sign a form.

Visits to lonely houses in the fens were time-consuming; addresses were vague. One morning I called at a remote farmhouse and knocked on the door. There was no answer. I let myself in and called a loud "Hallo." To be answered by, "I'm upstairs, darling." Nervously I climbed the stairs and entered the first bedroom where a heavily painted, negligee-clad lady of uncertain years lay on top of the bed. She looked startled and said, "Oh, I thought you were the baker."

NEXT TO NOCTON WAS A VILLAGE CALLED Potterhanworth whose squire was a man named Derek Olds. He had been born in and lived in the Manor House for all his eighty-eight years. He was not only congenitally rich, he had sold three thousand acres of prime agricultural land surrounding Nocton Hall to Smith's. He also owned the living of Nocton parish church. One Easter Sunday when I attended morning service, Squire Olds appeared at the entrance, leaning heavily on his shooting stick, about half an hour after the service had started. The organist stopped, the vicar halted the congregation in the middle of the hymn and stepped from the chancel. He walked the length of the aisle, greeted the squire and escorted him to his private pew next to the choir. The vicar returned to the chancel, announced the arrival of Mr Olds to the congregation, said how much pleasure his presence gave us and then the service continued.

Derek Olds was one of my patients. He had a chest problem, bronchiectasis. This is a condition in which the bronchial tubes are dilated, secretions pool in them and lead to recurrent chest infections. He was admitted a couple of times a year for antibiotic treatment and physiotherapy. He was tall with a shock of wavy white hair setting off his ruddy complexion. His nose was a prize-winner, large, purple, bulbous with dilated and broken veins coursing over it, witness to years of high living. He was loud, he was forthright and his gaze could be forbidding and disconcerting, particularly when he fixed you with his glass eye. Once, because he complained of headaches, we x-rayed his skull. It was peppered with shot and the artificial eye gave it a quizzical look. Rumour had it that he had been married four times but now he lived with his 'housekeeper'. Rumour further had it that at the start of the Second World War he had offered his manor house as accommodation for refugees, but on the understanding that they were all female – and young. This monocular old rogue still (literally) had an eye for the ladies and once when the pretty WRAF catering officer holding her menu list asked, "And what would you like today, Mr Olds?" she was seen milliseconds later, red-faced, rushing from his room.

I visited his home, the Manor House, several times. The walls were covered in huge oil paintings, mostly landscapes and each one, like his skull, peppered with shot holes. I asked what had happened. He said that for many years he had organised Boxing Day pheasant shoots for his pals and afterwards they would get together in his house and drink bucket-loads of champagne. Unfortunately some would bring in their guns and when they became boisterous they would let off a few shots.

"That damn fool, Sir Archie Willoughby from Gainsborough, took me bloody eye out, damn fool!"

MY SPECIALIST EDUCATION INCLUDED A SPELL at the RAF Chest Unit at the King Edward VII Hospital in Midhurst, Sussex. It had been built as a private hospital for 'cases of mild tuberculosis affecting the middle classes'. It was opened by His Majesty in 1906. Edward displayed great interest in the hospital and closely followed its construction, often spending weekends in hotels in Midhurst. At the time some observers claimed he deliberately delayed completing construction for over three years. Our Edward, affectionately known in the family as 'Bertie', was quite a lad and was always accompanied by one or other of his lady friends on those 'working weekends'. After a quick inspection of the building's progress, he would retire to the Spread Eagle or some other hostelry in Midhurst, enjoy a jolly romp, an excellent dinner and a good cigar.

The head physician was Sir Geoffrey Todd, an irascible Australian, short and loud with a pugnacious jutting lower jaw. He was a bachelor and had three favourite pastimes: eating vanilla ice cream, playing snooker and making sure his model railway ran on time.

Each day patients and staff would gather for lunch in the great hall of the hospital. The medical staff sat at a high table looking down on the patients. Came dessert time, he would ask the head waitress, "What do we have today, Doris?"

Doris would reply, "Jam roly poly, cabinet pudding or cream custard, Sir Geoffrey."

"What!" he would cry every day, "Don't you have any vanilla ice-cream?"

"Why, yes we do Sir Geoffrey."

"Well let's have that," he'd say and we all tucked into vanilla ice-cream. It was very good ice-cream, too.

After coffee we would retire to the snooker room, Sir Geoffrey would pick up his special cue and size up the potential competition. On my first day, he challenged me to a game. As a student I had been a competent player and reckoned I could give him a good run for his money, but I had been forewarned by the staff doctors, "Sir Geoffrey's going to ask you to play snooker with him but for heaven's sake please let him win. He's bad-tempered enough but if he's beaten he's insufferable." It took all my skill to line up easy pots for him. He could see I knew how to play and that made him all the happier to win.

On one occasion out of the blue he said to me, "Larkworthy, where do you get your shoes made?" I usually bought my shoes at one of the many high street shoe shops but, startled, I replied, "Poulson and Skone, Sir Geoffrey." This was because some years previously, in Germany, I had had a pair of their dress boots made for my mess kit. The shoemaker's representative had visited the Officers' Mess.

"Where are they?" he asked.

"Leicester Square, I think."

"But where exactly?" he demanded.

"I don't know," I said, "I get them to send their man to me."

In order to advance to become a consultant in general medicine, an essential qualification is the possession of the diploma of Membership of the Royal College of Physicians (MRCP), a tough examination. It is held in two parts. I took and passed the first part a year after arriving at Nocton Hall but it took me two attempts and two years further study to pass the second part.

Six

WITHIN A MONTH OF OBTAINING the MRCP diploma, I was graded Senior Specialist in Medicine and to my delight posted to a Royal Australian Air Force hospital at Butterworth on the west coast of the Malaysian peninsula, opposite the island of Penang.

The military base at Butterworth had been established in the Thirties by the RAF as a staging post between Singapore and Colombo. At the outbreak of war with Japan in 1941, it was reinforced with Bristol Blenheim bombers and Brewster Buffalo fighters, to little effect. When the Japanese invasion forces swept through the peninsula, Butterworth was attacked by Japanese bombers and Mitsubishi Zero fighters. The Blenheims were destroyed on the ground and the outclassed Buffaloes offered practically no resistance.

After the war, British forces re-established their presence in Malaya, as it was known until independence in 1957. I found it a fascinating country with marvellous cultural diversity. The late Sixties was an interesting time to be there.

Malaysia is a constitutional monarchy, a federation of independent states at the heart of Southeast Asia. Before Europeans started meddling in its affairs in the seventeenth century, it was a Hindu and Muslim country. The Portuguese, Dutch and British vied for control with, as usual, perfidious Albion coming out on top.

In 1786, Sir Francis Light of the British East India Company ceded the island of Penang from the Sultan of Kedah by offering him protection and lots of money. A few years later, land on the mainland opposite Penang was also ceded and became known as Province Wellesley. The Straits Settlements were formed by the administrative union of Penang, Malacca and Singapore. William T Butterworth was governor of Singapore and Malacca from 1843 to 1855 and the principal town of Province Wellesley was named for him, hence an extremely English name for a very Malaysian town.

Three miles off the coast and three-quarters of the way between Singapore and the Thai border sits Penang. Known as the Pearl of the Orient, it is an attractive island with the peak of Penang Hill almost permanently surrounded by a collar of orographic cloud. Penang's capital, Georgetown, was named for King George III ('Mad George', the one who lost us the American colonies). It became a thriving metropolis noted for its brothels and entrepot trade, including opium. Today it is a bustling, mainly Chinese, city of 400,000 with a booming trade in tourism.

Butterworth has a population of more than 100,000. In my day, forty years ago, Butterworth smelted tin, made biscuits and chilli sauce. It also had the smelliest drains in Southeast Asia and markets with smells to rival the drains. Piles of fly-ridden fish and prawns dried in the sun and in season the vile smell of the durian fruit pervaded the air.

Durian is legendary. Describing its smell gives rise to flights of noxious fancy: rotting pineapples in sewers, stale strawberry ice cream in a badly kept public lavatory, carrion in custard etc. And the taste? Sublime to those who can get past the smell.

The fruit is large, up to a foot long and weighing up to seven pounds; greyish yellow green, its husk covered in spikes and when sliced open contains seeds in a pale yellow flesh. To Malaysians the 'king of fruits', durians grow on trees and are aphrodisiac. When a ripe durian falls off the tree it hits the ground with a mighty thump which always provokes locals to say with a twinkle, "When the durians are down, the saris are up."

One of the greatest misfortunes in the durian season is to get stuck on a narrow Malaysian road behind a lorry loaded with durians and belching diesel fumes. By contrast, there is another 'laden lorry' that is fun to get stuck behind, the pig transport. The ever-ingenious Chinese solve the problem of taking large numbers of pigs to market in one lorry by getting them sloshed on mash spiked with alcohol. The tipsy pigs are put into separate sacks which are piled high in layers on a lorry. To drive behind a lorry load of drooling, inebriated pigs, their heads lolling and facing you in their sacks is, to say the least, a unique experience.

FOR MORE THAN A DECADE UP to 1960, Chinese guerrillas of the Malaysian Communist Party, under their leader Chin Peng, carried out a campaign of terror to take over the country. They had been well armed and air-supplied

Squadron Leader: senior RAF officer in Malaysia, 1970.

by the British during the war against Japan. After the war they became the target of Royal Australian Air Force (RAAF) Canberra bombers and F-86 Sabre fighters based at Butterworth which flew missions against the guerrillas, destroying them in their jungle strongholds.

In the Sixties, Australia became nervous of the increasing communist influence in Southeast Asia and needed a permanent base in the area. RAF Butterworth was turned over to the RAAF which installed a squadron of Dassault Mirage fighters to support Malaysia's defence against Indonesia, which had threatened to crush the newly formed Federated Malay States. A squadron of Lockheed C-130 Hercules transports was based at Butterworth to support the Australian military, by then involved in the war in Vietnam.

The RAAF medical branch was small and had no specialists in its ranks. Specialists for the base hospital at Butterworth were loaned by the RAF. I was sent to Malaysia as the senior medical specialist to the Australian armed forces. At the same time, holding the rank of squadron leader, I was the senior RAF officer Peninsular Malaysia and – to my astonishment – discovered that I held powers of subordinate command. This meant that I could hear charges and award punishments – something entirely foreign to my nature, especially as I hadn't a clue about RAF law.

In addition to the medical specialist services for the Australians and their dependents, I looked after all the other military forces in the area and their families, British and Gurkha. The 10th Princess Mary's Gurkha Rifles was based on Penang Island in Minden Barracks and another battalion at the Gurkha Training Depot at Sungai Patani, fifteen miles to the north of Butterworth.

Gurkhas are special. Although they're regarded simply as mercenaries by British civil servants, they are the most loyal and fearless soldiers Britain has ever had. Friendly and with a raunchy sense of humour, their discipline is impeccable. They come from hilly country in Nepal; they're short legged, tough and ideally suited to operations in rugged terrain. And they have their own special weapon, the *kukri*, a large curved knife which they use with consummate expertise.

Even as patients in hospital Gurkhas showed intense discipline. If a Gurkha did not jump out of bed and stand to attention, or at least come to attention in bed, you knew he was really sick. The enquiry *"Timi costa tcha?"* (How are you?) would invariably be met with *"Ram ro, sahib"* (I am fine) even if he was slipping into coma before your eyes.

One Monday morning a Gurkha warrant officer was referred to me with a wrist drop; his right hand was floppy and his wrist flexed, he couldn't raise his hand and to his distress he couldn't salute – a simple case of Saturday night palsy.

The name gives the clue to the cause. The palsy happens when, overcome with alcohol-induced fatigue (totally sloshed), the subject falls deeply asleep slumped in a chair with his arm over its back. The nerve that controls the muscles which extend the wrist runs in a groove down the inside of the humerus, the bone of the upper arm, and is compressed between that bone and the back of the chair. After several hours of unremitting compression, the nerve no longer works and when the hungover subject eventually wakes up, to his horror he finds his wrist paralysed. Invariably recovery is spontaneous, like a nerve of sensation which has 'gone to sleep', but a Saturday night palsy takes several days to come round.

After I examined him I said, "Warrant officer, were you drinking on Saturday night?"

"No, doctor *sahib*," he replied, apparently shocked that I should ask such a question. "Doctor *sahib*, I do not drink," he added.

I reassured him and told him that the paralysis would recover with no treatment and that I would see him in a week's time.

A week later the paralysis had gone and he was able to give me a smart salute. He stood before me holding his left hand behind his back and asked, "Doctor *sahib*, how did you know I drink? I lied to you; I had taken very big lot of rum." I indicated that we doctors know a thing or two and it is always a waste of time lying to us. He then produced a *kukri* from behind his back (he was the warrant officer in charge of equipment) saying, "This is for you, doctor *sahib*, you are clever man."

I still have that *kukri*. The sheath is made of ox hide, the handle of ox horn and there are two additional small blades incorporated in the sheath, one to sharpen the wicked blade and the other a small knife. Tradition dictates that, once drawn, a *kukri* cannot be re-sheathed unless blood has

Author sharpening memories: the warrant officer's kukri – bloodshed optional.

been shed, which is where the small knife proves useful, to nick a finger or thumb to draw blood.

It was not unusual to admit groups of Gurkha soldiers with fever after they had been on jungle exercises. The differential diagnosis was usually simple, one of three conditions: malaria, scrub typhus or leptospirosis. The challenge was to make the diagnosis quickly and to get it right as the treatment for each was different.

Apart from the east coast of Peninsular Malaysia where *falciparum* malaria (the very nasty form) existed, the malaria encountered in the jungle was the benign form, *vivax* malaria, which responded very well to treatment with chloroquine. Blood samples had to be examined rapidly in all cases of fever; malaria could be diagnosed and treated with confidence when the parasites were spotted in the blood smears.

As with the Lincolnshire butcher and the moonshine makers in the Seychelles with leptospirosis, the history gave the clue – the soldiers had been fording a river when one dropped his rifle and the whole platoon spent a pleasant interlude diving in the water and searching for it. But rats infest jungle rivers and infect them with their bacteria-laden urine. One of the features of leptospirosis is that it inflames the kidneys and a quick and easy microscopic examination of a specimen of urine reveals the presence of blood cells.

With scrub typhus, the usual story was that a platoon spent a night in a deserted jungle village. The illness results from the bite of mites infected with an organism with the euphonious name, *orientia tsutsugamushi*. The mites live on rats and other rodents living in scrubland and in the straw huts of deserted villages. Soldiers on jungle patrol find deserted villages a ready-made comfortable billet, unaware that they are providing supper for the infected mites. A diagnostic feature of scrub typhus is a black scab called an eschar. This is where the mites have bitten and is often found (if looked for) on the upper inner thigh.

The treatment of all three conditions was simple, they responded quickly to the correct medication, but the diagnosis had to be right from the start.

Other soldiers patrolling the jungle included the SAS who sometimes spent weeks in its depths searching for communist terrorists. Occasionally one would present with a fever which needed diagnosis but on one occasion three were admitted together. They had been ambushed and were brought in by helicopter. One had a large leg wound which even after only a few hours exposure was already crawling with maggots, another had a head wound which was not serious and the third had been shot in the chest but was uncomplaining. There was an entry wound at the top of his sternum but no exit wound and no indication of any injury to vital structures in his chest. I was told that the chest x-ray showed no abnormality but when I looked carefully at it and held it at various angles the bullet could be seen overlying his liver; the thickness of the liver in profile had virtually the same density on x-ray as the lead bullet, rendering the bullet almost invisible. The bullet had pierced his skin, struck the upper breast bone and tracked down under the skin for eighteen inches to lie over the liver. It had caused no serious damage and was easily taken out under local anaesthetic.

He was lucky he hadn't been shot with a high-velocity weapon; a bullet to the upper sternum would blast straight through and spell curtains for the victim. But in his case he had been shot by a tommy gun, a low-velocity weapon and a legacy of British generosity to Chin Peng during the Japanese War.

ONE OF MY MORE PLEASURABLE DUTIES was to visit a British military hospital in the Cameron Highlands. The hospital was for convalescent patients and the beautiful climate of the highlands, like a permanent English spring, contrasted with the ever-present heat and humidity that made life on the coastal plains tedious and enervating for Europeans. To get there from Butterworth would have taken a couple of days by road so my monthly visit was by helicopter. As the aircraft skimmed over the jungle canopy with wisps of cloud clinging to the trees, the beat of the rotors would startle exotic, colourful birds and less exotic, native villagers; short, brown, bow-legged people dressed in loin cloths — the *orang-asli,* Malay for 'the original people'.

The *orang-asli* hunted small animals with blowpipes but were just discovering a larger, more valuable prey: tourists. They use blowpipes up to three metres long to fire poison-tipped darts fashioned from sharpened slivers of bamboo. The rear end of the dart is inserted into a cork-shaped piece of wood, the dart is introduced into the blowpipe with a pledget of kapok behind, the mouth applied, blowpipe aimed and with a puff the dart flies up to twelve metres. Fortunately neither the indigenous primates, the

Ye Olde Smokehouse: a pleasant surprise in the rolling hills of Malaysia.

orang-utan, men of the woods, nor the *orang-puteh,* white people, are part of their diet but they quickly developed a taste for the cash of tourists..

Nowadays the *orang-asli* total about 140,000 and are scattered throughout peninsular Malaysia. Although marginalised by previous British and Malaysian governments, their native title rights have recently been recognised and as part of the racial unification of Malaysia they have been renamed *orang-kita,* our people.

At the military hospital, an army doctor looked after the patients so there was seldom need for my specialist services, but the change of climate was as delightful and invigorating as it must have been in 1885 when an English colonial surveyor called Cameron visited. He described the area as quiet jungle-clad rolling hills with a pleasing climate. Today that has given way to a thriving tourist industry, large tea plantations, terraced cultivation and vegetable gardens.

One particularly pleasant surprise was Foster's Smokehouse, a mock-Tudor style imitation English country house where one could enjoy Devon cream teas in the afternoon and roast dinners in the evening. Owned at that time by the eccentric Colonel Foster, it was a magnet for Europeans seeking relief from the oppressive climate. In later years, the colonel became very particular about his guests and long-haired, hippie-styled folk were shown the door, if necessary at the end of his twelve-bore.

On the return flight, especially if the pilot of the helicopter was in the Royal Malaysian Air Force, as we approached the Straits of Penang we would swoop close to the sea, startling fishermen who sometimes took fright and dived off their fishing *praus*.

The shoe was on the other foot when I had a ride in the back seat of an RAAF Mirage IIID, the training model of their ground attack fighter. As I sat there in flying suit, helmet and oxygen mask, the Aussie flight sergeant ground crew pleaded with me as he strapped me in, "Please, please sir, don't chuck up into the oxygen mask – it takes me four hours to clean the thing. If you are going to throw up, for God's sake whip off the mask."

It got worse. He leaned over into the cockpit, pointed down and said, "When you land, a parachute is deployed to slow your speed. Look down there to your left: you see that red lever? When the parachute is deployed, that little

Malaysian terraced cultivation, Cameron Highlands.

beaut shoots out – if your leg is in the way, you can say goodbye to your knee."
With those comforting words he climbed down and I closed the canopy.

We taxied to the end of the runway, sat there for a couple of minutes
revving our engine, waiting to be cleared for take-off. As soon as it came,
the pilot – an RAAF squadron leader, a jolly down-to-earth sort – released
the brakes and with what felt like an almighty kick in my back we bounded
forward and ascended almost vertically, did a couple of rolls at the top of
our climb then, with palpable relief for me, we flattened out and proceeded
like a bat out of hell on our mission at 35,000 feet. We were to inspect an
uninhabited island off the east coast of Malaysia that was regularly used for
practice bombing to make sure, before the action began, that no fishermen
had tied up there to have a siesta.

In half an hour, the pilot spotted the island and in a steep dive descended
to a thousand feet. "Look down, Bill, and let me know if you see any fishing
boats or activity on the island. We are going to do a few circuits to make
sure. Okay?"

"Okay," I said with confidence. My stomach had returned to its normal
anatomical position and I was starting to enjoy the trip. And then... he
inverted the aircraft; my eyes crossed; we flew upside down round and
round that cursed island; I tried to keep a look out but I couldn't focus and
then after six circuits the nausea started. It rapidly worsened. I remembered
the flight sergeant's parting words; I had to tell the pilot and managed to
croak, "I'm think I'm going to throw up."

"No problem, Bill, the island's clear, let's go home." With those sweet
words, he righted the Mirage.

As we landed, I remembered the flight sergeant's words again and my left
knee has served me well these past forty years.

PENANG NEVER FAILED TO IMPRESS ME with its variety of ethnic foods and
religious festivals; it had more than three dozen each year, Chinese, Tamil,
Hindu, Muslim and Christian. One of the most spectacular was Thaipusam,
a Hindu festival occurring early in the year and celebrating the day that
Lord Siva's son, Lord Meruga, banished three demons. A procession led by
a silver chariot would wend through the streets; coconuts would be dashed
to the ground (with Chinese children darting in to pick up the pieces) and
devotees walking barefoot in penance. Many carried *kavadis* which are box-

like structures attached to the body by chains hooked into the skin. Some *kavadis* are large metal frames and are similarly attached. Many in the procession would have small spears thrust through their tongues and cheeks with no bleeding and many would also have limes and lemons on chains attached to hooks through the skin of the chest and back. Most of the devotees appeared to be in a trance and those with metalwork thrust through their cheeks and tongues drooled incessantly.

It was claimed that no hypnotic substances were used and that the trance-like state and insensibility to pain was the result of forty days of fasting, praying and avoiding all temptations. However I noticed that the devotees were covered in a curious white powder, and when I stood in the temple before the start of the procession there were certainly some funny fumes wafting around which made me feel quite pleasantly giddy.

Curious, I asked a Chinese bystander what purpose the *kavadis*, spears and limes on hooks served. He told me that the penitents were either giving thanks for an important event in the previous year, recovery of a very sick child for example or in the hopes of good fortune in the coming year. Not so different from other religious displays, a view reinforced many years later when I visited Santiago de Compostela in Spain and Fatima in Portugal.

The Gurkhas had their own version of the Hindu festival, Dashera, in the autumn. It was very important as it would determine the regiment's fortune for the following year.

The ceremony was held on the parade ground at the Gurkha training depot at Sungei Patani. One morning in October, I was among the officers seated on a dais with the colonel commanding in the middle and the soldiers with their excited chattering families around the periphery. The focal point was a large stake driven into the ground. The ceremony involved chopping off the heads of various creatures, working up to beheading a buffalo. This would be the culmination: the neck had to be completely and cleanly severed with one blow. Failure – even a thin rim of skin connecting – would lead to a year of disasters, bad luck, illness and failure in any military endeavour.

A muscular Gurkha was selected to wield the sword. Muscles rippling, dressed only in a white loincloth, he was armed with what appeared to be an outsize *kukri*, a very sharp sword called a *kukruji*. To test the temper of the blade a large papaya on four wooden stilts was placed in front of the stake. The swordsman raised the *kukruji* and let it gently descend through the middle of the fruit, slicing through with no force. He then executed half a dozen chickens, whipping off heads at lightning speed and dropping the headless chicken to run amok to the delight of the shrieking Gurkha children. Ducks followed, not as much fun, but then we moved on to larger victims. A couple of sheep preceded several goats. The area around the stake was drenched in blood by the time we reached the finale.

Half a dozen uniformed soldiers dragged a buffalo into the arena. It was held by numerous ropes and the head tied to the stake. The soldiers at the rear pulled, the neck stretched, everybody held their breath, the sword flashed, the head was completely off in one blow and triumphantly the soldiers dragged the carcass around the parade ground; blood was gushing from the root of the neck in diminishing spouts. Happiness abounded, the colonel tied a ceremonial white turban around the head of our skilful sword wielder, drinks were handed round, toasts drunk and next year would be good for the regiment and everybody.

Not so for the Gurkha battalion on Penang Island. At Minden Barracks, the unthinkable happened: a botched job, two blows and everybody silently returned to their quarters. Misery hung in the air – but it wasn't to last.

At the time I had a young Gurkha, a girl of twenty-two, in my ward severely ill with *systemic lupus erythematosus* – a disease mainly of young women in which the immune system turns in on itself and causes inflammation of every part and system of the body. She was not responding to treatment, the illness was aggressive and had badly affected her heart, lungs, joints and kidneys. The poor girl died at four in the morning. She was the daughter of a sergeant at Minden Barracks, it was a disaster… but in one fell swoop her misfortune had consumed all the bad luck of the coming year.

About that time, I was to exercise – for the only occasion in my career – my power of subordinate command. One of our laboratory technicians had lost his 1369. The Form 1369 is an identity card which must be carried at all times. If lost it could fall into enemy hands and be used to infiltrate command headquarters. I wondered how a junior lab tech's 1369 could hold a key to the disruption of the military might of the Allies in Southeast Asia, but in any event it was an offence.

I read up what seemed relevant in the Manual of Law for the Royal Air Force and one afternoon sat in my airconditioned consulting room at the appointed hour. Promptly came the sound of clumping boots and "Left right, left right, left wheel," a loud knock on my door and in marched the flight sergeant in charge of discipline, two RAF policemen and the prisoner. "Hat off, attenshun!" yelled the flight sergeant. The prisoner, Junior Technician Evans, was well known to me, a happy-go-lucky Welsh lad and a very good laboratory technician. I sat there wearing my cap and attempting to look severe, but not entirely succeeding in erasing the smile on my face and squirming in my seat.

"Well Evans?" I demanded. "How do you account for this problem?"

"I can't, sir," he replied. "I found I'd lost my ID when I returned from a night in Penang, sir."

That appeared to be it, his record was unblemished and there were no other charges. "Will you accept my punishment?" I asked.

"Yes, sir," he replied without a trace of apprehension.

"Junior Technician Evans, I hereby admonish you for the loss of your identity card, form 1369, and I award you one month's extra duties." Evans accepted and signed the form.

"Hat on! Salute! About turn, quick march!" shouted the flight sergeant. I completed the paperwork and sent it off to headquarters in Singapore.

A week later I had a call from the provost marshal's office in Singapore. A very uptight legal wing commander demanded, "What the bloody hell are you up to, Larkworthy?" I asked him what the problem was.

"Problem?" he said, "Problem, you've gone and awarded two punishments for one offence; extra duties is a punishment and so is an admonishment. And what's more, you cannot award extra duties to an airman, only to boy entrants. The whole damn nonsense is quashed." With that he slammed down the phone and I felt abashed... just a little.

On the other hand, Evans was happy, no entry blotted his record sheet and when I told him he had no extra duties because of an 'administrative error', he grinned and said, "Me and the lads were wondering, sir, when we could have another court martial."

THROUGHOUT MY TOUR AT BUTTERWORTH, the Australians were fighting in Vietnam alongside the Americans. Each week we received a Hercules plane load of war casualties, mostly surgical cases needing rest and treatment to make them fit for the twelve-hour flight to Australia. At the same time, Malaysia was going through a period of turmoil. The mainly Chinese

Malaysian Communist Party (MCP) was provocatively planting red flags at road junctions, sometimes with bombs attached. Simmering racial tension between Chinese and Malays came to a head on 13 May 1969 after the federal elections. Riots broke out in the capital, Kuala Lumpur, hundreds were killed and millions of dollars worth of property destroyed. An emergency was declared, Butterworth was put on the highest alert and a curfew imposed for four days. Most of the rioting was confined to the capital but there were sporadic outbreaks in Penang where tension had been heightened by the murder of a Malaysian national party agent by Chinese youths on 10 May. For me, the tension was more imagined than real; rioters steer clear of military bases. A few months earlier, when the Gurkhas were called out to a riot in Penang, they simply lined up facing the screaming throng and drew their *kukris* – in no time the mob dispersed without a murmur.

In 1971, the Training Depot of the Brigade of Gurkhas was moved from Sungai Patani to Hong Kong and I was posted back to England. I attended the ceremonial Beating of the Retreat at Sungai Patani. This marked its closure. We sat on the same dais as we did for the Dashera. The Gurkhas marched, wheeled and saluted as only Gurkhas can. The Gurkha bagpipe band played mournful Scottish airs; in the far distance a train's whistle wailed and, right in front of me, the largest bee I have ever seen became entangled in the hair of the wife of the commanding officer. It was time to go.

Seven

RETURNING TO THE GREY SKIES AND grey people of England was a shock to the system after vibrant Malaysia but, no matter, a new and exciting chapter was unrolling. I had been given a year's study-leave. The head honcho of physicians, or more correctly, the Air Marshal Consultant Adviser in Medicine to the Royal Air Force, had decreed that his consultants should have training in children's diseases. Hence I found myself, at thirty-eight years of age, a hospital resident once more, living in decrepit Dickensian quarters in what was to become St George's Hospital, Tooting, South London, where the first half of my leave was to be spent in paediatrics before I could move on to my real interest, gastroenterology.

The original St George's had been built 250 years before in central London at Hyde Park Corner. With no room for expansion, a larger new site had been found at Tooting, where the Grove and the adjacent Fountain Fever hospitals stood. They had been built by the Metropolitan Asylum Board in a matter of weeks in the 1890s to accommodate the victims of waves of scarlet fever and diphtheria which afflicted London's children; diseases which scarcely exist these days in the developed world, thanks to antibiotics and immunisation programmes. The Grove and Fountain hospitals were to be demolished in a couple of years when the spanking new St George's had been completed.

I moved into St George's when it was in transition. Some clinics and the maternity services still carried on in the old hospital at Hyde Park Corner. Construction of the new hospital at Tooting had just started but the transferred hospital was housed in the old Victorian fever wards.

For six months, I lived in the old nurses' residence, a large block of discoloured ochre brick, black paintwork and curlicue cast iron guttering, flanked on one side by a busy London arterial road and on the other side by the twenty-four-hour ambulance entrance for emergencies. In its bowels an ancient central heating system clanked, groaned, occasionally exploded and regularly deployed an army of cockroaches which popped up everywhere; beneath pillows, between book leaves, in shoes. They especially enjoying the showers, where they marched in file across the ceiling, dropping off to be crunched under bare feet. Lovely.

I wasn't sure how I fitted into the paediatric scene, having recently returned from Malaysia where I had dealt with all kinds of diseases from the mundane to the exotic. Now I found myself looking after these small creatures, scarcely knowing one end from the other; moreover I was expected to teach senior medical students about them. I had to stay one step ahead: select a subject and bone up on it the night before to appear suave, knowledgeable and experienced the next day.

One of my duties was to care for newborns delivered by Caesarean section. The operations took place at Hyde Park Corner some six miles from Tooting – as the crow flies, but infinitely longer through the congested roads of Balham and Clapham. Occasionally there was good warning of an upcoming operation but both ends of a baby's nine-month sojourn, conception and delivery, are rushed jobs. I would receive the mucky, mewling infant, if necessary work on it to make sure it was in good shape and then order the transfer to the neonatal nursery. This was accomplished using a contraption constructed by Archimedes. The infant would be put in a cradle, the cradle placed in a hole in the operating theatre wall at the top of a shaft. Then an orderly would turn a large wheel adjacent to the hole; the unaccompanied baby would be wound slowly down the shaft from the operating theatre to the nursery. Meanwhile I would dash down four flights of stairs to receive – we hoped – an intact infant.

My boss, Dr Cyril Kesson, the senior consultant paediatrician, was a pleasant cove: old school, dapper, gold-rimmed half-moon spectacles perched on the tip of his nose. From time to time Cyril would take them off, and while pontificating twirl them around his fingers; now and again they would slip and fly across the room… he broke three pairs in my six months with him.

He was also an examiner for a qualifying body, the Conjoint Board of the Royal College of Physicians of London and the Royal College of Surgeons of England. The examination was known simply as the 'conjoint' and possession of it allowed one to practise. In that era, there were other qualifications equally recognised by the General Medical Council, the body which rules doctors qualifications, behaviour and fitness to practise. One was a licence granted by the Worshipful Society of Apothecaries of London that enabled the holder to practise medicine and also to drive sheep across London Bridge. A story, apocryphal I suspect, is that between the wars a Dublin college would grant a diploma, the Licentiate of Apothecaries Hall, to those who had taken a ferry across the Irish Channel, forked out generously and answered a few questions; all achieved in time to catch the return ferry. These were known as 'steamboat degrees'.

The conjoint became defunct in 1999 but when, over twenty-five years before that, Dr Kesson asked me to act as registrar for the conjoint examination, I readily agreed. It would be an interesting experience. My enthusiasm increased when he told me I would pick up a tenner for the day.

The examinations were held in Examination Hall in Queen Square, central London, a stone's throw from the British Museum. My job was to coordinate patients, candidates and examiners, the latter being the most difficult. Some of the patients were 'professionals' who had attended regularly for years, picked up a fiver for each session. They were so versed in their illnesses, their physical signs, the examiners' questions and the correct answers that, if kindly disposed to a nervous candidate, they could give *sotto voce* all the information that was needed to pass.

The candidates had forty minutes to take a history and examine a long case and would then be shown short cases which usually consisted of eliciting a physical sign, such as an enlarged spleen, a heart murmur, a lump in the belly or a skin eruption. They would then have to make a sensible stab at the diagnosis and discuss management.

As I stood directing the traffic, I well recalled my own experience a few years before when I was examined in the short cases for the MRCP at the old Charing Cross Hospital, a red brick building off the Strand. I was told to examine the eyes of three little old ladies sitting in a row. They were tiny, grey haired, sweet old ladies, draped in white crocheted shawls. The diagnosis was a pushover, their pupils were constricted, irregular, unequal in size and didn't react when I shone a torch at them but did react (accommodate) when I asked them to look at my finger held a few inches away.

"Well?" queried the examiner.

"Argyll Robertson pupils," said I.

"Cause?"

"Syphilis, sir."

"Quite right," said the examiner, "what are you going to do about it?"

"I'd give them a course of penicillin but it's a bit too late to expect any effect."

"Quite so," said the examiner, "on yer way, lad." I smiled at the three little old ladies and they beamed coquettishly at me, no doubt happily recalling their previous careers beneath the lamp posts of foggy London town... as I left one even winked, covering one of her irregular constricted pupils. 'Prostitute's pupils' is what Douglas Argyll Robertson, a Scottish ophthalmologist, called the condition he described in 1869 that was subsequently to be named as his pupils. He correctly associated them with syphilis of the nervous system. Later a wag was to remark that Robertson's original name was apposite since the pupils "accommodate but do not react".

But the diagnosis I made that really impressed the examiners – and here I make no apology for blowing my own trumpet: it was one of those satisfying triumphs that happen now and then – came in the second part of that clinical examination I took at the old Charing Cross. My examiner, tall, distinguished, grey haired, kindly and courtly, took me to see a young West Indian woman and handed me an ophthalmoscope to examine the interior of her eyes. In passing I noticed that the skin on her neck was abnormal, resembled that of a plucked chicken, yellow with little lumps. Examining her eyes, I found many curious streaks crossing her retinae.

"What do you think?" demanded the examiner.

Without hesitation I replied, "*Pseudoxanthoma elasticum*, also known as the Grönblad-Strandberg syndrome, sir." I was right and he was impressed.

"Why do you think she was admitted?" he asked.

I ventured that she might have had a haematemesis (vomited blood).

"Yes," he said, his eyes lighting up. Delighted, he put an arm around my shoulder. "Don't tell anyone else," he cautioned.

I had read about it but never seen a case of *pseudoxanthoma elasticum* (PXE). It somehow seemed that I had plucked the diagnosis out of thin air. PXE is a rare genetic disorder that affects the eyes, the skin of the neck and armpits, the heart and the stomach – from which bleeding commonly occurs, hence her admission with haematemesis. In forty-four years of specialist and general medical practice, I did not see another case.

Back to the examination hall in Queen Square. The morning session had passed uneventfully; most candidates had done well, the examiners were jolly and the subjects behaved well, apart from one, a cheerful Cockney in his sixties who seemed confused. The morning's candidates had left, fivers were handed out to the subjects and the examiners went off for lunch.

At two o'clock the show recommenced, patients reappeared, candidates nervously filed in and I began to allocate the long cases. One candidate, a loud irritating gentleman from the subcontinent, pushed himself to the fore, so I awarded him the confused Cockney. Within minutes peace reigned; the examinees were down to business of taking histories and examining their subjects. Suddenly there was an eruption, and the candidate examining the Cockney burst upon me.

"This is absolutely disgraceful," he shouted. "You have given me a lunatic, I cannot take a history, I cannot take this examination, I am insulted, I am leaving." With that he flounced out of the room.

Curious, I went to have a word with his subject. I hadn't realised that he had spent his morning's earnings in Peter's Bar in Southampton Row, just around the corner from examination hall. He reeked of booze and was tight.

I understood the candidate's confusion but not his action. He should neither have taken offence nor departed in such a huff. It's difficult to take a history from a drunk but in itself that's a very easy diagnosis and doesn't need medical training. Although he was drunk, it was simple to demonstrate the obvious physical signs of chronic liver disease.

If, when he appeared before the examiners, the candidate had said, "I couldn't take a history, the patient was drunk," he would have immediately scored. If he had then said, "But I examined him as best I could and he has a large irregular liver, his spleen is palpable, there is free fluid in his belly, his parotid glands are enlarged and he has numerous spider *naevi* (dilated spidery veins) on his chest and back. I could not examine his nervous system because he was uncooperative. In my opinion he has chronic liver disease, probable cirrhosis and the cause is most likely alcoholism," he would have sailed through the exam.

The next time I visited the examination hall, I was a candidate myself. Having completed six months paediatrics, I was eligible to take the Diploma in Child Health (DCH) examination. In the morning, the written part – multiple choice and short essay questions – seemed easy enough. In the afternoon I presented myself, suitably decked out in a dark three-piece suit, white shirt, college tie, polished shoes and stethoscope at the ready, for the clinical exams.

The senior examiner, a grumpy, grey-haired curmudgeon barked, "What's that tie you're wearing?" I told him it was the tie of the Royal College of Physicians of Edinburgh.

"Are you a member?"

"I am," I proudly replied.

"So why are you taking this examination?" he demanded. I told him I was in the Royal Air Force and it was thought I should have some experience in paediatrics and that the DCH would show that indeed I had.

He harrumphed and turned to the other examiner, a much younger paediatrician, about my age. Discomfited by his colleague's surliness, he looked sympathetically at me, smiled and said, "Tell me, since you are clearly more of a physician for adults, which diseases do children get which adults also suffer from?"

I looked at him, slightly stunned, and smiled back. "Well, it seems to me that children suffer from nearly all the diseases of adults. They can even suffer from some of the degenerative diseases we usually see in adults in old age."

He smiled again. "Y-e-s," he said. "Yes, that was a particularly stupid question wasn't it?" I smiled, he said, "So tell me about the complications to the foetus of rubella (German measles) in a pregnant woman."

MY DCH DIPLOMA IN HAND, MY STINT in paediatrics over, I was able to begin what I really wanted to do. This was to further my experience and knowledge in gastroenterology, the study of diseases of the stomach, intestines and liver. I'm not sure how I became so attracted to the subject but it held exciting possibilities and with the recent developments of the science of fiberoptics and the invention of marvellous flexible endoscopes, a whole new world opened up. You could now directly inspect, diagnose and often treat diseases of the gut from literally top to bottom – gastroenterology had taken, like the American astronauts said about mankind three years before, a giant leap forward.

When I was a junior specialist at Nocton Hall, I went to Addenbrooke's Hospital, Cambridge to learn the technique of taking a biopsy from the

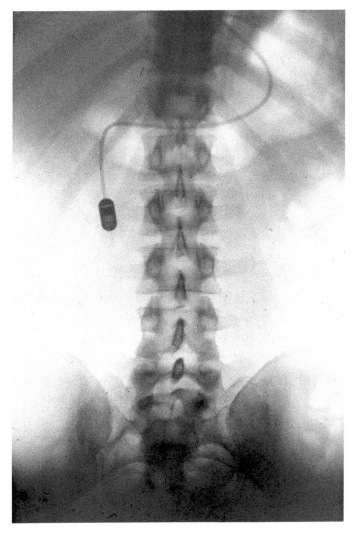

X-ray showing a small intestine biopsy capsule in the duodenum.

small intestine by using a metal capsule about the size of a boiled sweet attached to a narrow tube and swallowed by the patient.

A biopsy is a piece of tissue taken to help make a diagnosis, usually by microscopic analysis, of a disease. The small intestine (the part of the intestine concerned with digestion and absorption) has a special lining and by examining a biopsy of this lining, many diseases can be diagnosed. The capsule has a hole in its side and inside a blade triggered by a spring. When suction is applied to the tube, a small piece of intestinal lining is sucked in through the hole and bulges into the capsule, the spring is triggered and the blade swings around to cut off the projecting tiny piece of intestinal lining. The capsule is then hauled up like a lobster trap, the biopsy taken out and examined.

I was always of a practical turn of mind and the intricacies of assembling, loading, introducing, firing, retrieving and examining the biopsy appealed immensely, but not half as much as the thought that one was now able, for the first time, to access in the living body something that until now had been hidden.

Man has always been curious, wanting to know how things are structured and how they work. Up to the early twentieth century the only way he could effectively study the inner workings of his fellow creatures was by cutting them open, but this held a caveat: the subject had to be dead. As early as 400BC, in the era of Hippocrates, attempts had been made to peek inside. The Romans developed tubes for looking into the rectum and vagina. Such instruments, called *specula*, were found in the ashes of Pompeii, preserved for all time when Vesuvius erupted in the first century AD. But it was not until the second half of the twentieth century that flexible fiberscopes with adequate light sources (it's very dark in there; you need your own flashlight) were developed – and I was in at the start.

Fiberoptic endoscopy was in its infancy; indeed the clinical speciality of gastroenterology had yet to assume its current pre-eminent status. I was fortunate in once more being attached to that pinnacle of academic medicine, University College Hospital, and to another renowned centre, St Mark's Hospital in the City Road. But I would not be resident at those hospitals and first I needed to find somewhere to live.

There are plenty of accommodation agencies in London. I picked one in Oxford Street which directed me to an address in Golders Green, an area in London famous on two accounts: its crematorium and its large Jewish population. I was sent to a Mrs Rosen and was told by the agency staff that she was very particular about whom she accepted; she was.

She subjected me to a stiff oral examination lasting twenty minutes. When I told her I was a doctor, she demanded proof. I showed her correspondence in my briefcase and her eyes sparkled when she saw I would be attached to University College Hospital – UCH is popular in Golders Green. She showed me my bed-sit, a very large room overlooking a park, quiet, practically no traffic. I accepted her offer, she accepted me as a tenant for six months.

She invited me to take tea and we sat in her sitting room which reeked of lavender-perfumed furniture polish and so crammed with glittering expensive furniture it was difficult to negotiate. Mrs Rosen was in her seventies. She was short and bird-like; blue rinsed grey hair; but most striking were her bright and beady eyes, surrounded by large black circles like those of an unsuccessful pugilist. She was accompanied by a small poodle which barked, yapped and pranced around on its hind legs like a performing dog in a circus. It was called Trudy and every five minutes she picked it up, caressed it and kissed it murmuring, "Ach, Trudy, *meine leibling*, vat vould Mummy do wizzout her liddle darlink?"

"Doktor," she said, "I vunce had a doctor as a tenant, but he drank zo very heavy, he vould come in very late, vake up everybody und sometimes ve had to put him in ze bed! I had to tell him to go." She looked me in the eyes, "Do you trink?"

"Only in moderation," I assured her.

"Gut," she said. "Ve shall have a trink, shall ve?"

"Why yes," I replied.

She disappeared for a couple of minutes and returned with a dusty bottle and two large crystal glasses. "Zis is Neirsteiner Gutes Domthal Spatlese." She announced, "It is gut, *sehr gut*, it is spatlese. You know spatlese, doktor?" I confessed I didn't but said it sounded as though it might be a late wine.

She was pleased. "Zo you know Cherman?"

"A little," I confessed.

"Yes it is late, it comes from ze very last of ze grapes. Zey are allowed to stay on ze vine and shrivel."

We each took a sip. "For an aperitif zis is ze best," she pronounced. The wine was a pale gold, clear with reflections of light green. It tasted of peaches and apples and left a lingering taste of honey. It was delicious, not strong at 9.5 per cent alcohol.

After a couple of glasses she sat silent for a few minutes and then, evidently in the mood, she started to recount her story; told many times in the past and due for many more airings in the future.

"You know, doktor, I was born in Berlin, my family vas vealthy. Mein fater, mein oncles had vunderful businesses, the family vas so very rich, ve owned apartments, shops, buildings right in ze middle of Berlin.

"But zen came Hitler and ze hatred of ze Jews. Ve vere all going to be arrested; it vas... it vas, terrible. Ve had to escape. Mein fater knew Reichmarshal Hermann Goering very well. He bribed Goering who allowed us to flee."

She paused, she wiped a tear, embraced Trudy and took another sip of wine. "But," she went on, "it took all our fortune, ve left our homes, our bank accounts, our cars, everything, ve left with nussing. Ve came to England in 1938 vith nussing.

"And you know, doktor, ve left behind mein brudder, he vas fifteen years younger than me and Oh! Oh! I loved him so very much – but he wouldn't come, he vas young, he vas confident, he vas lawyer, he had been lawyer for a year, he vas doing so vell. I never saw him again; I never knew vat happened to him."

Mrs Rosen's father was a brilliant businessman. Although he lived in Berlin until 1938, he had made contacts and was already well-known in the Jewish community in Golders Green. His great reputation as a businessman helped when he needed to borrow to build a factory in north London. The factory made handbags that became fashionable and the family prospered. Then her father died, soon to be followed by her mother and all her other relatives apart from two cousins. So Mrs Rosen ran the factory. She married, but early in the marriage, her husband died suddenly of meningitis.

A couple of years after the war ended, she found herself immensely rich. Post-war reparations took account of her family's Berlin properties which had been confiscated by the Nazis. She told me she was happy with what she now had, but she mourned her lost family; all she had left were her two cousins, who had become very old, and her little dog, Trudy.

"And you know, *Herr Doktor,*" she concluded, "sometimes ven I vake up at night and I can't sleep for feeling sad and mourning my family I go to my safe, open it and count mein moneys, zen I know ze family would approve – und zen I can sleep."

Later Mrs Rosen told me that she attended a doctor in Harley Street. She told me his name and he was none other than an RAF acquaintance of mine from some twelve years before. We had worked together at the RAF hospital in Uxbridge. He was bright, a very good doctor, but abandoned his career as an air force consultant and took rooms in Harley Street. He was a first class physician but had fallen for the allure of dealing with the rich and famous.

Four years after my stay with her, I was in London and decided to visit Mrs Rosen. I took the tube to Golders Green station, walked the five-minute walk to her big house, rang the bell and to my surprise was greeted by a nurse in uniform.

I introduced myself and asked after Mrs Rosen. "Oh, I'm afraid she died two years ago," the nurse said. "She had a pulmonary embolism and do you know, scandalous it was, that doctor she had in Harley Street said he couldn't come to her because he was too busy."

Mrs Rosen's big house had been turned into a nursing home for Jewish ladies; she had endowed it generously. Saddened, I turned to leave, and as I did I glanced up at the bay window of my old room. Sitting there gazing out through the lace curtains was a distinguished white-haired old lady. She smiled gently at me and for a fleeting second I could have sworn I spied Mrs Rosen standing behind her with her beloved Trudy cradled in her arms.

Eight

EACH MORNING, WHILE I LODGEd with Mrs Rosen, I took the tube from Golders Green station, got off at the Angel and strolled down the City Road to St Mark's hospital. Inevitably, and like somebody afflicted by an obsessive compulsive disorder, I found myself humming over and over:

Up and down the City Road
In and out the Eagle
That's the way the money goes
Pop goes the weasel.

Like most nursery rhymes, there's a story behind it. At the bottom of City Road, in Shoreditch, there were many hatters workshops and shops; there was also a very good tavern or public house in the City Road called The Eagle. Hatters were fond of the drink and repaired to The Eagle as often as they could. If they were short of cash, they would go to a pawn shop and pop (pawn) their weasel (a hatter's tool). In those days, hatters had the reputation of being crazy – 'mad as a hatter'. They were tremulous, timorous, forgetful and staggered about – all attributed to mercury poisoning from the mercury salts that were used to give top hats a brilliant shine. Hatters ironed the salts into the hats, producing a mercury-rich vapour which they unconsciously inhaled... no doubt while anticipating their next trip to The Eagle.

But that had nothing to do with St Mark's which, when it opened, was the only hospital in the world specialising entirely in intestinal and colorectal surgery. Its founder, Frederick Salmon, declared it would be 'The Infirmary for the Relief of the Poor afflicted with Fistula and other Diseases of the Rectum' and indeed when I approached the hospital each morning I could read 'St Mark's Hospital for Rectum and Fistula-in-Ano' emblazoned across its façade. This did not conjure up visions of healing bedside angels mopping fevered brows but more of nasty smells and painful procedures. But needs must if your problems lie in the nether regions, as did those of a certain Charles Dickens, who attributed his problems to sitting at his desk for long hours. Happily Mr Dickens was cured by Mr Salmon's ministrations. In 1896, a new building was opened but had serious financial problems until Lillie Langtry, actress, beauty and mistress of King Edward VII, held a charity matinee at her theatre in Drury Lane and saved the day. History does not relate whether Lillie had also benefited from Surgeon Salmon's attention.

St Mark's stood on its own as a centre of international excellence. The Dukes' staging system for colonic cancer, now used worldwide, was developed by Cuthbert Dukes, surgeon from 1920 to 1950 to St Mark's. Sir Alan Parks in the 1970s developed at St Mark's an ingenious technique for fashioning a replacement rectum from the small intestine for patients who had had their diseased colons removed.

But throughout the medical world the most important advance has been the St Mark's polyposis registry established in 1924. The registry – possibly the world's longest running research project – records the relationship between colonic polyps and cancer. Colonic polyps are small growths that protrude from the mucous membrane, the inner lining of the colon; when polyps grow and reach a critical size they can become cancerous. Scientists at St Mark's identified the gene responsible for causing a familial condition in which there are many polyps in the colon which inevitably become malignant. Basil Morson, the hospital's consultant pathologist, defined the polyp-cancer sequence which has led to the saving of millions of lives worldwide, by the recognition that most cancers of the colon begin from small polyps which develop malignant potential when they grow. Christopher Willams, a physician at St Mark's, pioneered endoscopic surgery by removing the polyps through the endoscope – the colonoscope. Nowadays screening for cancer of the colon is universal and it has been well proven that the removal of polyps at an early stage prevents cancer.

I learned to drive endoscopes at St Mark's and to some extent at UCH; in those early days, much was self-taught and expertise came with experience.

Although the science of fiberoptics and design of endoscopes was largely attributable to the Western world, the production of these delicate and extremely expensive instruments largely fell to the Japanese. I worked with a Japanese surgeon who had come to St Mark's from Tokyo University. He was a man with a puckish sense of humour; when we spotted a polyp ahead of the advancing tip of the colonoscope, he would cry, "TORA! TORA! TORA!" I learned a few months later when a film of the same name about Pearl Harbour was released that this was Japanese for 'Attack! Attack! Attack!'

On one occasion we were to colonoscope the celebrated band leader Joe Loss, an extraordinarily pleasant and affable man. "Tetsu," I said, "this patient is very famous and we don't need any of your wisecracks."

So what happened? When our patient, a short, nervous little fellow, appeared at the theatre door, Tetsu turned to him with the colonoscope draped over his outstretched arms (it was two metres long), and said, "Herro, mista Ross, do you fink you could pray this instlumen?"

High fibre diets were hitting the headlines when I was at UCH and St Mark's. They were championed by Denis Burkitt, an Irish surgeon. Burkitt had already achieved fame by describing a form of predominantly childhood cancer which occurs in Africa. He identified it as a lymphoma, affecting white blood cells (lymphocytes) and the lymph glands. He also showed that it occurred in mosquito-ridden parts of Africa and that it was associated with a particular virus, the Epstein-Barr virus, infecting children whose immune systems had been weakened by chronic malaria. The exciting part of the story is that the tumour, which became known universally as Burkitt's lymphoma, was easily treatable with a chemotherapy agent, *cyclophosphamide*. In some cases just one course cured the cancer.

Burkitt had spent many years as a surgeon in Africa and he and another worker, a medical missionary called Hugh Trowell, together formed their 'fibre hypothesis'. They had noted that native patients in hospitals in Uganda seldom had colonic cancer, heart disease or *diverticula* (out-pouchings of the wall of the bowel) of the colon. Their diet was rich in fibre and unrefined plant foods.

In contrast, the British residents in Uganda who ate mostly the sort of diet they did at home – low in fibre, refined white bread and plenty of meat – displayed the diseases of the West so notably absent in the native Ugandans. Indeed, I remember attending one of Burkitt's lectures in which he said that when as duty surgeon he was called to a native with acute abdomenal pain, he would first advise emptying his pockets; if he had more than two shillings he was rich, no doubt eating a Western diet and he would almost certainly have appendicitis.

I also recall from Burkitt's lectures how he would hide behind trees to observe natives squatting to defaecate. He would then photograph the small mountain of stool, placing a ball point pen next to the pile as a measure. He showed several small mountains in the course of his lecture. Burkitt popularised the high-fibre diet, recommending generous quantities of whole grains, lentils, pulses, fruit, fresh vegetables and nuts. It was claimed that high fibre intake prevents heart disease (lowers cholesterol), stops *diverticula* forming in the colon (lowers the pressure inside and stops constipation) and avoids cancer.

Burkitt also achieved fame by his aphorisms: "America is a constipated nation... if you pass small stools you have to have big hospitals", "The frying pan you should give to your enemy. Food should not be prepared in fat. Our bodies are adapted to a stone-age diet of roots and vegetables" and "Diseases can rarely be eliminated through early diagnosis or good treatment, but prevention can eliminate disease".

In parallel, great interest was being shown in gut transit time, which is how long it takes for the intestinal contents to pass through the alimentary tract. I played a small, undistinguished and malodorous part in the research. The first problem was how does one study transit time? Obviously one had to give something by mouth and observe when it emerged at the other end... but what and how?

Plastic pellets were the answer. They could be swallowed and later spotted and counted by taking an x-ray of the stool. University College Hospital is now a huge gleaming new building in Euston Road but in those days it was housed in the old cruciform red brick building in Gower Street. Running beneath the old building, connecting various departments, were several tunnels which converged at a central point where a freezer for collection of specimens was located. The specimens I collected were from that ever-willing source of volunteers, medical students. A group of twenty was given packets of plastic pellets and plastic bags and asked to swallow fifteen plastic pellets. Over the next ten days, they were to collect their stools in separate bags and deposit them in the specimen freezer. Every three or four days, with bucket in gloved hand, I would collect the frozen samples, take them to the laboratory, weigh them and then off to the radiology department to have them x-rayed to count the number of pellets passed.

I don't suppose that many gentle readers have experience of frozen faeces several days old. The smell is formidable: think of your worst olfactory experience and treble it. Even ripe durian would be a distant second.

As I carried my bucket through subterranean UCH, people scattered holding handkerchiefs to their faces; when I approached the laboratory, technicians with horrified glances scurried away, leaving me strictly alone to handle and weigh my couple of dozen samples. When I got to the x-ray unit, sweet, pretty radiographers would hide, pushing one unfortunate forward to take the x-rays. I dread to think of the various nicknames my 'research' engendered.

As I came to the end of my study leave, the RAF promoted me to wing commander and I was summoned to London to appear before the Consultant Appointments Board to determine my fitness to become a consultant physician in the Royal Air Force.

It got off to a good start: the chairman of the board was the great Lord Rosenheim, president of the Royal College of Physicians... but more important to me, he was my professor of medicine when I began to walk the wards of UCH as a green medical student eighteen years before. He was attended by the big brass of the RAF Medical Branch who were impressed when Lord Rosenheim chatted informally to me for a few minutes, then turned to them and said, "I know Bill Larkworthy very well. He was one of my best students." Thereafter we coasted along.

I was posted back to the familiar haunts of Nocton Hall. It was a pleasure but now, seven years after I had been sent there as a junior specialist, I was the consultant in charge of the department of medicine with two junior specialists, thirty male beds, ten female beds and half a dozen on the officers' ward (in a military hospital, one separates the officers and other ranks).

The hospital was well-equipped but naturally lacked the one very important facility to me – an endoscopy unit. This had become my forte. I needed to exploit it. I needed space and I needed instruments. But fiberoptic endoscopes are expensive, complicated, delicate and easily broken if not handled expertly. I set about my task. First I commandeered a side ward, had the hospital carpenters build storage cupboards and work surfaces and then tackled the difficult task of persuading the Ministry of Defence (Air) to part with the money to buy 'scopes for the upper and lower gastro-intestinal tract.

I used duodenal ulcers for the economic argument, citing an imaginary pilot of a high performance military jet, who had been trained at a cost of a quarter of a million pounds, crashing his aircraft (worth several million pounds) because in the air he had been seized by a complication of his undiagnosed duodenal ulcer which could easily have been spotted in my endoscopy unit. In all I needed about £20,000, chicken feed in comparison to the cost of an expensive pilot crashing an expensive jet fighter. The MOD(A) is chronically short of funds but, to my surprise, my feeble argument won over their hearts of flint.

Soon the unit was in business and the more procedures I performed, the more its reputation spread. Those were still very early days in the endoscopy world. I had one of the first endoscopes in the UK sufficiently long to pass through the stomach and into the duodenum. People would come from miles to look with me as we passed through the exit of the stomach, the pylorus, into the duodenum. As we popped through the hole at the far end of the cavern-like stomach we entered a glistening pink tunnel and with a bit of manoeuvring could pass a few centimetres deeper. Much of the action lay in the part of the duodenum just beyond the pylorus, the duodenal bulb, where almost all duodenal ulcers occur.

I should mention that specialist general medicine was the work of my department lest an impression is given that it was solely for gastrointestinal disease. All manner of medical diseases were dealt with: thyroid disorders, heart problems, chest complaints, disorders of the nervous system, skin disorders; we had a coronary care unit with three beds and an intensive care unit; but of course, the icing on the cake was the endoscopy unit.

We generally think of most diseases as being present and of always having been present in exactly the same form as we see them today – but this is not so. Diseases, like civilisations and empires, rise and fall. Take for example the curious case of chlorosis, the lost disease of languid young ladies. Chlorosis, known as the 'green sickness' because the skin turned green, was first described as "peculiar to virgins" by a German physician, Johannes Lange, in 1554. It became common in the nineteenth century but disappeared in the twentieth. Herr Doktor Lange prescribed that sufferers should "live with men and copulate" – he'd be a celebrity these days. It is likely that chlorosis was a form of iron deficiency anaemia which occurred in young women when they began to menstruate; it responded well to less exciting treatment – iron tablets.

Ulcers, on the other hand, received little mention until the beginning of the nineteenth century although Hippocrates treated what were probably ulcer symptoms with alkalis (anti-acids) by having his patients swallow crushed and ground clam shells.

Napoleon led the way in 1821 by dying in the pain of peritonitis caused by a perforated ulcer. Other theories, like arsenic poisoning (from his damp mouldy arsenic-impregnated wallpaper) or gastric cancer, were suggested as the cause of his death on St Helena, a lonely island in the middle of the Atlantic where the British had incarcerated him, but a chronic ulcer which perforated fits the bill. A post-mortem examination, performed by an anatomist rather than a pathologist, revealed a perforated chronic ulcer and there is no record of microscopic tissue analysis.

In the early twentieth century, duodenal ulcer was more common in women but it became a disease of young and middle-aged men in the second half of the twentieth century and affected ten per cent of males. Years earlier, in 1910, a German surgeon called Schwartz pronounced what became known as his dictum, 'no acid – no ulcer'. This provided an explanation of the cause and a rationale for treatment – either neutralise the acid with alkalis (like Hippocrates did with the calcium carbonate of crushed sea shells) or reduce acid secretion. However, except where the secretion of acid was extremely high, there was no explanation as to why some people got ulcers and others didn't. Why, for instance, did ninety per cent of men escape?

A variety of causes for ulcers was proposed: stress, family history of ulcers, particular blood groups, smoking, alcohol, taking too much aspirin and drinking too much coffee or Coca-Cola. Certainly stress was evident in many sufferers, but there again ulcers themselves cause stress. Ulcers make people miserable. Patients endure frequent attacks of a nasty pain in the upper abdomen, provoked by hunger or coming out of the blue, repeatedly waking them from sleep. The pain could be relieved, but only temporarily, by antacids, food and milk. Life would be dominated by recurring bellyache throughout the twenty-four hours; some patients learned that self-induced vomiting might help – when that unpleasant manoeuvre transiently rid the stomach of acid. One of my patients, a consultant pathologist, would swallow a tube, pass it into his stomach and with a syringe suck out the acid... a drastic and heroic action but very effective when the pain was excruciating.

Generally, when patients could no longer tolerate their pain, physicians would admit them to hospital; confine them to bed, pass a tube through the nose into the stomach, anchor it there, and for twenty-four hours a day, for a week or two, drip soothing milk through it; sedating the bored and restless sufferers with phenobarbitone. Many ulcer sufferers experienced seasonal relapses in the spring and autumn; others had continuous symptoms. When patients had a sufficiently long history, suffered many relapses and moaned enough at their doctors, they would be deemed to have 'earned an operation'.

Surgery for ulcers was complex. There were no guarantees of success or that there would be no undesirable effects. The earliest operations were fraught with side effects; gastroenterostomy, when the stomach was joined to the small intestine (bypassing the ulcer bearing area), was abandoned because ulcers formed where the join was made; partial gastrectomy (when a large part of the stomach was removed) fell into disrepute when it became apparent that many patients were experiencing alarming symptoms called 'dumping'. Their symptoms, faintness, dizziness, abdominal distension and pain, happened when the stomach contents suddenly flooded the small intestine. Post-gastrectomy patients also suffered nutritional deficiencies. Operations to cut the nerve supply to the stomach, and so reduce acid secretion, became popular and were much less savage but even so some patients developed nasty diarrhoea.

As I considered the intriguing world of duodenal ulcers (boring and fruitless to many of my profession), there was evidently a virgin field of endeavour for me. The only absolutely sure way to diagnose ulcers was to see them through an endoscope and the only way to be sure that they had healed was to take another look to see if they had disappeared after treatment.

My first interest was liquorice. Napoleon (so often depicted with his hand inside his jacket massaging his sore belly) carried chests of the stuff on his campaigns. Liquorice had been used by the ancients but it had a nasty side effect: it raised the blood pressure, to disastrous levels in some. At that time I was treating patients with ulcers with a tablet which contained liquorice and an antacid. The results were good, the patients felt better and follow-up endoscopy showed that almost all had healed. I published a paper, much to the delight of the manufacturers of the tablet. There was one snag.

My studies were uncontrolled and I was making extravagant claims like some peddler of alternative medicine. It was time to do a proper study.

In my copious reading about ulcers, I came across an article by an Indian doctor called Malhotra. He was a medical officer for the Indian railways and so had access to the records of the network of railway hospitals throughout India with their large population of employees and families. He observed that the incidence of ulcers varied greatly in the subcontinent; ulcers were more prevalent in areas where the diet was sloppy and not necessarily, as one might think, where the diet contained the most ferocious quantities of chilli.

There was the clue, I reasoned... adequate chewing. Maybe our Victorian forebears were right; you should chew your food twenty times before swallowing. But why chewing? Chewing causes the saliva to flow, saliva contains an alkali, sodium bicarbonate, which neutralises acid. Saliva also contains a protective protein called secretory IgA – plentiful in mother's milk; it coats the newborn's innards like a lick of paint, protecting against infection. Bingo, I knew how to cure ulcers: make 'em chew liquorice.

I contacted the professor of Therapeutics at the University of Nottingham, Michael Langman, well-known for his research on ulcers and other gut diseases. I conveyed my enthusiasm and we together mounted a study.

On the market at this time was a preparation of liquorice in capsule form. The liquorice was deglycyrrhizinized; that is the element in crude liquorice which raises the blood pressure had been removed. This is what we should use. I contacted the makers and had several meetings with one of their clinical trial doctors. They agreed to supply their liquorice preparation and also supplied me with a back-up endoscope in case I had an instrument failure and couldn't perform follow-up examinations to assess healing.

How to make patients chew? Chewing gum was the obvious answer. I contacted the manager of Wrigleys at their factory in my home town of Plymouth and explained what I was up to and how it might benefit their sales. They were keen and supplied me with bucket loads of Doublemint chewing gum.

The design of the trial was simple. We would compare endoscopically the results of treatment of four groups of patients with ulcers. The endoscopists would not know which patients received which treatment. The treatment was divided into four groups: liquorice in capsules, lactose in identical capsules, liquorice mixed in chewing gum and chewing gum flavoured with aniseed. Patients would be allocated randomly by the hospital pharmacists and thus the trial would be double-blind; that is, neither the doctors nor the patients knew which preparation they were receiving. Treatment was for six weeks. The study took about a year to complete.

The results looked encouraging. Many of the ulcers healed, but which group(s) were they in? Excited, we cracked the code.

The results in a nutshell: liquorice didn't heal ulcers and chewing had no effect apart from showing that chewing gum for fifteen minutes five times a day can make your fillings fall out. What a shame! Dreams of medical glory evaporated. But the experiment demonstrated to me the value of double-blind studies, and it also showed an increase in the rate of healing of those who received placebo.

Nine

A NY DISAPPOINTMENT OVER THE outcome of the chewing and liquorice study was soon mollified by the appearance of a new group of potential anti-ulcer medications to be studied, the histamine H2 receptor blockers, in particular one called cimetidine. Work needed to be done to see how effective cimetidine would be in treating duodenal ulcers and soon I was in the thick of another double-blind therapeutic trial.

Histamine is well-known for its role in allergies but the histamine receptor sites involved in allergic asthma, hay fever and urticaria are called H1 receptors and are blocked by drugs called anti-histamines. The cells of the stomach which produce hydrochloric acid respond to histamine but their sites have different receptors, classified as H2. Anti-histamines do not block acid secretion but histamine H2 receptor blockers, such as cimetidine, do and thereby drastically reduce acid production.

Our first studies showed without doubt that cimetidine healed duodenal ulcers. The next question was what happens when the medication is stopped? We started a double-blind study with forty-two patients whose ulcers had been shown to have healed after treatment with cimetidine. The patients were randomly divided into two groups; one group continued to take daily cimetidine in a maintenance dose, the other group took a placebo. The results were striking; after six months nearly eighty per cent of those taking the dummy tablets developed new ulcers as opposed to only twenty per cent of those taking the maintenance treatment. We then followed both groups over a further eight months on no treatment, unless they had a symptomatic relapse. The relapse rate eventually became the same in both groups. Clearly, to prevent relapse, long-term, daily, continuous treatment was needed. Good news for the manufacturers.

During the clinical trials of cimetidine, and before the drug was released on the market, by chance I came across a patient with the most severe form of peptic ulcer disease known. It is a condition called the Zollinger-Ellison syndrome (ZES), named after the two American surgeons who first described it. The usual cause of the syndrome is a tumour in the pancreas which secretes large quantities of a substance called gastrin which causes the stomach to secrete acid. We all have gastrin, but in this condition there is vast overproduction and the patient's stomach secretes so much acid that ulcers occur in the stomach itself, the duodenum and the oesophagus.

My patient would be the first in the world to be treated with cimetidine. He was referred to me by one of the consultant physicians at Lincoln Hospital. He was a seventy-year-old watchmaker who had undergone surgery for severe ulcer problems seven years before. At that operation he had been found to have a tumour in his duodenum but unfortunately its nature had not been properly identified; ten per cent of ZES patients have tumours outside the pancreas. When I endoscoped the watchmaker, I found an enormous amount of inflammation and ulceration; there were several deep ulcers in his oesophagus, his stomach had a giant ulcer involving practically the whole of one wall, and where his stomach had been joined up to the intestine at the previous surgery the opening was surrounded by ulceration which extended way down into the intestine. What was also remarkable was that acid could be observed being continuously secreted, dripping from the walls of the stomach like water from stalactites on the roof of a cave.

He was given cimetidine and within hours his symptoms subsided and he became pain-free for the first time for years. When endoscoped again after a month, the ulceration had improved dramatically; when I examined him again after a year, only mild changes of inflammation could be seen. There were no ulcers. It was gratifying for me and fortunate for him that cimetidine had proved so remarkably effective but to prevent a relapse he would need to take cimetidine continuously.

There was another first in my endoscopy unit at Nocton Hall... and this was chance at play again. A seventy-six-year-old retired RAF officer (actually he had first served in the Royal Flying Corps, founded in the First World War, the forerunner of the Royal Air Force) was admitted having passed jet black stools – evidence of intestinal bleeding. He gave a history suggestive of a duodenal ulcer. At endoscopy there appeared at first to be a

Commissioned medical and nursing staff at RAF Hospital Nocton Hall, 1978.
The author is seated second left, front row. (Photo: Crown copyright).

narrowed pylorus (the exit from the stomach) but it turned out to be a circular scar at the far end of his stomach before the pylorus. No inflammation or ulceration could be seen until the aperture was, with difficulty, negotiated and suddenly the tip of the 'scope popped into a spherical chamber with a blackened disc that looked like a coin bobbing around in it. The sides of the 'chamber' were inflamed; the true pylorus could not be negotiated because it was scarred but an ulcer could be seen as one peered through the pylorus into the duodenum.

The foreign body would have to be removed; open surgery seemed the only answer. However, in discussion with the British agents for the Japanese endoscopes I was using, I discovered that they could make a pair of forceps with which I could retrieve the coin. I received the pair of special forceps in a matter of days. Meanwhile the patient was treated with cimetidine, his bleeding settled and we proceeded with the endoscopy. Passing the forceps through the endoscope, I was able to grasp the coin and extract it with ease, taking particular care not to let it slip from the forceps and drop into his lungs as I negotiated the endoscope past his larynx.

And what was the coin? It was a Queen Elizabeth sixpence dated 1953; not many were minted that year, the year of her coronation. Its market value as a 'fine' example would have been fifteen shillings, but exposure to acid over two decades had caused so much damage it had no resale value.

We asked our old warhorse if he could account for having a sixpence in his stomach for years. He was puzzled, thought at length, then a smile spread over his face. "I'm sure you chaps, being air force, know what goes on at dining-in nights. After dinner one gets down to idiotic amusements, be they mess rugby using a waste paper basket as a ball or climbing all the way around the circumference of the mess hall without your feet touching the floor. But twenty years ago, we had in my last mess a silly game in which one poked out one's tongue and put a sixpenny piece on the tip. The competition was not to be the first to drop or remove the coin. It becomes very tedious after a few minutes; needless to say the one who was the first to lose his coin bought the next round of drinks."

"And do you remember swallowing your tanner?" I asked.

"Well, no," he said, "but, as I'm sure you also know, a little amnesia can creep in at the end of mess evenings."

So that solved the problem of how the coin got into his stomach, but why did it stay there? Usually such a small object would pass easily through the pylorus and on down through the alimentary tract to be expelled in due course without causing symptoms. In his case, he must have already had a duodenal ulcer at the time he swallowed the coin; he did admit to occasional indigestion for many years. The ulcer narrowed his duodenum, the coin couldn't pass and for twenty years Queen Elizabeth's features bobbed around in his stomach.

When I mentioned the endoscopic coin exploit to one of the consultant surgeons at Nocton Hall, his eyes widened. "Remarkable," he exclaimed. "I've got a soldier with a two-shilling piece in his stomach. It's been there for three months, won't pass and I'm planning to open him up tomorrow and take it out. Would you like to have a go first?"

So I did. I took it out with no trouble. Alcohol was involved in this case just as in the first. The soldier had been out drinking with his mates and after several pints, he paid for his round. When he took the change from the barman, a wet two bob bit slid off his palm into his glass. The barman offered to change the glass but he said he would fish it out when he had drunk the pint – and forgot.

So not only did I use an endoscope to take the very first coin out of a

Wing Commander Larkworthy – flying endoscopist.

stomach, I took out the second as well. But these feats were nothing compared with a pal of mine, a fellow endoscopist, who managed to remove a sex toy from the colon using a colonoscope. He would delight in describing how, during the procedure, the patient's umbilicus – illuminated from within – could be seen vigorously vibrating.

MANY PATIENTS WERE REFERRED TO ME from other RAF hospitals but from time to time, usually when there were enough patients or the patient was one of the really big cheeses of the air force, it made sense for me to travel to them with my kit which consisted basically of the endoscope fitted in a large suitcase and a light source the size of a carry-on case to fit aircraft overhead lockers. There were a dozen RAF hospitals, half of them overseas, when I joined the service in 1959 but fifteen years later, only two remained outside the UK – one in Cyprus and the other in Germany.

Cyprus was always popular and I visited the hospital at Akrotiri two or three times a year. On one occasion, I was sleeping in my room in the Officers' Mess when I was awakened at six in the morning by an enormous explosion and to my surprise found myself lying on the floor. I had been thrown out of bed. Clearly some sort of disaster had occurred. I dressed in a hurry and dashed to the hospital where I discovered that an American spy plane, a U-2 based in Akrotiri, had crashed on take-off. The pilot and four Cypriot employees had been killed and seven RAF personnel injured.

The Lockheed U-2 was and still is a remarkable aircraft whose capabilities will always be overshadowed by one spectacular failure. It was originally developed for the American Central Intelligence Agency in the mid-fifties, but in 1960, it was the source of considerable embarrassment to the United States government. A U-2 piloted by Francis Gary Powers was shot down by missiles over Soviet air space. As the aircraft routinely flew at 70,000 feet, well exceeding the ceiling of conventional aircraft, the US believed it was beyond the range of Soviet interception. On this occasion, missiles exploding a hundred feet below it had caused such turbulence that the aircraft broke up. The US authorities announced that they had lost a 'weather research aircraft' which had accidentally strayed into Russian air space after the pilot had radioed saying that he was having "difficulties with his oxygen equipment".

The Americans could not conceive that the pilot had survived. Nikita Khrushchev, the Russian premier, announced that an American spy plane had been brought down but made no mention of the pilot. Most of the crashed U-2 wreckage was recovered and examination of the surveillance cameras of the so-called weather research aircraft showed it had been taking pictures of a Russian plutonium production plant immediately before it broke up. The Americans hotly denied any deliberate intrusion but a month after the crash Khrushchev announced that Powers had survived and confessed to spying. He had parachuted unharmed to the ground and had been captured. Russian money to the value of 7,500 roubles and jewellery had been found in his survival pack. Powers was imprisoned, sentenced to seven years hard labour but released after twenty-one months in exchange for a Russian spy held by the Americans.

The U-2 fascinated me. It is built like an enormous glider, packed with surveillance equipment, powered with one engine with a maximum operational height of 85,000 feet and an endurance of twelve hours. To save weight, the aircraft doesn't have conventional landing gear; instead it takes off from a 'dolly', a platform on wheels, and two wheels on long arms called pogos slotted into the mid-wings. As the plane takes off the dolly and pogos separate and fall from the aircraft.

Landing is difficult. Current models have landing gear but, because the aircraft is so large, as it lands a car with an experienced U-2 pilot accompanies it down the runway with the pilot in the car talking by radio to the pilot landing the plane to control the impact. In Akrotiri, I watched many times in fascination as the U-2 came in to land. Two RAF Land Rovers, one on either side, would chase it down the runway, catch up with it and position themselves under each wing; the aircraft would come to a gentle stop as its wings settled on the braking Land Rovers.

U-2s had been operating out of Cyprus since 1973 (the year of the Arab-Israeli war) to monitor the situation in the Middle East. After dinner one evening in the officers' mess, a fighter pilot gave me a different point of view about the U-2. "It is," he said, "a bitch to fly and a horror to take off and land."

The spy plane was housed in a large hangar, fuelled up. The pilot would have an extensive medical examination, don his pressure suit, climb with help into the cockpit and then start up the engine – still in the hangar. At full throttle, the plane would shoot out of the hangar, almost immediately assume a near-vertical attitude and climb away at an amazing speed. In the case of the aircraft that crashed on take-off in Cyprus on 7 December 1977, it failed to gain height, swerved and crashed into the Operations Room with a shattering explosion as the huge amount of fuel ignited.

WHEN I RETURNED TO NOCTON HALL, I learned that I was being sent as a UK clinical delegate to the Sixth SEATO Conference on Military Medicine in Bangkok, Thailand. Why me, I wondered? I was a general consultant clinician whose forte was passing endoscopes, but then perhaps my experience in Malaysia gave me the edge. SEATO was the South East Asian Treaty Organisation, founded in 1954 to contain communism in the region. It was not a success; the signatories squabbled and, after America withdrew from Vietnam in 1973, Pakistan pulled out. France followed in 1974 and in 1978 SEATO was disbanded.

As it happened, the SEATO military medicine conference I attended was the last. Although I contributed my fair share to the proceedings, I don't believe that the conference added much to the knowledge and understanding of military medical matters in Southeast Asia, but I had a good time.

I had never been to Bangkok. The very name excited me with its connotations of exotic food, bewitching pleasures, fascinating history and seductive tourist attractions, but my opinion was to be changed. For the most part Bangkok was crowded, hot, humid, meretricious, smelly and choked with diesel fumes. As I stepped from the aircraft at Bangkok's old Don Muang airport, I was greeted by the sort of stifling heat and humidity I had known in Malaysia. But I was no longer acclimatised and it was not until I reached my airconditioned room in Hotel Asia and stretched out on the bed for half an hour that I began to feel half human.

The telephone rang and a young female voice enquired, "How are you? Are you happy to be in our beautiful city? Would you care for a lady friend this evening to show you the sights?" Almost reluctantly I hung up without accepting the invitation. It rang again, a different but equally seductive voice wanted to know if I had everything I needed and "would I like a genuine Thai massage and any other attentions?" Again I hung up.

This was getting too much for my fevered flights of fancy and I got off the bed and walked to the large window overlooking the main road below. I could scarcely see a thing. The interface of the cold glass of the airconditioned room and the saturated humidity of Bangkok caused abundant condensation to stream down the outside of the window. I opened the window and looked down on the crowded pavements. The roads were stuffed with hooting cars, aggressive taxis, weaving scooters and buses and lorries belching dense black diesel fumes. Fifty yards away, at a crossroads, a white-helmeted, white-gaitered policeman stood swinging a white baton and constantly blowing his whistle at the near-stationary traffic. He was losing it and losing the battle. As I watched, he walked to the side of the road, hunkered down on the pavement's edge, took off his helmet, mopped his face and lit a cigarette – I swear the traffic started to move when he quit interfering.

At the conference, the UK had three representatives: a Royal Navy Medical Branch commodore, a Royal Army Medical Corps general and me, the ranking junior, a wing commander in the RAF. The meetings, held in an auditorium on a large military base, reintroduced me to my old friends leptospirosis, scrub typhus and malaria, among other topics. A new problem, but not a new disease, was a sudden large increase in the incidence of Japanese B encephalitis (a virus infection causing inflammation of the brain, transmitted by mosquitoes with pigs as the animal reservoir).

The control of malaria was the most important topic. We were taken to the Thai National Research Centre to observe how the Thais were approaching management of the disease. Controlling the mosquito population is key to success; stopping mosquitoes breeding is a fundamental approach. The next approach is to kill them with insecticides; next to stop them biting and injecting the parasites (which are harboured in their salivary glands) into human blood streams; then, the final step, to use drugs to destroy the malaria parasites once they infected humans. I mentioned to my companion, the general (who was incidentally a psychiatrist: a psychiatrist? Why a psychiatrist when we were discussing tropical diseases?) that in my time in Malaysia the British Army soldiers firmly believed that drinking Tiger beer from sunset to midnight would stop mosquitoes biting, but no controlled trial had been carried out... possibly because it would be impossible to produce placebo Tiger beer. The general looked me over and with his psychiatric expertise concluded I was daft.

The Thai researchers had a novel way of studying the first part of the reproductive cycle of mosquitoes – the mating. It is impossible to get male and female mosquitoes to mate in captivity; put males and females together in a large airy cage and their libido plummets. What the clever Thai researchers had discovered was that the male mosquito would ejaculate at the point of a violent death.

We entered a large room where, sitting at laboratory benches, were half a dozen pretty young Thai girls. In front of each girl four living female mosquitoes, lightly anaesthetised with ether, were pinned to cork mats, accommodatingly on their backs. The girls would take a male mosquito from a jar, hold it delicately with forceps and with another pair of forceps whip off its head, legs and wings at lightning speed – instantly applying the abdomen of the ejaculating multiple amputee to the supine passive female. Scarcely *un mariage d'amour*... but this brutal method produced thousands of fertilised eggs which yielded larvae for research into practical ways of interrupting the mosquitoes' life cycle with larvicides.

In many species in the animal world, it's the female which is dangerous and such is the case with the anopheles mosquito, the carrier of malaria. It takes a knowing eye to distinguish male from female... and the same can be said of the night life of Bangkok. Inevitably the three of us sampled it.

Downtown Bangkok centres around an area called Patpong, and that's where we found ourselves, on our second night in the city, attracted like a female mosquito to human blood. We drank beer, watched many so-called erotic shows which regretfully for us were more of the variety which would appeal to young men just launched into the hormonal maelstrom of puberty.

We ended the night in an establishment run by an Englishman and called Pete's Bar. We found Pete sitting in a corner too sloshed to appreciate the bar girls (his employees) draped over him. Other English lads were concluding their evening in a similar fashion in various depths of coma. But the beer was cold, the glasses frosted, the taste enticing and our thirsts enviable. Come three in the morning, we thought about leaving. My senior companions pulled rank and ordered me to get a cab. I lurched into the street and flagged down a car cruising by. We piled in, I commanded "Hotel Asia" and fifteen minutes later we were there.

As I got out, I asked the driver, "How much?"

"Fifty baht, please," he said.

It was then that I noticed he was wearing a leather shoulder strap, a leather belt and a gun in a holster; he also had a black uniform cap with a silver badge. I had hired a police car. I paid him, got my senior colleagues to their rooms and as I fell asleep reflected how it would have been if we three sloshed senior officers had piled into a police car in a Muslim country.

The following day I took a trip to Ayutthya, the royal capital of Thailand (Siam as it was then) from 1350 until it was taken, and largely destroyed, by an invading Burmese army in 1767. Many structures remained, enormous monasteries, reliquary towers called *prangs*, numerous statues of the Lord Buddha including one giant seated example with a very disapproving frown. My guide, no doubt with some financial reward in mind, took me to an antique shop where the owner offered sixteenth century suits of armour at knock-down prices, relics of nobility and Ming bowls.

The bowls caught my eye. Just before I left England, I had read in a newspaper of a slightly damaged Ming dynasty vase which had sold for £70,000. Here in front of me were two bowls for 200 baht (£4). Naturally I bought. I could sell these at one of the great London auction houses, retire to cruise my yacht on the blue Caribbean or maybe watch hula girls in Hawaii... whatever. I wrapped these treasures securely and guarded them against damage until I could collect the cash.

IMMEDIATELY I RETURNED TO NOCTON HALL, I had a call from an old RAF friend, a specialist in diseases of the eye who had left the service two years before, emigrated to Canada, to a place called Moose Jaw, and established a practice which was successful. He told me that the surgeons at the Moose Jaw hospital were keen to appoint an endoscopist and suggested that I should come over to have a look at the place. He would arrange for me to be appointed as locum tenens physician for a month; the hospital would purchase an endoscope for me. A month would give me enough time to explore the possibilities of the hospital and the place.

And where was it? It was in Saskatchewan. Ever since then when I talk to Canadians about where I spent time in their country, they break into big smiles when I say, "Moose Jaw."

I flew to Canada on a British Airways Boeing 747. I boarded at Heathrow and took my seat at the very back of the aircraft. As boarding continued I noted with pleasure that the seat on my right, next to the window, had not been taken. Doors closed, still no neighbour. I moved into the empty seat, then a delay was announced. After half an hour. a man in overalls appeared, I could watch him from my window seat. He carried a ladder and a spanner, placed the ladder against a wheel, climbed to the top, did something for all of thirty seconds, climbed down and walked away with his spanner and ladder. A few minutes later the captain announced that we would be rolling for take-off in ten minutes.

Then the doors reopened and down the aisle came the fattest man I had ever seen (I hadn't yet visited North America). He struggled towards me clutching his boarding pass in his podgy hand, drew level with me and told me that I was in his seat. I got out to let him past and with much heaving and puffing, he eased his bulk through and sat down, overflowing across the arm rest into my territory. He grunted a greeting and pulled out a large brown paper bag full of very ripe pears. He ate every one before we took off, slushing, slurping and sloshing with juice running down his chin on to his already spattered waistcoat and tie. He burped a couple of times and was sound asleep before we reached cruising altitude.

He was not a tranquil sleeper. He snored, he muttered, even though he was sitting upright he clearly had the sort of airways obstruction that afflicts very fat people. Time after time he would almost waken with a start and a loud snort; but worse, he threw his arms about. They were the size of a sumo wrestler's legs. His left arm would suddenly shoot across my chest and for a couple of minutes, until the next apnoeic episode, I was pinned against the back of my seat, scarcely able to breathe.

I called the stewardess, explained the situation which she immediately appreciated but could do nothing about; there were no vacant seats. Sympathetically she brought me a gin and tonic and a tiny packet of peanuts.

Eventually my neighbour woke. He turned out to be a very pleasant chap, a vicar in the Canadian Anglican church. We chatted and he told me joke after joke after joke, none risqué of course.

The best concerned a family from Newfoundland (he told me that Newfies were commonly the butt of Canadian jokes) who were sitting around the fire in their log cabin one winter's night, Pa gently rocking in his chair, smoking his pipe and occasionally spitting in the fire; Ma darning holes in socks and son, as usual, gazing vacantly into space. Pa cleared his throat and a minute later said, "Son, now that you're thirty-five, perhaps you should be thinking about getting a job."

Minutes passed then son sighed and said, "Well Pa, I guess you're right, but what can I do?" After several minutes of silence, son's face suddenly brightened and he said, "I tell you what, Pa, I'll grow chickens." They all thought this was a great idea.

A year passed, again we find the family sitting around the fire, Ma sewing, Pa smoking and spitting and son staring. Suddenly Pa said, "Son, I don't recall us getting any eggs or chickens to eat. What happened about this chicken growing business?"

"I dunno," said the son, "somethin's gone wrong."

"Well," said Pa after a few minutes, "why don't you write to Guelph; they'll help for sure." (Guelph, I learned, was home to Canada's top agriculture college.)

The son wrote, weeks passed before he got a reply. That evening, again around the fire, Pa said, "What did them clever fellers in Guelph say?"

"Well Pa, I wrote and told them that I had tried planting the chickens head-first and planting them tail-first but none growed."

"Yes, I know," said Pa impatiently, "but what did they say?"

"Send a soil sample," said the son.

Welcome to Canadian humour.

MOOSE JAW IS A PRAIRIE TOWN OF some 40,000 inhabitants in southern Saskatchewan; to the west of Regina (original name: Pile o'Bones Creek; renamed Regina for Queen Victoria's Diamond Jubilee), to the east of Medicine Hat and not far from Red Deer. It was first settled in 1882 and grew as a divisional point for the Canadian Pacific Railway.

Other notable features are that it was heavily involved in bootlegging and gambling in the 1920s; a network of tunnels used by the bootleggers is a major tourist attraction today. Al Capone is said to have fled to Moose Jaw when the heat was on in Chicago. Another celebrity refugee was the great Sioux chief, Sitting Bull (son of Jumping Bull), who after defeating Lieutenant Colonel Custer at the Battle of Little Bighorn in 1876, retreated into Canada to escape the avenging American military and established a Sioux village four miles south of Moose Jaw.

Because of its gambling and drinking, Moose Jaw became known as 'The Red Light on the Prairie'. When I was there, you could buy reminders of those bawdy days when raunchy lads came to town looking for relief from the mind-numbing boredom of life on the prairie. The souvenirs were metal discs, two inches in diameter, stamped on one side $2 and on the obverse, 'Good for one Screw'.

The denizens of Moose Jaw were pleasant, honest, open-faced, friendly and tough with a remarkable hubris for their small city. They had to be tough to survive the harsh extremes of the climate of the wide open prairie, exposed in winter to freezing blasts from the Arctic and in the summer to extreme heat and mosquitoes... boy, did they have mosquitoes, some as big as bumble bees. There's a lake near Moose Jaw infested with mossies in the summer. On one occasion, an old couple picnicked on the lakeshore and all that was found of them next day were their bones and dentures... I made up that bit, but Moose Jaw mosquitoes are truly formidable.

A large number of very, very old people lived in Moose Jaw. In my first outpatient clinic, I saw a man who looked about seventy. He complained that he had become extremely tired. "Doctor, normally I get up at five, feed the chickens, milk the cows, then have my breakfast and work all day in my fields. I get home at seven in the evening, have supper and I'm in bed by nine. But now I'm so tired, I don't get up until six, I come home in the afternoon and if there's a problem with my tractor and I have to get under it, when I stand I'm dizzy."

I asked him how old he was. "Ninety-eight," he replied. I examined him; he was pale beneath his weathered leathery skin and a blood count showed he was mildly anaemic. I treated him with iron. When I saw him a couple of weeks later, he beamed; he was back on his old routine.

During my time in Moose Jaw, I admitted four patients well past a hundred years old. They were dying, but not of any acute or specific illness; their various systems were worn out and just packing in.

Although the hospital had bought an endoscope for me to use, there weren't many opportunities to do so. Serving a total population of some 50,000 does not produce a deal of clinical material. I was given accommodation in the hospital but I was alone. There were no other residents. I had time on my hands and touring the flat, featureless local countryside held no appeal. In the evenings I could eat a steak that overlapped the edges of the dinner plate and wash it down with a wine like Bubbling Duck or Cracklin' Rosé, but often I was left to my solitary thoughts.

I had become uneasy about the future of the RAF medical branch and my career in it. Ever since I had joined, getting on for twenty years before, each year had shown progressive contractions in personnel, budgets and facilities. In time of war, armed forces flourish, but now the country was at peace and the government wanted to spend more on vote-catching welfare schemes than on the military. And, let's face it: the Medical Branch was not at the sharp end of a fighting service. More cutbacks were in the pipeline. RAF hospitals would close and the service, particularly the Medical Branch, would get progressively smaller until it no longer existed. Maybe amalgamation of the army, navy and air force medical services was around the corner.

What of Moose Jaw? Pleasant though its people were, it held the disadvantage, nay terror, of long, desperately cold winters. I felt more comfortable in hot climates. Almost without exception the locals told me, with a certain glee, how in winter car engine blocks had to be plugged into mains electricity overnight to keep them warm enough to start. And when moving off after being parked, there would be a bump-bump-bump until the flattened frozen part of the tyre which had been in contact with the ground regained some malleability. What's more, "don't drive your car without having a candle, matches and a tow rope in it. If you get stuck in a snow drift, don't get out and walk, you'll be dead in twenty-five yards. Stay in the car, light your candle and that will give just enough heat to keep you alive. Wait and pray for rescue." This of course was before mobile phones. I didn't need that sort of life.

I needed to review my future; that would be my priority when I returned. But I had another priority on my mind: the Ming bowls I had bought in Thailand and the fortune in store for me. At the first opportunity, when I had to attend a meeting at the RAF Central Medical Establishment in Goodge Street, off Tottenham Court Road, I found a couple of hours to go to Christie's, one of the big London auction houses. At the reception I stated my case; the bowls were taken from me and I was asked to sit and wait. Fifteen minutes later, a studious, bespectacled elderly man appeared and asked me to accompany him to his office. He sat me down, smiled and said, "These are indeed Ming Dynasty bowls and are good examples in fine condition. Look, you can see the small transparent areas where grains of rice were inserted when they were made." This was good news, I had hit the jackpot!

"But," he went on, "they are what we call Domestic Ming; that is, they were rice bowls used daily by the Thai peasants and there are literally thousands still in existence." I tried to hide my disappointment. Sympathetically he went on, "I could sell these for you. This one would probably make £12 and the other £10." I thanked him and took my bowls... I would have to continue working, thoughts of idle Caribbean days on my yacht faded, but there again I thought, I'd soon get bored and driving endoscopes was so much more satisfying than eating the fruit of the lotus.

In the corridor in Nocton Hall, I bumped into our consultant radiologist who had returned from a locum tenens post in Jeddah, Saudi Arabia, a few days before I returned from Canada. We exchanged experiences; he was not enthusiastic about Jeddah; it was so primitive. But for some time it had been on my mind that there were opportunities in that magical kingdom. I had heard of an excellent specialist hospital in the capital, Riyadh. It had opened two years before. I contacted the Hospital Corporation of America, the company which ran the hospital, and arranged a six-week locum as a visiting gastroenterologist.

Ten

Six hours outbound from London Heathrow, the Lockheed Tristar in the dark green livery of Saudi Arabian Airlines (soon after renamed Saudia) gently banked as it joined the circuit over Riyadh. The movement barely registered in first class where I continued sipping 'Saudi champagne' – apple juice and fizzy water – from a crystal flute.

It was one in the morning, local time. For the past two hours, the view from the cabin window had been a uniform jet black as we overflew the vast empty spaces that made up most of the Kingdom of Saudi Arabia. Suddenly myriad twinkling lights appeared below and as we descended, villas and palaces could be distinguished, each festooned with fairground lights; the streets looked crowded with speeding cars and swirling dust devils obscured patches of the panorama before me.

Immediately the aircraft touched down, the intercom broke into agitated Arabic, a harsh unfamiliar guttural language, punctuated by clicks, groans and glottal strangulations. Then, in English, it welcomed us to Riyadh; it told us the local time, that the outside temperature was forty-two degrees Celsius and that we must keep our seats until the aircraft came to a complete stop. "Complete stop?" I remember thinking, "what's an incomplete stop?"

The instruction to remain seated clearly did not apply to all passengers. As one, the Saudis got up, took their cases from the lockers and jostled towards the front to the dismay of the impotent Lebanese air hostesses – my first encounter with the soon-to-be-familiar law that Saudis come first, don't have to follow the rules and can do as they please.

It had been a strange experience, my first of many flights on Saudia. At Heathrow, a number of beautiful young Saudi girls dressed in designer jeans, designer belts, designer shoes, dripping in gold and sporting standard-issue gold Rolex watches had boarded. They all disappeared an hour before we were due to land at Riyadh. One by one, they made their way to the toilets and emerged after a few minutes covered in *abayas*, the black all-enveloping cloaks, with black head scarves; some beauties sported *burqas,* face masks. Meanwhile, their fathers or husbands remained clad in their Savile Row suits and Jermyn Street shirts.

We deplaned into airconditioned buses for the short drive to the arrivals lounge, where we were divided into Saudis, Europeans and others. My bags were searched diligently by a young bearded customs officer with an irritating sniff and a suspicious eye. Going over my belongings like a forensic scientist investigating a murder, he at last came upon the only vile pornographic material I was carrying. It was a *Punch* magazine I had bought at Heathrow and on the inside of the back cover was a photograph displaying a half-page advertisement by that well-known purveyor of smut, Kodak. The advert showed scantily clad maidens draped around the rippling blue waters of a swimming pool.

"Ah, ha!" he cried triumphantly, having discovered one more evil person entering his sin-free sacred kingdom. He turned to me; raised his eyes, fixed me with a disapproving stare and said, "This is bad things. You know you coming into the Kingdom of Holy Places and such badness is not allowed." With that, with his left thumb he scrunched the advert, then tore it out, dropped it on the floor, glared at me and said, "For this I could send you to prison but, *Allah kareem* (God is generous), I will not, but next time I will."

I was shocked and wryly amused by my first encounter with such a censorious attitude. He chalked my bags and I moved to the exit where I was met by a driver holding a large board which read, 'Doctor Lark'.

The driver was a young Saudi who wasted no time telling me that normally he didn't do driving but he was here tonight as a personal favour to me. His English was pretty good and as we drove we chatted about this and that. I was agog to learn as much as I could about this magic kingdom I had just entered.

Suddenly he asked, "How old are you?"

"Forty-five," I replied.

Bluntly he demanded, "Can you still get it up?"

While I considered whether I would reply or ask him for the Arabic equivalent of 'piss off', he went on, "You are very old and you are not young like me. I am wonderful with the ladies; very wonderful, they all love me. I love them too, especially Egyptian girls, they know all about making love, Filipinas is good too but your English and American womens are just silly."

He became silent, ruminating no doubt on his good fortune at being such a Saudi stallion, and what might be waiting for him after he had dropped me at the end of the journey. I also lapsed into silence and briefly thanked him when he deposited me at the door of the small two-up, two-down house in which I was to live for the next four weeks. As I climbed the stairs, I heard a gentle snore.

Up early next morning, anxious to see what excitement the day had in store, I met my house companion. He was Mike Franklin, an ENT surgeon, and he was doing his third locum at the King Faisal Specialist Hospital so he knew the ropes. Over a freshly brewed coffee, he gave me a lot of useful advice.

I reported at nine in the morning to the hospital reception and was directed to what was called the Amenities Center for orientation. It was a large building, a recreation centre with a small library, pool room, a hall and an Olympic-size swimming pool. Squash courts with stone floors and tennis courts were nearby. There was everything a person could desire with the exception of the equivalent of a medical students' bar.

I joined a group of a dozen new arrivals and a tall, tanned, slim young American lady, sporting at least a dozen gold bangles on each arm, told us how privileged we were to have the privilege of working in this wonderful kingdom. That we would be privileged to have excellent accommodation, excellent restaurants and have the privilege of meeting the wonderful Saudi Arabians. While privileged to be here, we must remember to obey all the Saudi rules and codes of behaviour and dress modestly. Males mustn't wear shorts in public (Saudi men were easily turned on by male thighs, it seemed) and we must at all times treat our hosts with respect.

Ah yes, our hosts. Cultured they might be, but it was hard to understand how certain nuances of dignified behaviour that I considered universal after my many foreign postings had passed them by. Such habits as the deep probing of the nostrils and vigorous scratching of the genitals in public were not my idea of performance art. And as for the lewd staring at Western women... perhaps we should have sought reciprocity but in truth, there was not a great incentive to ogle the local ladies, who mostly appeared as black blobs. I must admit, however, there were one or two on whom a

Main entrance, King Faisal Specialist Hospital, about 1978.

carefully draped black *abaya* and head scarf could emphasise a seductive figure and *kohl* bedecked eyes could convey promises of ecstasy.

After a conducted tour of the hospital we ended up in the medical records department where a lady of uncertain years and a mask-like face, evidence of repeated and not particularly successful plastic surgery, guided us through the complexities of recording clinical notes and dictating letters, and proudly displayed the hospital's computer. Remember, although not so very long ago, that these were early days in computing. The computer occupied a large airconditioned, dust-free room. Its guts were visible in a number of free-standing glass-fronted cabinets in which large spools whirled. She explained the various uses the hospital was making of the computer, one of the first in the world. It was impressive but took up an awful lot of space. "Perhaps one day computers will be made smaller," she added. Indeed. I imagine that the desktop model I am sitting at now could do at least twice as much and at ten times the speed of the first King Faisal Specialist Hospital computer.

Later that day I met the chairman of the Department of Medicine, Dr Robert Butler, an American dermatologist. Short, somehow penguin-like, he was affable and instantly likeable. After a brief description of the department, he handed me over to a senior resident for a conducted tour of the hospital.

And what an Arabian treasure trove of medical delights: superb laboratories with apparatus which could perform all the tests known to man. Some vast machines blinking and beeping away would be loaded with a specimen of a patient's blood and, after the sample travelled through the machine for a few minutes, the results of twenty different tests would be printed out. The laboratory boasted three haematologists, several specialists in microscopic pathology and an electron microscopy unit.

The radiology department had all the most up-to-date equipment; a radio-isotope department, wonderful ultra-sound scanning as well as three, yes three, computerised scanners. The operating suites were as large and well equipped as would be found in a couple of teaching hospitals at home. The library, with its twenty-four-carat gold leaf ceilings, had such extensive facilities one could possibly access all the medical literature published in the twentieth century.

One snag was that those who built the hospital had constructed only 134 single patient rooms and no open wards. This meant there was always a serious shortage of beds with an unheard of doctor/patient ratio of perhaps

KFSH Amenities Center, about 1978: everything but a bar.

one doctor to two inpatients. In addition, this was a royal hospital; there were always rooms and suites which had to be made available for the legion of major and minor royalty.

Admitting ordinary Saudis could involve pleading, fighting, bribing and sometimes deceiving colleagues by promising to have a patient discharged in a day or two, knowing full well that it would not be possible. Only Saudis and members of the hospital staff were eligible for admission, unless a person had *wasta* – influence. I was to encounter *wasta* again and again. It was the lubricant that kept the wheels of society moving and was a daily demonstration of power and position.

And what about the endoscopy unit? There wasn't one. Their gastroenterologists predated endoscopy; it had passed them by.

The surgeons had bought endoscopes which were all said to be stored in the operating theatres suite, but most couldn't be found. This great hospital had only one upper gastrointestinal endoscope and it was a side-viewing duodenoscope, an instrument which normally has one use: it is passed deep into the duodenum to search for the tiny outlet of the bile and pancreatic ducts, then through it is inserted a tiny tube to inject x-ray contrast material to display the gall-bladder, the major bile ducts and the duct of the pancreas.

I was used to driving a forward-viewing 'scope to inspect the gullet, stomach and duodenum; forward-viewing is easy, you see where you are going and you look ahead. A side-viewing endoscope is difficult. It's like going into a room with one's face pressed close to the wall and then examining the room by sliding sideways facing the walls. But I had to adapt and performed all my upper gastrointestinal examinations using the duodenoscope.

They had a colonoscope, but one of the earliest models which didn't look as though it had ever been taken out of its case. I was also shown a brand new bronchoscope, never used. Bronchoscopes are designed for examining the interior of the lungs. Having learned the technique at the Royal Brompton hospital in London, I had performed many bronchoscopies in my unit at Nocton Hall. Bronchoscopes are very narrow flexible instruments and are passed through the nose. Using local anaesthetic, sprayed through the tip of the advancing 'scope, the larynx can be entered and traversed to reach the bronchial tree. But I couldn't use this one. In replacing it in its metal case, some idiot had trapped the tip between the lid and the base. All the optical fibres had been broken – a beautiful instrument ruined by carelessness.

I made the best of the paucity of endoscopes and was able to show my colleagues in the Department of Medicine that to function properly in the late twentieth century one could not practice without endoscopy. I demonstrated with the colonoscope that one could diagnose tuberculosis of the *caecum*, the distant first part of the colon, delving two metres with the scope and taking biopsies. With the duodenoscope, I was able to carry out ERCPs (endoscopic retrograde cholangio-pancreatograms) diagnosing diseases of the gall bladder, biliary system and pancreas. By making practical demonstrations (all the more impressive to the uninitiated) and recounting the future possibilities of fiberoptic endoscopy in a series of lectures to the assembled medical staff, I had opened their eyes to a new world.

IN MY SECOND WEEK, MIKE, MY HOUSE companion, the ENT surgeon locum, over breakfast one morning said, "How about a trip to Chop Chop Square on Friday? Should be very interesting."

I had heard of Chop Chop Square. It was in the centre of old Riyadh and was where executions by beheading and amputations of limbs were carried out after Friday prayers.

Mike told me a hospital employee had been executed there a month before. "He was this huge Somali guy and he had tried to rape the wife of one of the hospital doctors."

"That's surely serious," I allowed, "but execution is drastic."

"Not only drastic," he said, "there was a certain sardonic humour."

He told me the story. The Somali had been employed since the hospital opened in 1975 and was entitled to a month's wages for every year he had worked. That would amount to a nice little sum for his family in Somalia.

"And the humour?"

"Well, the terminal benefits here are known as 'severance pay.' The condemned chap was brought from jail to the hospital accounts department on his way to Chop Chop Square so that he could sign a form to say that he had received his severance pay."

"So, Bill," he said, "think about it; should be interesting. We'll need to leave early. One of my British male nurses will take us in his car."

I gave it a lot of thought; I wasn't sure that I wanted to have the image of a crude and barbaric execution engraved on my brain for the remainder of my life. But the more I thought about it, the more I thought I should go, if only to witness something that the rest of the world condemned and would surely be stopped within a decade.

Friday morning was clear, sunny and cool. We drove to the centre of Riyadh, parked the car some two hundred metres from Chop Chop Square and walked the crowded streets, past open shops displaying sacks of colourful spices, past several shops selling gold, the scent of frankincense and myrrh in the morning air. We walked past a clock tower and the restored Musmak Fort, a national treasure commemorating ibn Saud's assault and conquest of Riyadh at the turn of the last century.

Friday prayers were not yet over when we assembled in the square. Crowds were milling around and an ambulance and a couple of police cars were parked near the Grand Mosque. We waited; I was absorbed in my thoughts. Was this really where I wanted to be? Did I really want to see a fellow human being have his head lopped off? The crowd grew restive, prayers had ended and the mass of worshippers streaming from the mosque added to the congestion. Suddenly, with wailing sirens, the ambulance and police cars drove off. Today's execution had been cancelled; the disappointed crowd dispersed. I breathed a sigh of relief. "We'll have to try again next week," said Mike.

THERE WAS NO 'NEXT WEEK' FOR ME. I decided not to go, but Mike and his friend went. There was indeed an execution that Friday. When Mike returned late in the afternoon he was shaken, he was pale and uncommunicative... in fact he spoke barely half a dozen words over the next two days. When he eventually described the event, I was even more relieved that I had not witnessed it.

They had joined the crowd in Chop Chop Square as on the previous Friday. The ambulance and police cars rolled up and parked. As before, the crowd was swollen by several hundred worshippers from the Grand Mosque. The police cleared a space in front of the mosque; they held the crowds back but Mike was suddenly seized by a bearded, scraggy, hawk-nosed *muttawa*, a religious policeman, and forced to the front of the throng – he didn't know that habitually the *muttaween* would push any foreigners in the crowd to the front, ostensibly because if the last sight of the dying man was an infidel, he would not go to paradise.

Suddenly a van drove into the cleared area, the back doors opened and out staggered a young man, blindfolded, manacled and obviously drugged. He was made to kneel in the centre while an official, who had emerged from the mosque, read the charges. Then a very large, very black man with a scimitar appeared from behind the kneeling man. With the tip of the scimitar, he pricked the condemned man in the lower neck which caused him to jerk his head up, the sword flashed and blood spurted. But the job was not done properly; with his neck half severed, the victim keeled over, he moaned pitifully. Assistants straightened him so that the executioner could complete the job. He took another two swings, the head separated, blood continued to jet and when it subsided a doctor approached the headless corpse, felt for a pulse and declared the criminal dead.

The crowd cried, "*Allahu akbar*" (God is the greatest) over and over. The body and head were thrown on a stretcher, put in the van and driven away. The police retreated and the ambulance drove off.

And then Mike saw the most sickening end to the affair: the crowd milled around, trampling in the pools of blood, to and fro, to and fro, getting more and more frenzied and all the while chanting, "*Allahu akbar.*"

Mike was silent for ten minutes; I was shocked... his description was so vivid. Mixed with my feelings of horror I felt relief that I had not witnessed this ghastly display of primitive religious fervour.

FORTUNATELY THERE WAS MORE TO the place than that. During my locum, I had a couple of trips into the desert, one of them an overnighter with friends. The desert is awe-inspiring, beautiful, has its own surprisingly diverse ecology and the sight of the desert sky at night is unbelievably impressive. If the moon is full, it is enormous and seems close enough to touch.

My appetite was whetted by both the hospital and the desert. I needed to return; I made enquiries. The locum I was doing was to replace the staff gastroenterologist who was elderly and on leave but wasn't showing any indication of quitting despite approaching his seventies. I expressed my interest to the chairman of the Department of Medicine. Next day I was on the return Saudia flight to London.

RAF Hospital Nocton Hall was something of an anticlimax after the exotic King Faisal Specialist Hospital and Research Centre, but it wasn't to be for long. Inside three months, I received a call from the office of Hospital

Escarpment in the Saudi Arabia desert: awe-inspiring beauty.

Corporation of America: Would I be interested in a permanent post at the King Faisal Specialist Hospital?

Not wishing to appear too enthusiastic, I said I would make up my mind and call back in a couple of days. I did and was invited to London, to (would you believe?) University College Hospital, to attend an interview board. The board consisted of one of my old teachers, Dr John Stokes, the epitome of the elegant London consultant, and an old pal of mine who was now a consultant at UCH. We had played rugby together as students over twenty years before.

We chatted about the King Faisal Specialist Hospital. Having done the locum and being familiar with the local problems were very much in my favour. Then, I guess as a test, I was shown the x-rays of an ERCP (endoscopic retrograde cholangiopancreatogram). It showed the outline of the biliary tree and to me an obvious diagnosis, it was full of blood. What did I think?

"Haemobilia," I said. Blood in the bile ducts.

"Yes," said Dr Stokes, "do you know whose x-rays these are?" Naturally I said I didn't. "They are of Sir William Bentley-Purchase who fell off the roof of his house and damaged his liver when he climbed up to try to realign his television aerial. Fortunately he recovered without needing surgery."

I knew the patient; he had been our lecturer in forensic medicine and also was Her Majesty's Coroner for King's Cross, a red light district just down the road.

Sir William was a tall man with a deep voice who laughed loudly, especially at his own jokes. For some reason I instantly recalled one of his many stories he told us students more than twenty years earlier. He had recounted how he was once called to a large green playing field to investigate the murder of a young woman. She lay there, strangled and dishevelled, with her skirt around her neck. The detective with him said, "No English murder this one."

"How can you possibly know that?" asked Sir William.

"Take a look at where we are," said the policeman. The body was lying mid-way between the wickets of a cricket pitch.

"Very unBritish," agreed Sir William. The murderer, arrested a few days later, was Polish.

Sir William also had no time for the jury system. "Twelve good men and true, phooey! Four are deaf, four are so dim they don't know what you're talking about and four have already committed the crime themselves."

Forensic medicine lecturers are popular; Sir William's lectures were always crowded as were those of visiting lecturers who gave us inside knowledge of famous murders. Like for instance, the Home Office Pathologist, Dr Francis Camps, who delivered an hour's lecture on the macabre serial murderer of Rillington Place, John Christie. He had specialised in young ladies and as a souvenir of their encounters kept a small tuft of each one's pubic hair in a battered green and yellow tobacco tin. The tin was passed around the lecture theatre, 'Sunrise Tobacco – gives you a lift!' proclaimed the lid of the tin.

Sir Keith Simpson was another popular forensic lecturer. He had written a textbook for medical students, the frontispiece of which showed a picture of a woman with an axe buried in her head, severe lacerations of her exposed chest and abdomen, clear evidence of sexual assault and a scarf knotted tightly around her throat. The picture was captioned... 'Injuries arousing suspicion'.

Sir Keith always started his lectures by warming up the audience. He would show a black-and-white photograph of the entrance to Bow Street police station. "What do you see?" he would demand.

"Nipples, sir!" the *cognoscenti* would in one voice cry out.

"Yes" he would reply and explain to those who weren't in the know that a man crazed with what we now call recreational drugs had bitten off the nipples of a lady who plied her trade in Covent Garden, ran to the nearest police station and spat them on the pavement as he rushed in to confess. Sure enough, on closer inspection, two black dots were visible on the pavement beneath the blue lamp.

But I digress with these titillating if morbid memories.

I was accepted for a staff appointment. My predecessor had retired and I was to take over as Chief of Gastroenterology at the King Faisal Specialist Hospital and Research Centre. I was eager and anticipated my new job with relish. The clinical material would be fascinating; the hospital was the major referral centre for the whole of the kingdom and had the most modern facilities in the world. The country and the culture would be new and interesting.

The only drawback I could see was that the *modus vivendi* of the average Saudi might offend my liberal spirit. During my month's locum, I had seen how Saudi women lived in subservience to their domineering husbands and male relatives. The nub of the matter seemed to me to be an entrenched male insecurity mixed with machismo, emotional immaturity and pathological jealousy all masquerading as religious dogma. Women had to be covered at all times outside the house lest they provoke lust in strangers. They were not allowed to work. They were not allowed to drive. They could not travel unescorted and had to have their husband's permission if they were leaving Saudi Arabia without him. They were segregated at home, unseen by male eyes other than those of close family members... but would this matter to me in my new life? Were the checks and balances adequate?

I could adapt to irritating aspects of life in Riyadh, the call to prayer five times a day which caused shops to close for twenty minutes, times varying day by day with the time of sunrise, but guaranteed to happen at the precise moment I entered one. The banning of other religions had no personal impact apart from its overt intolerance; I could live with interdictions on public gatherings, pork, alcohol and cinemas and I had no need to witness the activities of Chop Chop Square.

I could even come to terms with the sight of young, heavily perfumed Saudi men in their pressed and brilliant white *thobes*, constantly readjusting their red-and-white check *goutras*, or headdresses, kissing each other in greeting and holding hands as they mooched away their idle lives. I could tolerate the climate, the very hot summers made less demanding by zero humidity, and the delightful winters – the temperatures of an English spring with an occasional frost. Having grown up in the constantly wet south-west of England, I felt no burden from a lack of rain and sand storms could be avoided. All in all, the balance was in favour but an ability to endure without open criticism would be crucial to survival.

I had reasons enough to take up the post of consultant gastroenterologist and chief of service at the King Faisal Specialist Hospital in Riyadh. The future of the Royal Air Force Medical Branch was not bright. RAF hospital closures would be inevitable. I wanted to continue working as a clinician and not end up in the RAF Central Medical Establishment in London doing what amounted to insurance medical examinations. Saudi Arabia beckoned; wonderful clinical material, excellent colleagues and a magnificently equipped hospital. Moreover the kingdom was intriguing in many ways; there was promise of excitement and not least a good and tax-free income.

I resigned my commission in the RAF and put my affairs in order in England. On 19 September 1978, I flew once again on a Lockheed Tristar to Riyadh. It may have been that very aircraft which three years later burst into flames on the runway at Riyadh when a Bedouin passenger lit his oil stove in the aisle to warm up stewed goat to feed his numerous wives and children.

This time I had a trouble-free passage through customs and a driver who could not speak a word of English but knew the way to my new home.

Part Two

The 'magical' kingdom: Saudi Arabia

'Bayti baytak wa baytak bayti'
(Your house is my house and
my house is your house).

– ARABIC PROVERB

The man from Tihama: a colourful hitchhiker (see page 175).

Eleven

THE KINGDOM OF SAUDI ARABIA IS BIG; France, Germany, Britain and Spain combined would make up only half its surface area. Roughly rectangular in shape, it occupies most of the Arabian Peninsula, bounded on the west by the Red Sea, on the east by the Persian Gulf, to the south by the Oman and Yemen and to the north by Egypt, Jordan and Iraq.

Apart from the mountainous regions in the west, the coastal plains and the oases dotted around, it is a barren land containing the world's largest continuous sand desert, the Rub al Khali – the Empty Quarter. Saudi Arabia is hot and dry; many desert areas do not see rain for years on end. The dreadful summer heat in the central areas would make it the largest sauna in the world if it was accompanied by the high humidity encountered in the littoral regions. The winters are cool by day with very cold nights, even frost at times.

It was quite unlike anywhere else I had lived and worked, and remains so.

Saudi Arabia holds a quarter of the world's oil reserves, mostly in the Eastern Province along the Persian Gulf. The discovery of oil dragged a feudal, medieval Islamic nation into the twentieth century in less than four decades. Like people, countries need time to grow, time to mature and time to assimilate civilisation. Saudi Arabia suffered by its precipitate entry into modern life. The explosion of wealth delighted the Saudis. They could build highways, import American cars, crash them willy-nilly and leave wrecks by the hundred scattered around city roads or angled against lamp posts with their noses pointing towards the blistering sky. Even after they erected traffic lights at junctions, it took months for the Saudis to realise what they were for, and even longer for them to appreciate that they were not there to control only foreign drivers.

By importing skilled and unskilled labour, the Saudis had little need to exert themselves. Foreign architects and manpower could build hospitals, schools, universities; oil money could attract the best minds with generous salaries. Not only did they have vast oil wealth, theirs was the land in which Islam was founded and they were the guardians of the Holy Places, Mecca and Medina. Saudis, not surprisingly, became arrogant.

For all that, Saudi Arabia is fundamentally a young country, unified in 1932, and to this day is still tribal. It has come a long way but has a long way to go to win universal respect.

The history of Saudi Arabia is intimately and inextricably bound with the story of Islam. Centuries before Islam, the tribes of the Arabian Peninsula were pagan and later many converted to Christianity and Judaism. The peninsula has been populated for three millennia. It was home of the Semites, those who spoke a Semitic language, notably Arabic, Hebrew or Aramaic. The Semites were traditionally the descendants of Shem, son of the biblical figure Noah. What became Saudi Arabia was punctuated by oases, each forming a centre where several tribes lived together. Internecine fighting would break out from time to time between the tribes and all were preyed upon by the fierce, nomadic, desert-dwelling Bedouin. The larger oases grew into towns and were often staging points of caravans carrying frankincense and myrrh to the eastern Mediterranean from the south, Yemen in particular.

Muhammad, destined to be the Prophet of Islam, was born in Mecca in 570AD. Mecca was already an important city with a pagan shrine, the Kaaba, which brought in much of its revenues through visiting pilgrims. Legend has it that the Kaaba, a large cubic stone building, was originally constructed by Adam and rebuilt by the great patriarch of monotheism, Abraham, and his son, Ishmael.

Muhammad married into a wealthy merchant family and lived a quiet well-respected life within the religious community of Mecca. At the age of forty, he had a vision in which the angel Gabriel appeared before him while he was on retreat in a cave in the hills north of Mecca. Gabriel told Muhammad that he had been selected by God as his chosen messenger and he was commanded to preach. Muhammad received many revelations and recorded them as the Koran. He converted his wife and family and then began preaching the new religion to the public in Mecca. This alarmed local religious leaders as an attack on local religions was an attack on the prosperity of Mecca. Muhammad's life was threatened and he fled to a city two hundred miles north of Mecca called Yathrib at the time but later renamed Medina in his honour.

The flight of the Prophet to Medina in 622AD is called the Heggira and is the date at which the Islamic calendar begins. Muhammad consolidated his power base at Medina and by 630AD the Muslims were strong enough to attack and capture Mecca. He cleansed the Kaaba, removed the idols and ordained the building as a house of God. Muhammad died in 632AD, by which time the whole of the Arabian Peninsula had converted to Islam.

Mecca has remained the spiritual focus of Islam because it is the destination for the haj pilgrimage. The haj is the fifth of the five pillars of Islam; the faithful must make at least one pilgrimage to Mecca in their lives to visit the Kaaba and perform the rituals initiated by Abraham and Ishmael many centuries before.

The haj is the largest annual pilgrimage in the world; full of symbolism, it unites the followers of worldwide Islam. But is the world of Islam united? I remember holidaying in Kashmir, sitting one night drinking a cold beer on the roof of a houseboat on beautiful Lake Nageen, near Srinagar, and hearing what sounded like fireworks across the water. I thought the locals were enjoying a festival but when I enquired the next day, I learned that it wasn't fireworks I'd heard but gunfire. The local Shia and Sunni Muslims were shooting at each other; that night eleven had died.

Ninety per cent of the world's Muslims, of which there are more than a billion, are Sunni and the other ten per cent, Shia. Shiites are concentrated in Iran, Iraq and the Yemen. The division dates back to the death of Muhammad and the question of his successor. A major cause of the schism was the murder of Hussein, the grandson of Muhammad, son of Ali (who was Muhammad's son-in-law and at the same time his cousin). The Imams of the Shiite are regarded as being divinely appointed and infallible.

The Christian wars of religion are long over; let's hope it won't also take the Sunnis and Shiites another four hundred years and a few million deaths to achieve harmony.

As for the kingdom itself, it's a family affair on a grand scale. King Abdul Aziz bin Abdour Rahman al Saud, commonly referred to as ibn Saud, was the founder, first monarch and father of Saudi Arabia. Not only that, he fathered all the kings of Saudi Arabia who have succeeded him since he died in 1953. The top job is open to his grandsons too under the Saudi Basic Law passed in 1992.

Ibn Saud probably had twenty-two wives, although never more than three or four at a time as allowed under Islamic law. He had thirty-seven sons of which Saud, Faisal, Khalid, Fah'd and Abdullah became king. The reigning monarch, Abdullah, was born in 1924. He is vigorous and a just, wise and sensible ruler not given to the excesses of some of his predecessors.

THE POWER THAT RELIGION WIELDS IN society is a defining characteristic of Saudi Arabia. It perpetuates a pact dating from mid-eighteenth century which was conceived as a means of quelling lawlessness under a consolidated leadership.

The Saud family has followed the Wahhabi movement of Islam since the eighteenth century. Wahhabism is an austere form of Sunni Islam which insists on a literal translation of the Koran. Strict Wahhabis hold that those who do not follow their beliefs to the letter are heathens, even those who regard themselves as orthodox Muslims. Wahhabis believe they have a divine right to kill all non-believers, including Christians, Jews and Shia Muslims.

Wahhabism has grown explosively since the 1970s, fuelled by Saudi funding of religous schools called *madrassas* and mosques throughout the world, from Karachi to London, from Islamabad to New York. It is regarded as a major factor in the rise of Islamic fundamentalism, producing such organisations as the Taliban, the followers of al-Qaeda's Osama bin Laden and the Egyptian Muslim Brotherhood.

The union of the Sauds and the Wahhabis began in a town near Riyadh, called Dariyah. In 1744, Muhammad Ibn Abd-al-Wahhab sought refuge there, having caused widespread antagonism throughout the Nejd, the traditional power base of the Sauds, by his extremist views. At this time the Saud family also held Dariyah and the surrounding country. Wahhabi support legitimised the Sauds (in their own eyes) as political leaders; they in turn upheld Wahhab's claim to the religious leadership and attacked other Muslims to promote the true faith. By 1788 the Wahhab-Saud alliance ruled much of the Arabian Peninsula. Throughout the nineteenth century the Wahhabis power fluctuated, they took the holy cities of Mecca and Medina, destroyed shrines and holy books, dug up graveyards and banned the haj – all in accordance with their extreme interpretation of Islam.

At the beginning of the twentieth century a rival tribe, the Rashidis, ruled Riyadh and much of the Nejd. In 1901, leading the Wahhabi-Saud alliance, ibn Saud attacked the Rashidis with great success, securing masses of booty and many camels. Encouraged, in January 1902, ibn Saud attacked Riyadh with a party of about sixty. He and twenty followers took the Riyadh fortress, killed the Rashidi governor as he was fleeing and established for himself a magnetic reputation as a conqueror.

During the next thirty years, ibn Saud fought battles against the Turks, the Rashidis and other tribes of the Hejaz. By 1932, with most of the Arabian Peninsula under his control, he named the conquered lands Saudi Arabia and proclaimed himself king.

Kings need money to support their ambitions, to protect themselves with armies, to keep the hoi-polloi happy and under control. Ibn Saud was doing reasonably well from British subsidies and taxing the 130,000 pilgrims performing the haj, but the Great Depression exerted its toll and the number of pilgrims dropped to 40,000. His salvation was to be oil, but ibn Saud had to wait a few years.

Oil had been discovered in Iran and by 1911 a British company, the Anglo-Persian Oil Company, was producing oil in commercial quantities. The British also found oil in Iraq after the First World War and in 1932 the Standard Oil Company of California (SOCAL) found it in Bahrain. SOCAL obtained a concession in Saudi Arabia in 1933, paying ibn Saud a quarter of a million dollars, and in 1938 discovered huge oil reserves in Dhahran on the Gulf coast.

The oil of eastern Saudi Arabia is present in enormous quantities, located at shallow depths in flat lands with no vegetation and near enough to the sea to make transportation easy. From the beginning, Saudi Arabia was – and remains – the cheapest place in the world to produce oil.

By 1955, Saudi Arabia's income had reached $2 million a day compared with half a million dollars a year in 1935. There was enough money not just to satisfy the needs of the Royal Family: there was enough for some of it to filter through to the people, to improve their lot and fund a construction boom. Of greater impact was the growing dependence of the United States and the West on Saudi Arabia as the world's largest single oil producer, the source of twelve per cent of global production.

The Saudi Royal Family grew in parallel with the burgeoning oil production. Royal polygamy and an insatiable appetite for copulation saw the family grow and grow through the 1990s. A prince might sire forty children. Reliable statistics are not available but these days there are perhaps 4,000 princes and more than 30,000 members of the Royal Family. To the mounting dissatisfaction of increasing numbers of ordinary Saudis, to say nothing of the ever-vigilant Wahhabis, the royals are always first at the feeding trough.

Ibn Saud was succeeded in 1953 by his eldest son, Saud, who reigned until he was replaced by his younger half-brother Faisal in 1964. Although he reigned for eleven years, one doesn't hear much of him. He was politically inept, squandered tens of millions of dollars, appointed his own sons to ministerial posts, whether competent or not, married more women than his father and was said to have quite an appetite for boys.

The House of Saud became concerned; Saudi Arabia was being weakened by a simple-minded profligate and it was feared that King Saud, who had a poor grasp of state and foreign affairs, was bringing the country to financial ruin. In 1958, the Royal Family and the religious leadership, the *ulema*, pressured Saud into appointing Faisal as prime minister. Faisal set about reforming the country's finances and cut much superfluous state spending. In 1962, when Saud had gone abroad for medical treatment, Faisal formed a cabinet which included his half-brothers Fah'd and Sultan. He excluded Saud's sons and proposed various reforms, including abolishing slavery. On return, Saud rejected Faisal's new plan, but Faisal mobilised the National Guard against Saud. With pressure from Faisal, the cabinet and other senior members of the Royal Family, particularly the ferocious Prince Muhammad (of whom more later), Saud agreed to abdicate. He went first to Geneva, then to other European cities and died in Athens in 1969.

After his abdication, Saud was no longer mentioned in Saudi Arabia. Institutions named after him were renamed, his reign does not feature in history books and his sons were removed from their government posts.

King Faisal, the third son of ibn Saud, had an abundance of energy, wisdom, intelligence and diplomatic skills; qualities notably lacking in Saud. He rescued the nation's finances, introduced reforms, many of which, like the abolition of slavery and introduction of girls' schools, were applauded by the outside world. During the 1973 Arab-Israeli war, Faisal withdrew Saudi oil from the world markets in protest over the American support of Israel. This action provoked an oil crisis, quadrupled the price of oil and gained him enormous prestige among Arabs and Muslims worldwide. The huge financial gains led to an economic boom in Saudi Arabia and allowed Faisal to give aid and subsidies to Egypt, Syria and the Palestine Liberation Organisation.

This era of enlightenment ended abruptly when Faisal was assassinated in Riyadh by a nephew, Prince Faisal bin Musa'id, in March 1975. It happened at the king's *majlis*, the traditional assembly where a tribal or other leader receives petitioners. The king leaned forward to greet his nephew who pulled out a pistol and shot him under the chin and then through the ear. King Faisal was taken to the newly opened King Faisal Specialist Hospital but died.

Prince Faisal was seized and questioned. The motive for the assassination has never been clear. Islamic scholars contended that the young man had been exposed to an excess of malevolent Western ways. He had been educated under the evil influence of universities in the United States, he had grown his hair long, smoked marijuana and sold LSD – he had been arrested for drug sales in 1969 but released after making a confession. He was deranged; doctors and psychiatrists confirmed that he was mentally unbalanced. Nonetheless he was tried, found guilty of regicide and publicly beheaded in Chop Chop Square.

Faisal was succeeded by his half-brother Crown Prince Khalid.

THE KING FAISAL SPECIALIST HOSPITAL and Research Centre was one of the late king's ambitious dreams. He donated about half a million square metres of land in the north of Riyadh and laid the cornerstone of the hospital in 1970. In 1973, Hospital Corporation of America was awarded the contract to operate the hospital, a contract which it held until the operation was taken over by a Saudi team twelve years later.

King Faisal's aim in establishing a high-powered hospital was to bring to Saudi Arabia the medical expertise of the West and thus to avoid forcing members of the Royal Family to travel to Europe and the United States for specialist treatment. This did happen, but to a limited extent, even when the hospital was fully staffed and operational.

So often when a member of the Royal Family was seriously ill, particularly if a grave prognosis had been given, relatives would tote the unfortunate around the world, on the basis that somewhere there had to be an exceptionally clever doctor who could effect a cure and it was just a question of finding him. Unlimited funds meant that hopeless cases would be badly handled. Instead of being treated with the kindness and the compassion the terminally ill deserve, patients who were really too sick to be moved would spend their final days being dragged around in a search for the non-existent cure. It seemed difficult for the Saudis to accept the evidence before their eyes and it may be that there was an underlying feeling that to give a grave prognosis might be usurping the Almighty in determining an individual's fate.

An advantage for the relatives accompanying sick patients was that they had an opportunity to escape the rigours of the climate, the austere life of the kingdom and to enjoy the fleshpots which abound in London, Boston and elsewhere – to the glee of tabloid journalists.

Another distressing aspect was the Saudi attitude to unfortunates who were brain-dead through stroke, accident or illness yet were kept alive by modern technology. These poor creatures often occupied precious beds in the Intensive Care Unit for months and although demonstrably dead were maintained indefinitely on life-support systems.

King Faisal's wish for a specialist hospital in Riyadh was realised by his successor, King Khalid, who officially opened the fully functioning King Faisal Specialist Hospital and Research Centre in 1975. Three years later, I joined the consultant staff.

Twelve

CULTURE SHOCK, EVERYBODY TALKED about culture shock. The difference between the Saudi culture and the culture of the West was extreme. Everybody was affected but scarcely anybody admitted their emotions had been at all disturbed.

For me, the manifestation was a sudden, out-of-the-blue self-questioning, "Why am I here, what am I doing in this strange place?" This uncomfortable doubt crept up on me several times a day, gradually disappearing as I settled in and became absorbed in the work.

But unexpected events could trigger the old feeling, a feeling that I was living a weird experience and really didn't know why. For instance, one morning when I strode into my consulting room, my eyes were greeted by the sight of a little old Bedouin lady sitting cross-legged on the examination couch. She was unveiled, disaster in front of a man, but not just a man, a man from heathen Europe. In a flash she pulled up her cloak, her black *abaya*, and covered her face with it. Beneath her *abaya* she was naked, she was wearing nothing below her waist, but her modesty was spared; she may have been exposed to the world – but she had covered her face.

Many a time I found myself asking an old lady lying in bed how she was – the reply, even if she was desperately ill, would be, "*Alhamdulillah*" (thanks be to God) – and if she had no veil or *burqa* she would anxiously drag the bedclothes across her face. No matter how old and no matter how wrinkled, a Saudi woman's face has to be covered when a stranger hoves into view.

Saudi Wahhabism impinged on life in many ways. Churches were not allowed, informal Christian services were forbidden and one could be jailed for importing a Bible.

In my first year at the King Faisal Specialist Hospital and Research

Centre, an edict was issued ordering Christian members of staff not to hum carols. As if we would...

Ugly, bad-tempered, hook-nosed religious police, the *mutawwa*, patrolled the streets and shopping malls in their dark brown robes and often burst into restaurants frequented by Westerners. They were on the lookout for Western women accompanied by men who were not their husbands or who had not covered their hair – or even sometimes women who had covered their hair, because the religious police thought that as non-Muslims they were mocking the Saudi dress code. Women wearing short skirts, short sleeves or with bare wrists were fair game. A *mutawwa'in* would think nothing of thrashing a woman with his camel stick for any of these offences.

The *mutawwa* are attached to The Committee for the Propagation of Virtue and the Prevention of Vice. There is a network of these volunteer ultra-pious types throughout the kingdom. They have powers of arrest and are in cahoots with the police. Apart from keeping their eyes open for real or imagined sexual offences, they make sure that the official ban on other religions is enforced, that fasting is observed during daylight hours in Ramadan and that shops close during prayer times. They are not just fervent religious killjoys... they can be killers.

In March 2002, a girls' school caught fire. The *mutawwa* prevented pupils leaving if they were not properly dressed, if they were not wearing headscarves and *abayas*. Fifteen died, fifty were badly burned. No doubt the *mutawwa* involved still consider that they did the right thing, that the fate of these improperly dressed girls was preordained. The rest of the world was aghast... for a few minutes: does anyone now recall that event? Or has it been forgotten like so many Saudi tales?

But there were amusing aspects. An American physiotherapist, known to all as 'Betty Boobs' for two good reasons was disciplined for 'immoral jogging'. She liked to keep fit and to the pleasure of all, except the hospital security guards – ever vigilant to protect our morals – jogged around the compound in which we lived in a loose track suit.

Some months later, as I was walking to work, I was some yards behind our buxom Betty when towards us swished a big American car driven by a Saudi... who could not take his eyes off Betty's prized features. He swivelled his head as he passed, lost control, the car veered to the side and overturned. He wasn't injured and as he got out dusting himself off and straightening his *thobe* and *goutra*, he smiled, no doubt still having Betty's boobs imprinted on his mind.

Censorship of all material brought into the country was severe. References to Israel were torn from newspapers and periodicals. World atlases had the state of Israel heavily blacked out with a permanent marker. Advertisements for ladies' underwear particularly aroused the ire of the sensitive censors with their red-hot permanent black markers cholerically criss-crossing the offending ladies.

Customs officers at all points of entry are empowered to censor and confiscate all foreign books, publications and video cassettes. Often material is confiscated simply because the customs officer can't read English and anything in French is automatically regarded as too racy for naïve and innocent Saudi souls. When I was in Saudi, short wave radios were banned; listening to world broadcasts from the BBC or Voice of America was an offence. Naturally history books were rewritten and when later the story of the First Gulf War was told, the Saudi armed forces played a remarkably large role.

So HOW COME I TOLERATED SUCH a repressive regime? Many reasons: the clinical material was excellent, colleagues of high calibre, facilities superb, the country interesting and trips to the open desert uninhibited by fences. And of course the pay was good, free of tax, housing was free and the holidays generous.

Being attached to the only referral hospital at the time in Saudi Arabia, you could expect to see a great variety of interesting cases. Surprisingly, some conditions common in Europe, inflammatory bowel diseases such as ulcerative colitis and Crohn's disease, occurred only rarely and were absent for no obvious reason. Liver disease was common and the effects of chronic liver problems, cirrhosis, bleeding from veins in the gullet and primary liver cancer were all too common. Duodenal ulcers, gallstones, tumours of the stomach and colon had an incidence equal to that seen in Europe.

By far the commonest problem seen in gastroenterology clinics at home were cases of a functional disorder labelled the irritable bowel syndrome, very real, poorly understood and defying remedy. It also occurred in Saudi Arabia, but far commoner was simple constipation – not surprising in such an arid country – and in males usually accompanied by the TATT syndrome

("Doctor, I'm 'tired all the time'...") with a limp-wristed gesture signifying feeble or non-existent erections.

Erectile function in Saudi males is a matter of intense pride; the old fellow of ninety who can sire a child or two is hailed as a hero. When it came to the ears of ibn Saud in his declining years that some had said he was losing his potency, he immediately gave the lie to this calumny by deflowering a young maiden of the family making the accusation. Luckily for me, I was able to skirt around the problem in my clinic by explaining that erectile dysfunction was not a gastroenterological problem. I would then refer the patient to the urologist for perhaps the implantation of some mechanical device or to the endocrinologist if there was a whiff of testosterone insufficiency. We were in the pre-Viagra era; I am quite sure that the advent of Viagra and similar drugs has brought inestimable joy to the House of Saud in particular and the kingdom in general.

WHAT SURPRISED ME, IN THIS LAND where alcohol was totally and absolutely forbidden, was the incidence of alcoholic liver disease. Believe it or not, I saw more in my clinics in Saudi Arabia than I encountered elsewhere.

From whence came the booze? Of course you quickly learn that knowing the right contacts, you could buy a bottle of ordinary whisky for the equivalent of £150. You would really have to have a great taste for the wee dram at that price. But how did it get in? The clue was that newly purchased, unopened whisky bottles had a strong smell of diesel fuel. The whisky had been loaded in returning empty fuel tankers after they had delivered fuel to neighbouring countries. No doubt there were Saudi customs officials getting fat by turning blind eyes at the border crossings.

Another source was *siddiqui*. *Siddiqui* is Arabic for 'my friend', and in this context was commonly abbreviated to 'Sid'. It was made by fermenting a sugar and water solution and then distilling the resulting liquor to produce what was thought to resemble gin. Indeed, mixed with a slice of lemon, ice and tonic water, a glass of really good Sid could almost pass for a Christian gin and tonic at sundown.

But one had to be careful; the quality of Sid varied enormously. The litmus test, or rather the flame test, was to ignite a teaspoonful of Sid with a match and if it burned with a uniform blue colour, all was well and any ill effects next day would be dependent on the quantity of Sid taken. However, if the flame was yellow, beware; too much methyl alcohol, horrible hangovers, visual problems and even a touch of death.

When the Arabian American Oil Company (Aramco) built houses for its employees in the Eastern Province of Saudi Arabia, it added small quarters for the servants and would routinely install a copper still in a separate annexe; separate because of the danger of explosion when a volatile liquid is distilled. The Aramco employees became so good at making 'the stuff' that they produced a recipe book which naturally they entitled, *The Blue Flame*. I once saw a copy. It contained all the information a deprived Westerner could desire, like how to make your Sid taste like sherry, or brandy or even cointreau. There was a story, also credible I'm sure, of some Americans who became so addicted to Sid that they had to smuggle the stuff out whenever they took leave.

But I was less inclined to make Sid with the hazards of distillation and I soon swore off it when, following modest consumption, my 'morning after' included tingling fingers and ringing in the ears. Local manufacturers of Sid included a Filipino called Art who came around with his car boot full of plastic containers and delivered Sid, much as the milkman delivered milk in the old days in England. Art came to a sticky end. He got involved in distributing funny tobacco and pleasing pictures of lady friends. When Art was rumbled by the Saudi police and they searched his house, they found not only his reserve supply of Sid, they found a pistol. One suspects Art ended up tipped out of an aircraft somewhere high over the Empty Quarter after having had various bits chopped off.

Another great source of Sid was a large local British company whose employees topped up their generous salaries making and flogging it. But they made the mistake of getting overconfident. Routinely they would bulk-buy sugar from supermarkets and cart home several pick-up trucks full of sacks of sugar. Not surprisingly, this aroused Saudi curiosity. The entrepreneurs were arrested and thrown in jail; all had sentences of indeterminate length.

On one occasion, a local supermarket filled a shelf with gripe water. Most people are not aware that the way gripe water works on a colicky baby which is irritating its parents to distraction is by giving it a slug of alcohol. Clearly visible in the contents listed on this well-known British brand was '5% alcohol'. When the news got out, the packed shelves emptied as quickly as the streets of medieval London when a leper taking a stroll tinkled his bell.

Nevertheless, even devoid of gripe water, the supermarkets held all the necessities for the production of wine of acceptable quality. They had shelves stacked with grape juice, conveniently segregated into red and white; other ingredients could be found and even, until the authorities tumbled to the fact that the wicked expatriates weren't buying it to make their own bread, tins of baker's yeast.

First you had to assemble the apparatus; not difficult. Take a five-gallon plastic container, drill a hole in the screw cap and insert a length of transfusion tubing. Make sure it's well sealed in the cap, with a short end inside to collect the carbon dioxide and leave enough tubing outside to feed well below the surface of the water in a bottle standing next to the container. Twelve bottles of red or white grape juice, a kilo of sugar, the juice of a lemon, a cup of tea, top up with water, add the yeast and off you go. Within a few days, a merry bloop-bleep-bloop-bleep sound indicates that bubbles are rising in the water bottle and wine is in the making. After about six weeks, the wine is ready for racking – drawing off from the sediment in the container.

The young wine was poured into bottles: those the grape juice came in were the most convenient because they had flip tops which made good seals. Racked at least once again into fresh bottles, the wine would be left to mature just as long as possible. Some days, depending on the ratio of supplies to thirst, this could be a matter of a few hours. Of course ostentatious oenophiles who wanted to display their knowledge would add the odd bottle of red currant juice, or cherry juice or even raspberry juice so that after swilling it around in the glass, sniffing, judging its robe and taste, they could remark on its fruitiness and pontificate about a specific flavour.

Once I had an original idea, went to the huge vegetable market on the Mecca road and bought a large quantity of black grapes. I took them home, put them in a big black plastic rubbish bag, tied the neck and then walked up and down treading on the bag on the floor: traditional *methode française*. When I was sure I had made a mush, I opened the bag and poured its contents into a bucket and left the bucket in my wardrobe. After a few days, a remarkable crust had formed, the surface of which bore brilliantly coloured fungal colonies. I perforated the crust, gas escaped – Eureka! I left the bucket a few weeks, then bottled the liquid contents. I tasted the young wine: it was a cloudy rosé and was disgusting; I racked it into new bottles, left it another six weeks; it clarified itself and a bottle opened with a nice little pop. It looked and tasted like that Portuguese rosé we plied our girl friends with in our teens... Mateus Rosé.

Supermarkets also contained the makings of beer. You could buy jars of malt; water, sugar, yeast added and within days, *voilà*, beer... usually in a large plastic rubbish bin. The supermarkets also sold alcohol-free beer which you could modify by added a few grains of yeast and recapping.

So confident were we in our skills that we decided to pit them against each other in a wine festival. At the time, we had a visiting French Professor of Neurosurgery and somebody had the bright idea of asking him to be our judge. He agreed with Gallic enthusiasm. The rules were simple; each competitor submitted two bottles of his wine, one bottle for immediate general consumption, the other for judging and subsequently drinking when the competition was over.

I would very much like to record that I was a winner; certainly my wine was infinitely better than that of the American pathologist who walked off with the *médaille d'or* (I still believe that he got up to something in the laboratory – after all, he had access to pure alcohol) why, I had even gone to the trouble of designing my own label on which it was stated that the wine had been *mis en bouteilles dans ma salle de bains*. What was surprising – maybe I mean unsurprising – was that the bottle which took second place had been entered mistakenly and contained home-brewed beer.

We used the yeast over and over; it could be kept going for months by careful and clean housekeeping, but eventually it became fatigued. New supplies were always welcome. On one occasion, as I was coming through the airport, the customs officer up-ended my shoulder bag and out fell several packets of beer yeast. Each packet had on its front an illustration of a foaming tankard. "What's this?" demanded the man.

"Yeast," I replied (perhaps he could read English.)

"For making alcohol?"

"No, certainly not. It's vitamins which I take; it's a medicine."

He was not satisfied and called his supervisor who inspected a packet and then said, "I will taste it, I will put it in water." He returned a few minutes later with his face screwed up in disgust, "It is medicine, it is terrible, give it back."

Thankfully I was off the hook, and who knows? Perhaps that customs officer is still, to this day, making gas in his yeast-populated colon, enough to outstrip any cud-chewing cow in an English meadow.

Saudis are not blessed with tough livers. They get all sorts of problems. Hepatitis in its various forms was common in my day. Their livers could be affected by parasites and alcohol seemed to play havoc. The hepatitis B virus could lead to chronic inflammation, which usually would go on to the scarring and fibrosis of the liver called cirrhosis. But even if the virus came to terms with the liver, and just lived there in a carrier state, it could end up causing a primary liver cancer.

Naturally your Saudi man in the street was not prone to alcoholic liver disease. Usually he couldn't lay his hands on the stuff and if by chance it came his way, he couldn't afford it. Moreover, the average Saudi was more likely to respect Saudi laws and Islamic teachings, unlike those who were able to travel abroad and get into evil ways, i.e. members of the Royal Family and rich Saudi merchants.

One Saudi prince, with advanced liver disease, recounted to me in a matter-of-fact way that he kept his whisky in the refrigerator and when he was thirsty would pull out a bottle and take a swig. He also mentioned that he started his day with a bottle of champagne (Dom Perignon, naturally) and a bowl of Beluga caviar for breakfast.

Another alcoholic Saudi prince was a puzzle to me. I had to admit him several times with what appeared to be coma induced by liver failure. He usually responded quickly to treatment and would come round no worse for the experience. The number of his functioning brain cells had already been reduced to below the minimum necessary for leading an independent existence and he totally depended on his servants. One afternoon when I was passing his room I saw through the open door his hand searching and waving above the bed rail (there to stop him tumbling out of bed). As I watched, the duty servant picked something out of his pocket, put it in the prince's hand and the prince transferred it to his mouth. I called for a security guard who searched the servant and found a large quantity of strong tranquillisers in his pocket. No doubt the duties of all the servants were less onerous with their royal boss snoozing his life away.

An extraordinarily pleasant Saudi in his fifties told me he was not only a general in the army, he was also head of the secret service. He had a big,

Dear Dr. Lark

I send you this picture for memory and in appreciation for your faithfulness and your good progress.

I present to you my simple present, my picture in my domain at work, my office, behind a set of pens and an enveloppe opener.

I would be very pleased if you would accept my modest present.

Wishing you all the best in your holiday.

Regards

Major General Huzaim
Tel 63418
P.O. Box 3698

A grateful patient: the 'extraordinarily pleasant' Major General Huzaim.

irregular liver, swelling of the legs and jaundice. I managed to get him to stop drinking (I think), treated him and he got better. At one consultation he said to me, "Doctor Lark, I have at home a very valuable watch, I want to make you a present of it."

"No, general," said I, "you mustn't do that, it's not right."

"But Doctor Lark, you are my brother and my friend, you have made me better."

"That's true of course," I said, "but you must not give me gifts."

"But cannot a man give his friend a gift; cannot a man give his brother a gift?" countered the general. I ignored that and said, "I will see you again in a month."

A month later he was still doing well. I thought he had forgotten our conversation but when that consultation was over and he got up to leave, he put something in my hand saying, "It rings you know, it rings."

I pocketed it in my white coat and when, later and alone, I pulled it out of my pocket I discovered it to be a wind-up travel alarm clock, evidently much used by the scratches on its face and back, and available for thirty shillings at any branch of Boots.

One of my patients proved to be a Sharia judge. He had great difficulty in accepting that what he had was alcoholic liver disease but I put it to him as gently as I could that his liver biopsy was totally consistent with that diagnosis. I pondered on whether his sentences were more or less severe when he had a hangover.

FAMILIAL CONDITIONS WERE COMMON in Saudi Arabia. The custom of marrying blood relatives provided fertile ground for those who wished to study the medical effects of consanguineous marriages. One such disease is called Wilson's disease; a rare congenital disease which requires that each parent carries the gene which leads to a disorder of the way the body handles copper. Copper accumulates in various tissues, especially in the liver, brain, bones, kidneys and the cornea (the transparent bit in the front of the eye). Deposition of copper in the cornea leads to the appearance of distinctive rings of copper around the periphery of the cornea; these were named Kayser-Fleischer rings after the discoverers. The liver was affected by inflammation, which would eventually lead to cirrhosis, and the copper deposits in the tissues of the brain would lead to disorders of the nervous system such as dementia, difficulty in walking, jerky movements, impairment of speech, confusion and tremors of the limbs.

I had a case of Wilson's disease under my care. He came from a large Bedouin tribe; there was a history of similar illnesses in several deceased family members. One afternoon as I passed his room I heard him shouting angrily. I stopped and popped my head around the door; he was shouting at the top of his voice into the phone – but he was holding the phone upside down and shouting in to the earpiece. Not only that, he also had great difficulty in holding the phone anywhere near his mouth because his hand was jerking around. I took the phone from his hand, turned it around and held it correctly aligned to his mouth and ear. A smile lit his face; he could hear his relatives and they could hear him. He held my hand tightly as I held the phone to his ear for what must have been half an hour: I swear he spoke to every member of his tribe.

The good news for him was that there is effective treatment for Wilson's disease. Excess copper can be removed from the body with drugs, by a process called chelation which turns copper into a form which can be excreted by the kidneys, and passed in the urine. Over a period of months, his condition improved but he never became totally normal because permanent damage had already been inflicted.

The liver is a big organ, weighs about one and a half kilogrammes and sits in the right upper abdomen immediately below the diaphragm. It has many functions: it helps fat digestion with the bile it produces, deals with the nutrients and toxins absorbed from the intestine into large veins called the portal veins. The liver detoxifies drugs, manufactures proteins and enzymes.

One enzyme in particular, called alcohol dehydrogenase, deals with alcohol, breaking it down to water and carbon dioxide. If, however, the quantity of alcohol drunk on a particular occasion exhausts the liver's current supply and temporarily exceeds the liver's ability to manufacture more of the enzyme, the excess alcohol will be metabolised by other less efficient routes. These lead to nasty by-products including acetaldehyde which, together with dehydration, are partly responsible for hangovers, and in the long term for serious liver, brain, muscle and heart damage.

When the liver goes wrong many things can happen. If the bile the liver makes is not excreted because there is a stone blocking the bile duct, or if the liver cells are damaged by inflammation or other disease and are incapable of passing on the bile, the patient turns yellow, becoming jaundiced. If the liver is so diseased it is unable to make the protein substances concerned with blood clotting, there will be a bleeding tendency. If the liver is not able to detoxify oestrogens (female hormones, which males also have) men will grow breasts (*gynaecomastia*) and their testes shrivel.

If the liver is not able to deal with toxins absorbed from the gut, the patient will develop hepatic encephalopathy, a situation in which the brain is affected by the toxins absorbed from the colon into the blood. The patient may slip into coma; an early sign of impending coma is that the patient develops a curious tremor of the outstretched arms, a flapping tremor like the way a seagull's wings beat and smelly breath (*foetor hepaticus*) likened to the smell of a freshly opened corpse (not pleasant, take my word).

Cirrhosis develops because the inflamed liver lays down fibrous tissue. The liver has remarkable powers of regeneration when it is inflamed from any cause, be it alcohol, virus infection or other insult. But once the liver develops a lot of tough fibrous scar tissue within it, the process of cirrhosis begins and is usually irreversible.

With cirrhosis the pressure in the veins which bring seventy-five per cent

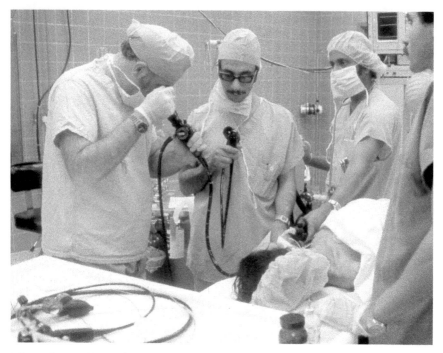

The author in theatre beginning a session of injecting oesophageal varices.

of the liver's blood supply, mainly from the intestine and called the portal system, rises. At half a dozen sites the veins of the portal system connect with systemic veins, which are those which bring blood from all over the body back to the heart. At these connecting sites the increased pressure transmitted from the liver can make the veins bulge; their walls become thin and tortuous, just like the bunches of varicose veins one sees on the legs of fat ladies.

One of these sites is in the rectum. Haemorrhoids (which are dilated rectal veins) are common in cirrhotics. Another site is around the umbilicus where the dilated veins cause an appearance called the *caput medusae* – Medusa's Head – with dilated tortuous veins wriggling away from the belly button. But the most serious situation lies in the oesophagus, where the dilated thin-walled veins (called oesophageal varices) can rupture, leading to devastating bleeding. Because advanced liver disease was common in the kingdom, this complication was common, and patients with bleeding oesophageal varices presented in the emergency room at least twice a week.

I learned about the serious problems I would face with bleeding varices when I did my month's locum. Before taking up the permanent post at the

King Faisal Specialist Hospital, I studied the way bleeding oesophageal varices were handled at King's College Hospital in London whose Liver Unit is famous. There I learned and practised the technique of injecting the veins to stop bleeding. The substance used was exactly the same as used by surgeons for injecting varicose veins of the legs. The object is to cause local inflammation and thrombosis, and when the inflammation subsides, there would be scar tissue which would prevent recurrence. But injecting leg veins is a totally different matter to injecting fragile, briskly bleeding veins in the lower end of the gullet.

One particular patient was a young man of twenty-five who presented almost drained of blood, exsanguinated, to the emergency room. We put up three transfusions, pumped blood into him and took him to theatre when he was sufficiently resuscitated. I then injected his varices and the bleeding was controlled. Subsequently I injected his varices on three occasions, each a month apart. Endoscopic examination after the third showed no evidence of varices but unfortunately the poor chap had such advanced liver disease that he died some months later of liver failure. But there was something memorable about him. His enlarged spleen, in the left upper quadrant of his abdomen, was outlined by healed burns, the scars of cautery.

Cautery is a traditional treatment in Saudi Arabia. It involved burning a particular area of skin with a poker or hot iron to treat a specific illness. Normally cautery was applied to the back, chest or abdomen but I have seen it on the scalp. Remarkably it appeared that those who practised cautery could distinguish between obstructive jaundice due to a gallstone or tumour and jaundice due to liver disease itself. The first would be treated with cautery to the wrist and the latter with cautery to the base of the little finger nail.

Our young man with the cautery over his spleen told the story that one night, many months before, he had been sitting around the camp fire in the desert with his companions when an old Bedouin rode up on his camel and sat with them drinking coffee. Our patient had a sudden small *haematemesis*... he vomited a small quantity of blood. The visitor examined him and then cauterized his abdomen, and as we saw, the cautery accurately outlined his enlarged spleen.

Nowadays liver transplant offers hope of a cure. But you have to be cautious with alcoholics who may, despite solemn promises to eschew the demon, regard a new liver as allowing the beginning of a new drinking career.

ANOTHER COMMON CLINICAL PROBLEM we had was bleeding from the intestinal tract, usually from ulcers, but one very unusual case occurred in an infant less than a year old. This child, from a remote desert village, had suffered several episodes of bleeding presenting as the passage of jet black tarry stools. The paediatric department asked me to see her. Physical examination was unremarkable but when I endoscoped her under general anaesthesia, as I looked at the walls of her stomach, I could see small quantities of blood oozing from many areas scattered throughout the middle of the stomach. Tests of her blood had shown that she did not have a primary bleeding disorder and so I was able to take biopsies. These showed multiple, minute telangiectases, collections of abnormal tiny blood vessels. Clearly surgery was the only option.

At surgery it was demonstrated that the blood vessel abnormalities extended throughout her stomach, from its entrance at the oesophagus to its exit at the pylorus. The whole of her stomach had to be removed and the oesophagus hooked up to the small intestine. I, the paediatricians and the surgeons thought that the removal of all her stomach would have a devastating effect on her health, her growth and her development. But miracles happen: she thrived. We made sure that she suffered none of the deficiencies which could affect patients who had lost all their stomachs. She gained weight and was an active, happy and delightful little girl. When I last saw her, some two years after the operation, she was to all intents normal for her age.

Thirteen

IN JULY 1977, A SENIOR SAUDI PRINCE had his granddaughter, a young princess, publicly executed in a parking lot in Jeddah. The Saudi prince, Muhammad ibn Abdul Aziz al Saud, was a nasty piece of work; alcoholic, sadistic and violent. He was the sixth son of ibn Saud and had been in line for the throne. But he had voluntarily stepped aside from the succession. It was generally thought that he did so because ascending the throne of Saudi Arabia would cramp his unrestrained, debauched lifestyle.

When his older brothers died, Muhammad became the elder of the clan. Because of his fierce temperament, the Saud family chose him to put the frighteners on King Saud, the second Saudi king, to force him to abdicate after ten years of wanton spending and less than regal behaviour. Muhammad's younger brother, Khalid, became crown prince when Faisal succeeded to the throne.

Muhammad was loathed and feared but because of tight Saudi press restrictions, the outside world knew nothing of him until the news of his granddaughter's murder, an act of primitive tribal vengeance, reached a worldwide audience through a British drama-documentary, *Death of a Princess*. The princess was not named in the film but it became common knowledge that she was Princess Misha'al bint Fahd al Saud.

Like so many stories coming out of the Kingdom of Saudi Arabia, there was haziness of detail and the truth was muddied as accounts passed from mouth to mouth. Of course there was no report of the event in the Saudi press.

The story begins with Princess Misha'al being educated in Beirut, Lebanon, where for the first time she was exposed to the world outside Saudi Arabia. At the age of seventeen, she was given in marriage to a first cousin, but the marriage failed and she was divorced.

She travelled around Europe and met and fell in love with a young

Lebanese. Her family refused to allow her to marry him. Using a false name, she met her lover in a hotel in Jeddah. They were caught and her grandfather ordered their imprisonment. He demanded that Khalid, by then king, sentence them both to death; the king declined. He then turned to the head imam of Jeddah and made the same demand, but the imam wanted to order an inquiry. Muhammad lost patience and ordered the Jeddah executioner to do the job, but he expressed doubts.

Finally Muhammad ordered his personal bodyguards to execute the pair of lovers. The couple were taken to a parking lot on the outskirts of Jeddah. She was veiled and covered in black. He had his hands tied behind his back. In front of a rapidly assembled crowd, the princess was shot twice in the head and died in front of her lover who was forced to watch the killing. He was then beheaded and dismembered. She was just nineteen years old. It had been put about that she had confessed to having committed adultery. The existence of a confession was vital; otherwise, according to Sharia law, four males would have to testify that they had witnessed the act.

Photographs of the executions were taken by a British carpenter who happened to be staying nearby. They were published in the British press.

Death of a Princess took eighteen months to make and was shown on Independent Television London on 9 March 1980. Some weeks later, it appeared on the American Public Broadcasting Services television network. The Saudis were outraged by the film; they tried to get it banned, failed and expelled the British ambassador. American oil companies got jittery, suspended donations to the Public Broadcasting Services and published full-page spreads in newspapers criticising the film.

As usual the furore died down, shoulders were shrugged, and in the minds of the West it became another example of Saudi ways, but it touched me personally a couple of months later.

A colleague who had been looking after a member of the Saud family had to take compassionate leave and asked me to replace him as the patient's physician. At first the prince would have nothing to do with me because I was British and therefore associated with the notorious film. He had an inflamed gall bladder full of stones. It was infected and he needed my services. I treated him and his condition improved. Some weeks later he was well enough to have his gall bladder removed by one of our surgical teams. So grateful and surprised was the prince to be restored to excellent health that he made gifts of Chevrolet cars to the surgeon, the anaesthetist and my colleague who had briefly cared for him, but for me, the Englishman – nothing. Frankly I had no yearning for a Chevy but I did feel offended when he left the hospital without as much as a *shukran* (thank you) or a *ma'salaama* (goodbye).

At the same time I had under my care another princely Saud who had been admitted as an emergency with a catastrophic bleed from his stomach. He had what is called a *leiomyoma* of the stomach wall. *Leiomyomata* are tumours of muscle, well-recognised as occurring in the stomach but not common. The tumours, which are not cancerous, are very dangerous because they are riddled with blood vessels and can ulcerate with profuse bleeding. He had been transfused with blood, his general condition was good and I discussed surgery with him. He would not entertain the idea of an operation even though I explained the danger and likelihood of a further haemorrhage. If he persistently refused surgery, I should by rights have discharged him, but I couldn't; he told me he was buddy-buddy with the crown prince who had said he could stay in hospital for as long as he liked.

Every day I had a chat with him and described over and over the danger he faced; every day he refused surgery. Eventually one morning he announced, "You may operate."

"Good," said I.

"But," he said, "not on my stomach, on my liver."

I paused, startled by this piece of logic. I said I would ask my surgical colleague to see him. It was agreed that he should go to theatre the next day; the surgeon had managed to get him to consent to having surgery on his stomach if at operation he found that there was no problem with his liver. The surgery was simple; the tumour popped out like a pea from a pod and the prince was home in a few days.

She swept into my consulting room on a gust of the most exotic perfume I had ever inhaled; she was forty-four; she looked twenty-four – with her doe eyes, perfect figure and generous painted lips she looked like a suicide bomber's promise of paradise. She swept her black cloak around her, crossed her legs revealing a tantalizing glimpse of a black stockinged knee, and sat next to my desk. She smiled a heart-stopping smile and said, "Good morning, doctor."

She was followed by a Saudi dressed in an impeccable white *thobe* and a red-and-white check *goutra* sporting a gold watch as thin as a postage stamp and gold cufflinks each weighing about an ounce. He was also densely perfumed; she motioned him to sit next to her.

She had a serious problem. She had well-established liver disease and had been referred to me for advice concerning contraception. Oral contraceptives were out because of her liver problem and she did not want any mechanical devices fitted. As far as I could see, the only alternative was that the husband should undergo a vasectomy, which is a small operation to tie his spermatic cords and render him infertile.

Now this had to be tackled very gently; Saudi males don't go for this sort of thing. I discussed it with him. Not surprisingly he became agitated. As the discussion continued, he became more agitated – he got up, he paced the room, up and down, up and down, muttering, "Why me? Why, Me?" Finally he turned to me and exclaimed, "But why me, doctor? I'm her son."

AS INDIVIDUALS, SAUDIS ARE VERY HOSPITABLE, a legacy of the ancient tradition of desert dwellers. However, their hospitality could be embarrassing, at times tedious, but impossible to refuse. Many times I was invited to share an evening meal with a Saudi family (men only of course) and the pattern of the evening was the same, unless the host happened to be one of those thirsty royals who liked his guests to share a few bottles of whisky with him.

I would be collected at the hospital in the early evening and taken to the host's villa or palace, perhaps a stone's throw away from the hospital, perhaps twenty miles into the desert. After introductions, we would squat in a circle on the floor around a large baby-pink plastic sheet with bowls of fruit and plates of flat Arabic bread. The evening would begin with dates. Saudis are experts on dates and the ones they grow are delicious. We would eat dates and drink Arabic coffee from tiny cups, with murmurs of pleasure, for half an hour. We only moved on when I had swallowed enough dates to last a lifetime and then more and the delicious things were losing their appeal. I would try to refuse, but dates galore would continue to be pressed on me as the honoured guest.

"Doctor, do you not like our dates?"

"Oh, but of course I do."

"Well then, doctor, why not have some more?"

"But really I have had enough."

"Had enough? But they are so good, just eat a few more."

"Very well, thank you," I muttered as I forced yet another into my gagging mouth.

Arabic coffee seems slightly bitter at first but delicious when you have acquired the taste. It is made from coffee beans picked green, roasted and flavoured with cardamom. It is offered in tiny cups with no handles, slightly bigger than egg-cups, and it is customary to accept two cups. In order to signal that you'd drunk enough coffee, you would hold out the empty cup towards the coffee bearer and wobble it from side to side; without the wobble he would refill the cup *ad infinitum*. Many a Western guest, unaware of this tradition, would find himself awash with coffee, to the barely concealed delight of the coffee bearer.

At this early stage of the evening, feeling as though I had a solid column of dates extending from my incisors to my already groaning stomach, the main course would arrive. It would be either a whole roasted goat or sheep resting on a bed of fragrant rice on a huge platter. We sat around helping ourselves, but always the ever-attentive host would complain that I, the honoured guest, wasn't eating enough and he would pile more of everything onto my plate. I am happy to report that I was never, in five years, offered the eye of a sheep or goat.

On one occasion a squat, cross-eyed and obese son of the host, sitting on the floor opposite me some two yards away asked, "You liver specialist?" When I said, "Yes," he got up, waddled over to the cooked carcass, pulled up his right sleeve, delved deep into the goat's abdomen, felt around for a moment and yanked out the liver. He then waddled over to me and plopped it onto my plate saying, "*Hinna tahassusi fil cabed*," (Here you are, specialist of the liver) thinking no doubt it would be a great treat for me. However the liver, being deep in the recess of the goat's abdomen, was only partly cooked and – horrors – the gall bladder had not been removed, had been nicked and had leaked bile. The liver looked awful, its surface stained a nasty shade of green. It crossed my mind that perhaps Saudi goats also suffer from liver diseases.

As a good guest, there was nothing I could do but eat some of the ugly organ in front of my hosts. I took a slice, forced it into my mouth with an exclamation of, "*Laziza* – delicious!" During the course of the meal,

I managed to secrete slices of liver in the scattered fruit bowls and slip them under the tablecloth, or under neighbours' plates, not caring what the servants would think when they cleared the meal. I knew that before that happened, we would have adjourned to the nearby *majlis*, a large meeting room where people sat and sometimes made important decisions but more often just chatted and smoked hookahs. Just once I tried a hookah. I was surprised; the smoke, cooled and perfumed as it passed through the water in the base, tasted delicious; usually the 'tobacco' in hookahs has a basis of dried fruit.

Often the conversation would turn to the marvels of Islam and the Holy Koran. My hosts seemed to think that I might instantly convert to Islam when I was enlightened by their learned discussions. They went to great pains to convince me that their holy book contained all the knowledge of the world; everything from the past and the present, in the old world and in the modern world, from jumbo jets to nuclear bombs. I soon learned to agree and not raise points for discussion, such as the inhibition of women in their society or intolerance of other religions; to do so would provoke fierce, endless, arguments.

Then came the *pièce de résistance* and I would have to sing for my supper.

My host would signal a servant who would leave the room and trot back with a couple of bulging shopping bags, each full of medications. The contents of one would be tipped onto the floor between us and bottle by bottle, packet by packet, we would discuss each medicament.

"What is this doctor?"

"It is Inderal," I would say.

"Is it good for my heart?"

"Could be," I would reply. "Who prescribed it?"

Pause for thought, "My doctor in London."

"And do you take it?"

"*Yanni*, sometimes. But tell me, doctor, who is the best doctor in London to take my blood pressure?"

We went through a similar performance with each drug, then he would pack up the first bag and tip the contents of the second bag onto the floor, announcing, "These are my wives' medicines." Once again we would go through them drug by drug. Often a servant would be sent to the women's quarters to get the answer to a question I had asked about a particular drug.

Eventually I would be released and driven home, vowing in the future to avoid such tedious evenings.

On one occasion a family invited me again within a few months of my first visit. Hoping to cut short the evening, I arranged for an Irish colleague, John Froude, to call me at about ten o'clock in the evening on my locator. Spot on time he bleeped; we were halfway through the drugs questions-and-answers routine. I answered, listened to the message and made my excuses. I said I had to go because there was a very sick patient in the hospital that I had been called to see.

"Go!" exclaimed the host. "Why go?"

I explained again that I had been asked to see a very sick patient. He was genuinely puzzled, "But you are the head doctor. You have other doctors. Tell them to see the patient. Now these tablets were given to me in Germany, or was it Amerikee? Are they good for my *imsac* (constipation)?"

Eventually I got away and was driven home. I had promised my Irish colleague who paged me that I would have a nightcap with him on my return. I rang his bell; he lived just a few doors from me. John opened the door. He was unshaven, unkempt, sweating freely and stark naked except for a guitar slung across his lower abdomen.

"Hi Bill, hot night." He welcomed me in as he strummed his guitar. His wife, he informed me, was upstairs in bed, close to term in her second pregnancy. "But," said he, placing a plastic jug of wine on the table between us, "although I was thinking of taking her to the hospital, her contractions are far apart and irregular so let's drink a little wine and you can tell me all about your fascinating evening."

I went home at midnight and was asleep as soon as my head hit the pillow.

I was woken at two by the shrill ringing of my bedside telephone and the anxious voice of John, "Come quickly, Bill, the head's presenting." I dashed to his house and, sure enough, the head was being delivered. The bed was drenched in amniotic fluid, the labour was precipitate and things were moving fast. John looked up at me and agitatedly said, "What about the cord? How am I going to cut it? I don't have any clamps!" I raced home to get some rusty Spencer-Wells artery forceps I had in my do-it-yourself kit.

But it was all over by the time I returned. John had cut the cord using a razor blade and tied knots in the severed ends in the time-honoured way. There had been no time to call the obstetrician until after the baby had arrived. He came just in time to deliver the placenta and said that mother, baby and placenta must go into hospital to deal with any complications from such a speedy delivery.

"I'll take her," said John, and we drove off in convoy with John, wife and new baby leading in his clapped out red Volvo. The obstetrician followed in his sunny yellow Volkswagen beetle and I, who had been given the placenta wrapped in a white towel, followed in my ancient powder-blue Lada, with the placenta resting on the passenger seat.

We pulled up at the luxurious front entrance of the King Faisal Specialist Hospital, the Royal Hospital. The guards, more accustomed to seeing Rolls-Royces, Mercedes and the like, told us to park elsewhere but we pulled rank and left our three tatty cars where they were. We processed down a very long hospital corridor with mother in a wheelchair holding the baby, father pushing the chair, solicitous obstetrician at her side and me, again bringing up the rear, holding the wrapped placenta (the towel by now saturated with blood) in my outstretched arms and leaving a trail of drops of blood down the length of the corridor.

Next day, to my horror, I found that the passenger seat of my precious Lada had been soused with placental blood, had turned black and become rock-hard. And that's the way it remained, under a smart seat cover that I bought in a souk, until I sold the car to one of our pathologists a few months later.

But my little car had served me well. Although an object of derision to my colleagues who possessed smart four-wheel-drive cars that they proudly drove on desert outings, my Lada was light and bounced over the desert like thistle-down, sometimes leaving them behind and stuck in the sand. Then I would jauntily drive back and proffer my shovel to help with the digging out.

On one occasion when I returned from leave I found dents in the roof, bonnet and boot of my long-suffering Lada. Eventually a friend confessed that in my absence a few 'Lada parties' had been held, the object being to see how many people could balance on the car. This needed several record-breaking attempts, usually towards the end of an evening of wine testing and tasting. I think the record was a dozen. This was remarkable considering the small surface area of the car and the wobbly balance of the contestants. One morning when I departed for work I found that some wag had erected a transfusion stand next to my poor little Lada and fed tubing under the bonnet.

Eventually I surrendered; although nippy in the desert, my car was very small and had no airconditioning. I sold it to a brilliant medical scientist called Edward, who came from Nigeria. He got it for song. For some reason, I don't know why (it had always gone well for me and I never bothered with having it serviced) he had a car mechanic overhaul it and take it for a test drive. It caught fire and was destroyed. Edward came to see me and told me, in my view with unnecessary aggression, what had happened. I offered my condolences and said, "But Edward, the insurance will cover that." Through clenched teeth he muttered what I thought was, "I hadn't got it insured yet."

So going from the ridiculous to the sublime, I bought a Range-Rover. A powerful beast in the desert, it could almost climb the wall of a house, cross the roughest ground and the softest sand. What's more, it had ample floor space for sleeping and highly efficient airconditioning. But it was thirsty… thirsty? In Saudi Arabia, petrol was infinitely cheaper than water and I could fill the tank for the price of a ham sandwich at home.

AT THAT TIME, THE MINISTER OF Information was Sheikh Muhammad abdo Yamani. He was a respected scholar and an extremely intelligent, educated, affable and modest man. He smiled easily and was pleasant to all. He was not related to Zaki Yamani, the celebrated successful arbiter of Saudi oil. One morning at prayers with King Khalid, he knelt, stood up, and fell over in a dead faint. He was admitted under my care.

Muhammad Yamani was very pale. He gave a history of indigestion for many years. Upper abdominal pain would waken him regularly at two in the morning. It could be relieved by a glass of warm camel's milk and he volunteered that over the past six weeks he had passed jet black stools from time to time. His haemoglobin (think of it as the redness or strength of his blood) was in percentage terms down to about thirty per cent. It all added up to a chronic ulcer that had been bleeding intermittently.

Endoscopy showed a duodenal ulcer and smack in the middle of the floor of the ulcer was a jet black area which indicated recent haemorrhage. He was treated with anti-ulcer medication, iron tablets and rest. His indigestion went away in a matter of a day or two and he began to feel better than he had for many years. I visited Sheikh Yamani in his hospital room every day. He was making excellent progress and we got to chatting. "So, doctor, as a complete outsider what do you think of my country?" he asked.

"Well, Your Excellency..." My reply was guarded – it would not do to dwell on negative aspects. "It is certainly very different to any country I have visited in my travels, but it is interesting and irresistibly attractive. My colleagues and I find that our expeditions into the desert are fascinating. I never knew the desert had such a varied ecology, such grandeur and is so enchanting at night."

I couldn't resist telling him that I had recently bought a marvellous desert vehicle, a Range-Rover, and that I was hoping that we could extend our travels beyond camping at weekends.

"Ah doctor," he smiled, "so you want to be a Saudi tourist. We don't have many of those." I agreed and he said, "But where would you like to go?" I said I would have to talk to my camping companions but that I thought a cross-country trip to the Red Sea, a tour down the coast, south-west into the mountains and finally back to Riyadh skirting the Empty Quarter would be good for starters, and perhaps we could visit other regions later. He was enthusiastic. "What a nice trip. If you like I can help you." I said it would be an honour and thanked him.

Six weeks later, Sheikh Yamani attended as a day case for a follow-up endoscopy to make sure that the ulcer had healed. He was obviously restored to full health and brushed aside the preliminary injection of a sedative, saying, "I have a royal cabinet meeting in two hours and I must be fully alert for that." I passed the 'scope under local anaesthesia; the ulcer had healed without even a blush of residual inflammation.

As the minister jumped off the examination table, he looked at me with a twinkle in his eye and asked, "So what about the tourism?"

"I've talked to my friends," I replied, "we're all keen."

"Same route?" he asked. "Leave it with me." We shook hands, he gathered his cloak and his retinue and departed with a smile.

A week later, a courier from the Ministry of Information arrived at the hospital. He handed me a bundle of letters tied together with green ribbon. The letters were written by Sheikh Yamani; each was addressed to the governor of a province we would enter on our trip. "His Excellency wishes you a good journey," he said, adding that we should not hesitate to use the letters at police checkpoints and present them at governors' palaces.

I called my usual camping buddies with more than the usual level of excitement and we immediately got down to organising the trip.

Fourteen

W̲E HAD ALL READ *ARABIAN SANDS* by the celebrated Arabist and explorer Wilfred Thesiger and envied his freedom. It's hard to imagine anyone not being inspired by his account of crossing the Empty Quarter in 1945, his visit to the little-known south-west corner of Arabia, to the Hejaz mountains and to the Tihama region:

> …the hot plain that lies between the Red Sea and the mountains, passing through villages of daub-and-wattle huts reminiscent of Africa. The people here were of uncommon beauty and pleasantly easy and informal in their manner. We watched them dressed in loincloths and with circlets of scented herbs upon their flowing hair, dancing in the moonlight to the quickening rhythm of drums at the annual festivals when the young men were circumcised.

If ever there was going to be an opportunity to experience a glimpse of that Saudi Arabia, this was it. So much had changed in the intervening thirty-five years. Everything about our normal situation now kept us apart from the Saudi hoi polloi. We lived in guarded hospital accommodation; our only social intercourse was through our patients and their relatives, and although some might be described as 'ordinary', even they had to have some degree of wasta to get through the portals of the royal hospital. My Arabic was pretty much limited to medical phraseology – not all that useful haggling in the souk or camel market.

Our route would take us to Mecca, Jeddah, the Tihama coast, then the Asir mountains and back to Riyadh skirting the Rub al Khali, the Empty Quarter. Altogether we would take ten days; the intrepid, tough Thesiger – who some years later would be a patient of mine – took months on camel

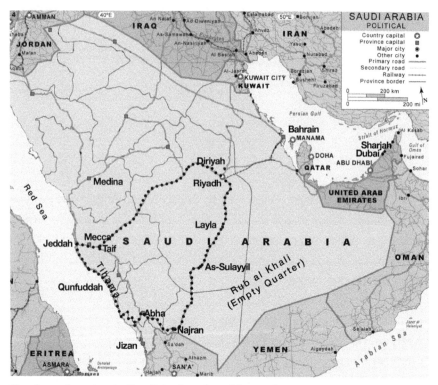

Ten days of tourism in Saudi Arabia (dotted line indicates tour route).

and on foot, barely surviving the searing heat and láck of water in the desert. We were softies: we had four-wheel drives and as much food and water as we wanted. We had tents, sleeping bags and even hot water bottles – it was mid-November and nights could get cold. Nonetheless we were privileged to be doing what few other foreign workers in the kingdom had been able to enjoy.

We were nineteen in all, eleven adults and eight children, and enough medical expertise between us to staff a UN field hospital. We had two obstetricians, Don McDonald and Ulla Sieck, but did not anticipate calling on their professional services on the trip. Likewise with David Lewall, the chief of radiology, and the three internists, Nick Woodhouse, Sean Sieck and myself. It would be a pleasure to be temporarily divorced from our normal activities.

With undisguised excitement, we set off late on a cool afternoon from Riyadh, taking the Taif road in the direction of the setting sun. As we passed through the outskirts of Riyadh, through the usual landscape of wrecked cars, scattered rubbish, blue plastic bags adorning skeletal trees like bizarre ripe fruit and goats enjoying their usual diet of cardboard cartons, we heard the call to prayer resonating from a hundred minarets. Outside mosques, camels with disdainful, superior expressions were couched in the back of parked Toyota pick-up trucks waiting patiently for evening prayers to end before being driven by their owners to market.

Darkness fell abruptly soon after six but we continued for another two hours. By the time we stopped, it was impossible to pick a good camp site so we drove what we thought was a few hundred yards off the main road. We stumbled around in the dark until we had lit our hurricane lamps and started a fire. Huddling together for warmth, we scoffed our sandwiches, by now sandy and gritty, boiled water to fill our hot water bottles (I dread to think what Thesiger would have made of that) and turned in for an early night, adults in the back of the four-wheel drives, children in tents. But sleep did not come easy and throughout the night huge lorries rumbled by. We had in fact travelled at an angle to the main road and were closer to it than we thought.

Dawn came not a minute too soon. We set off with the rising sun on our backs. I'd like to recount the beauty of the drive, to say how refreshing we found the early morning air and the glory of the countryside in dawn's early light – but the air was choking with dust and redolent with diesel fumes and

Beings in nothingness: Convoy en route to Taif.

the vista was not pleasing at all, more of a rocky barren moonscape than rolling red sand dunes.

After a few miles the air cleared, the visibility was good and we were humming along... until our lead car disappeared in a cloud of steam. It was Don's GMC Suburban. When the steam had cleared and his engine cooled, we inspected the radiator. Sure enough, there was a crack in the base. We could see a village on the horizon of the flat plane we were traversing, so we refilled Don's radiator and gently drove to the village hoping to find a garage...

We were out of luck but the villagers must have thought they'd hit the jackpot. Soon we were surrounded by cavorting, excited, chattering locals who hadn't had so much excitement since Uncle Abdullah's stallion camel broke loose and tried (unsuccessfully) to mate with a donkey. We stood around and scratched our heads.

"I guess we'll have to head home and just take it very slow," said Don to loud choruses of "No!" from his wife and three children.

Then a bright young lad took Don by the hand and led him to the village shop. In the spice corner, he pointed to an open sack of turmeric and indicated that this was what we should use. Don bought a bag of the stuff and under the supervision of his young mentor, added water to a generous quantity of it, poured the thick yellow mixture into his radiator, topped it with fresh water and started the engine. He ran it for twenty minutes and then switched it off and breathed a silent prayer. Anxiously we waited for it to cool; Don opened the bonnet and we all, together with what seemed like a hundred villagers, craned our necks to look at the radiator. Amid cries of "*Alhamdulillah*," "*Allah mowjood*" and "Bloody marvellous", we observed that the crack was now a thin yellow line and not a drop issued from it.

Don bought Pepsi and ice creams all round for the villagers and off we drove to cries of "*Jimshi imshi*" (GMC goes). The radiator held out all the way back to Riyadh and didn't need another dose of the yellow miracle.

THAT EVENING WE PASSED THROUGH TAIF and camped on Mount Arafat, about ten miles from the holy city of Mecca. Mount Arafat isn't much of a mountain, in reality a hill of some 150 feet surrounded by the gravelled plain of Arafat. It's significant because it is where the Prophet Muhammad delivered his farewell sermon to the faithful who had accompanied him on his last haj when he was close to the end of his life. At another time of year, the plain of Arafat would have thronged with Muslims performing the vigil which is a vital part of the haj ritual. As it was, we had the place to ourselves. The morning dawned delightfully cool and clear; the air, despite the locale, had the quality of fine champagne.

On the way to Jeddah, we passed the entrance to Mecca. We didn't linger. An enormous notice in front of a forbidding military checkpoint screamed, 'ONLY MUSLIMS ALLOWED FURTHER.'

The nearer we got to Jeddah and the coast, the more humid the air became. Jeddah is known as the Bride of the Red Sea, but this bride did not welcome us into her cool boudoir with open arms and all the perfumes of Arabia; she was hot, humid, sweaty and dusty. Her road network was a work in progress. We sought directions to the coast, where we planned to camp for a few days, but might as well have saved our breath. So often a metalled road would take us back out into the desert where, after a dozen miles, it ended abruptly in the sand.

Eventually, by trial and error, we found a good road running parallel to the sea and followed it for about fifty miles to escape the detritus of civilisation. By mid-afternoon, we had found a crescentic bay with limpid, inviting, blue water surrounded by dunes and palm trees. We pitched camp, as usual forming a circle like the covered wagons of the old frontiersmen, but we didn't need protection against marauding Red Indians. Our hazards were more mundane: snakes and scorpions (fortunately rare) and mosquitoes (all too abundant). For the rest of the afternoon, we swam and snorkelled. Nick Woodhouse found oysters and gathered a bucketful. They were good: as good as any fresh French oysters from Normandy.

That night we sat around a fire built of driftwood. The temperature had fallen several degrees and it was pleasant to gaze into the fire and chew the fat. When a poker school started, I excused myself – the game has no interest; I've never played – by saying that my temperament was too straightforward and my face too honest, and turned in.

There's nothing like settling down, pleasantly fatigued by the day's exertions and excitements and dropping off to a sound sleep with the stars of Arabia twinkling above, the moon turning night into day, the air cooled by a breeze off the Red Sea and the gentle murmuring of the water lapping on the nearby shore.

I was awakened at dawn by shouts. Nick and Don had spotted a couple

Nick Woodhouse's Red Sea oyster harvest.

of fishing boats a hundred yards offshore and were trying to get the attention of their crews so they could buy fresh fish. But it was only when Nick pulled out his wallet and waved a few fresh fifty *riyal* notes that he got his message across. The fishermen pulled in their nets, gunned their engines and raced to the shore as if pursued by a tsunami.

They quickly had a crowd of us around their boats, and after a great deal of semi-serious haggling we bought the whole catch at a price that satisfied vendors and buyers. It seemed ridiculously low to us but they were pleased; we had far exceeded the price they would get in the local market.

Don, an accomplished fisherman, rapidly cleaned the fish in the shallows of the Red Sea while others organised barbecues. The delightful aroma of the cooking fish was outdone only by its succulent taste. I asked Don, "Do you think a sprinkling of turmeric would enhance the flavour?" The sideways look I received in reply said it all.

OUR ROUTE TOOK US ALONG THE COASTAL plain of Tihama. As we travelled further down the Red Sea, we passed houses constructed solely of flattened large tin cans, the cheapest and most readily available building material. The Red Sea was on our right and as calm as a mill pond. It was a deep blue... so why 'Red'? Several theories have been advanced, the most plausible being that the seasonal blooming of a pigmented bacteria, *trichodesmium erythraeum*, colours stretches of the sea red.

Suddenly a hundred yards ahead a black figure stepped out into the middle of the road, right arm raised. We stopped, I dropped my side window. "*Salaam aleikoum,*" (Peace be upon you) I said, to which he courteously replied with a smile, "*Aleikoum salaam,*" (Peace be upon you also) and then, "*Qunfuddah?*" That was where we were heading, some fifty miles further on, so I motioned him into the car and he jumped in with alacrity. We exchanged further greetings; my Arabic was exhausted and we fell to silently enjoying the drive and curiously, and discreetly, examining each other.

What he made of me I don't know. In this remote area, I may well have been the first living white man he had ever seen. He would certainly never have seen one dressed, as I was, in an operating theatre green scrub suit (a cool and comfortable dress we all adopted after one of our surgical companions had liberated a supply from the hospital operating suite).

This man of Tihama was just as Thesiger had described them – only more so. His oiled and perfumed skin was mahogany and glistened. His hair was in ringlets topped by a circlet of flowers; his eyes were abundantly made up with khol and appeared twice as big as normal; his whiter-than-white teeth flashed a ready smile; his feet were bare and he wore a black loincloth with red, white and gold stripes and a black long-sleeved shirt. Soon the car was filled with the over-powering musk-like smell of his perfume. But this was no effeminate dandy: he held his rifle comfortably like an old friend and at his waist was a large *khanjar*, the J-shaped dagger of the southern peninsula. He looked almost piratical and certainly not one to argue with.

Before we reached Qunfuddah, he motioned me to stop at a small village, probably his home. He jumped out of the car, thanked me, blessed me for my help, "*Allah ye barak feek,*" and loped off towards one of a score of huts – again just as described by Thesiger: beehive-shaped daub-and-wattle constructions with roofs of *barasti* or woven palm fronds, reminiscent of parts of Africa. But there were a couple of notable differences. The camel that

Village by the beach: beehive huts just as Thesiger had described.

in Thesiger's day was hobbled in the shade by the hut had been replaced by a Toyota pick-up, and each domed roof sprouting a TV aerial.

Qunfuddah, which we reached in the middle of a hot afternoon, was a disappointment. Maybe we had a coastal resort with a corniche and beaches backed by a thriving town in our minds. Perhaps we expected too much. Although it was only 250 miles from Jeddah, it was too remote for even the rudimentary development of the Bride of the Sea to reach it.

Qunfuddah had the look of neglect. Everywhere there were sheep and goats with matted fleeces; ragged children with equally matted hair and running noses ran up to us with outstretched grubby palms. The town was strewn with rubbish and blighted by the ubiquitous blue plastic bags – surely one of the least welcome gifts of the modern world. And smell? Very much so. I can only hope that Qunfuddah has improved since then.

We bought bread with a degree of confidence, having observed that the bakers' ovens were too hot to allow survival of the hardiest bacteria. We also wanted ice, but that was a different matter. They brought a huge chunk of dirty ice out of a cold room and smashed it to pieces in front of us. It would be okay to use to cool our bottled water but no way could we put it in our drinks. We badly needed to top up our drinking water supplies and inspected the village well; it was deep, the water was gin-clear, it tasted good and, although dirty, the townsfolk were healthy. We risked it – after all, we had a supply of antibiotics that would deal with any enteric infection, and in any case we would boil the water.

I was keen to take photographs but when I got my camera out, Don tugged my sleeve, "Don't Bill. Look at these folk: they're still living in the Middle Ages. They might attack us if we take pictures." He was right: we moved on with just our memories.

THE NEXT DAY WE TURNED INLAND. JUST before we joined the road to Abha, we hit a police checkpoint. The magic of Sheikh Yamani's letter and the official ministry stamps worked like a charm. The captain in charge emerged from his airconditioned office to wish us a pleasant journey and the smiling police waved us through.

What a contrast, the road to Abha: it twisted and turned as it rose steeply through the stunning scenery of the Asir mountains which peaked at 3,000 metres. The temperature fell progressively; it rained for the first hour as we passed terraced farms. There were trees, mostly juniper and wild olive; large grassy patches appeared and mountain streams tumbled. "O Allah," I

Mountain road to Abha.

mused, "I'm ascending to your paradise, now all I lack is a bottle of wine and seventy-two doe-eyed virgins… perhaps, *Inshallah*, around the next corner?"

The next corner was a hairpin bend, and the new vista appeared abruptly: a scattered troop of pink-faced, big-nosed, purple-bottomed baboons gazed at us with little curiosity. Judging by the troop's goings-on, there were no virgins there. Half an hour later, the startling sight of goats – scores of them – balancing precariously on their cloven hooves on the branches of trees while they stripped them of their leaves greeted us. How they got up there and how they stayed up there was beyond me.

We reached Abha by late afternoon. There, above the rain, the air was clear, the sky a rich blue. Vultures with wing spans of six feet sailed in lazy circles.

News of Sheikh Yamani's letter to the governor, Prince Khalid bin Faisal, had been telephoned through to the town police. At the town entrance, they directed us to the Intercontinental Hotel where we found that the governor's office had reserved rooms for us. It was just like any Intercon the world over, *sans* bars. Once inside, you wouldn't know if you were in London, Paris or Abha; they had the same smell and décor. At this stage, the familiar provided a welcome respite.

Prince Khalid had sent English-speaking guides to take us on a tour of his domain. Offered a visit to newly created national parks or a valley where cave dwellers had lived for several centuries, we chose the latter. A bumpy journey of thirty kilometres across rocky desert brought us to the deserted village of al-Habala. Far down an escarpment four hundred metres deep with almost vertical sides we could see a few tumbledown rough stone houses. They were the remains of a community which had first settled there in the seventeenth century. One of our guides recited what was a well-rehearsed account of the history of al Habala, clearly not for him the first time:

"Eleven generations ago a pest was sweeping the country* killing more people than it left alive. The head of a family of a mountain tribe in Abha took his family – brothers, sisters, cousins and their children – to this valley to which there was no access except by climbing a perpendicular mountainside. Animals and seed were brought down by ropes. Since then sixty families making up the Habala tribe have made their lives in this valley,

* Most likely this was the Great Plague (*la grande peste*) which arose in Asia, spread far and wide and swept through Europe. In 1665 it claimed 100,000 lives in London alone.

Deserted houses and terraced gardens of Al-Habala.

only climbing up for necessities. The children were about seven years old when they first learned to climb. The oldest man to climb out of the gorge was seventy and blind. A year ago the sixty families were brought up by government decree so that their medical and educational needs could be better looked after."

Our guides took us to the new King Faisal village in which the families from Habala had been resettled. We were invited to take tea with them; segregated, naturally. They were shy and quite unused to tourists – photography was out of the question – but the headman was forthcoming, "We miss our old homes, our solitude, our gardens. Our women are especially unhappy even though the houses are new and have water and electricity."

Later, one of the women in our group said the headman's wife appeared to be in her late twenties but didn't really know her age. She had borne him six babies; the first three had died between the ages of one and two but three children survived and were in good health. All the villagers bore a remarkable resemblance to each other, hardly surprising as every marriage would be to a close blood relative. They had identical upper lips, thin, flat and lacking a bow.

Today, some thirty years on, al-Habala is again inhabited and is a local tourist attraction with a cable railway, clinics and schools. Even a theme park has been installed. Somehow, however, I don't think Disney needs to worry.

That evening we were royally entertained, literally. We were invited to the governor's palace and on arrival separated. The children were taken to play with the palace children and the adults joined the male and female members of the family and their retinues.

Prince Khalid wanted each of us to tell him how we came to be working in Saudi Arabia. He was intrigued to learn that I had moved to the King Faisal Specialist Hospital in Riyadh directly from the Royal Air Force. "Surely, doctor, there's a world of difference between English military medicine and the Royal Hospital in Riyadh?"

"I agree, Your Highness," I responded, "but you know beneath the skin the human body is the same the world over."

He smiled, then asked, "How come my good friend Sheikh Yamani is involved? He's from this region, you know." I explained that I had treated His Excellency for an ulcer problem. "And is he now well?" enquired the prince.

"Quite well," I reassured him.

"*Alhamdulillah*," said the prince and in a conditioned Saudi reflex, each of us murmured *alhamdulillah*.

He wanted to know about our tour, where we had been, if we were enjoying ourselves and if we had met friendly people. His eyes lit up when we told him one of the highlights had been the visit to al-Habala that very afternoon.

"Ah, al-Habala! You know those people had been living primitive lives for hundreds of years; they were remote from the world. Getting in and out of their village was so difficult they had to use ropes. In fact they were known in the region as the 'Rope People' – *habala* is Arabic for rope."

He paused, took another tiny cup from his coffee bearer, swallowed the single mouthful and went on, "They said it was unkind to uproot those people who claimed that their lives were happy where they were, but the final straw for me was when a young woman died in obstructed labour when she would most likely have survived if expert medical help was at hand." Another small coffee and he continued.

"It wasn't easy. They resisted and I had to use the National Guard to move them. They were so used to their lives on that vertical mountainside – I suppose it's like transferring mountain goats to the pastures of the plain. And, you know, they are still drawn back to their vegetable patches."

At ten o'clock, we adjourned to a large dining room with a huge glass table supported on gold plated legs and stretching the length of the room. The silver was Christofle, the crystal glasses the finest Waterford and the crockery the best Japanese porcelain. This was not going to be the usual goat-grab on a carpeted floor – much to my relief as I still hadn't acquired the ability to arrange myself comfortably cross-legged.

The food was exquisite and was served by waiters dressed in black pants, white shirts, starched white jackets with gold epaulettes and white gloves. Dish succeeded dish, maybe twenty in all. Bloated, we retired to a large sitting room where we drank Arabic coffee and tea and talked about the local history, the construction of the Najran dam in the mountains, the development of national parks and the modernisation of farming.

As we were driven back to the hotel in limousines, we reflected that Prince Khalid was evidently a benign ruler with the best interests of his people at heart. He was also a generous one, as we discovered the next morning when we tried to pay our bills. The prince had picked up the entire tab.

Prince Khalid wanted us to see two national parks created under his direction and sent his guides for us. Then they took us to the city of Najran, the provincial capital, where they handed us over to new guides. And were they different?

Our new guides were a dozen *askari* (soldiers). They sat in three red open Land Rovers with mounted machine guns. They were armed to the teeth with crossed bandoliers of ammunition, modern rifles and the ubiquitous *khanjars*. They were some of the personal guards of the governor of Najran province and turned out to be a jolly bunch of young men beneath that forbidding appearance.

They led us to a secluded orange grove where enormous carpets had been spread and – to my discomfort – we were invited to squat in a large circle. Servants arrived with jugs of water, soap, towels and bowls. We washed our

Reservoir high in the mountains behind the Najran Valley dam.

hands and minutes later the same servants reappeared bearing four huge platters of rice on each of which rested a cooked young goat with its head lolling to one side. Numerous side dishes of salads, hot peppers and fruit accompanied the goats. Our guards joined us for this traditional goat grab. It was fun with the *askari* joking and joshing each other. The fruit was delicious, the best being the large juicy oranges freshly picked in the orange grove.

After the meal we headed out to see the Najran Valley dam, a local feat of construction built high in the mountains. Driving in convoy, with two military Land Rovers leading our five cars and the third Land Rover bringing up the rear, we mounted an assault on the mountain – there's no other way of describing it. The roads were steep, tortuous, had no safety barriers and all too often perilously close to heart-stopping precipitous drops. Our guards drove at reckless speed; it was difficult to keep up. We shot through a couple of checkpoints with sirens screaming, the guards at the barriers jumping for their lives. To our relief we finally rounded a mountain bend and screeched to a halt amid clouds of dust and flying stones. There before us stretched a glistening expanse of water filling the valleys between erstwhile mountain peaks which now projected like conical islands.

The dam had been completed recently and was obviously viewed with great pride by our guards, although I thought it unlikely that a single Saudi hand had been involved in the labour of its construction. The dam was huge and would provide irrigation for a vast area; the reservoir it created held more than two billion gallons of water and would be replenished by the twenty-three inches of rain that fell each year on the Asir mountains – the highest rainfall in the whole of the Arabian peninsula.

The next day our guides announced that they were taking us to an archaeological site several miles south of Najran to a place called Ukhdud which dates back to 500BC.

Ukhdud had been an important town on the so-called 'frankincense trail', the trade route from Yemen through the Hejaz to Egypt and the Levant. The archaeological dig was at an early stage when we saw it, but even so, houses and pagan temples had been unearthed. The ancient walls bore Thamudic (old Arabic) inscriptions and carvings of snakes and horses. In pre-Islamic times, it had been a centre of Christianity until its inhabitants were massacred by a king of Yemen in the sixth century. Ukhdud is mentioned in the Koran, the city having been destroyed because its occupants had killed 'believers' by burning them in a pit.

On that upbeat note, our guides left us and we began the long journey back skirting the Empty Quarter. Only the oasis towns of As-Sulayyil and Layla lay between us and Riyadh.

Several hours of daylight remained. After stocking up with fuel, water, bread, cooked chickens and fruit, we considered our route. Driving discipline was vital as we skirted the Rub al Khali; tragedies can occur easily and mostly when travellers get separated and are on their own. Each driver, except the last, had to keep an eye on the car following and if it was no longer in sight, he alerted the others and the convoy would stop. If the straggler did not appear after a few minutes, two cars would retrace the road to find out what had happened.

The road was rough but not bad and we made good time to As-Sulayyil. Despite being so close to the largest sand desert in the world, it is one of the richest farming areas in Saudi Arabia. A few years after we passed through the town, it became important militarily. The Saudis bought a hundred 'East Wind' intermediate range ballistic missiles from China and deployed them at As-Sulayyil. They had conventional warheads and a range of 1,500 miles; unsurprisingly they were pointed at Israel and Iran. Nowadays, with its

Sean Sieck supervising at the last filling station before the Empty Quarter...
note precarious roof rack.

strategic importance, it is unlikely that a bunch of western 'tourists' would be allowed anywhere near the town.

We didn't linger. We topped up our fuel and water supplies and pressed on to Layla. The road was disconcertingly empty; we met no cars and saw no houses and no trees. It was desolate, isolated and the occasional mummified corpse of a camel or an abandoned car remarkably well preserved in zero humidity caused a shiver of apprehension to run down our spines.

Halfway to Layla, the sky in the west suddenly darkened, became pitch black. A fierce hot wind hit us, rocking the cars; and then came the sand – we were in the middle of a raging sand storm. We pulled off the road and waited for it to pass. Despite tightly closed windows as the wind roared around us, the sand got everywhere: noses, mouths, eyes – this could explain the mummified camels. A miserable half an hour later, the storm passed as quickly as it had arrived and after a lot of nose-blowing and gargling, we continued our journey.

Layla is about 200 miles south of Riyadh. It is the largest town of al-Aflaj oasis and until 1997 had the largest permanent lake in the Arabian peninsula. Originally more than a mile long and half a mile wide, it was kept filled by the rain that fell on the Asir mountains far away in the west, replenishing the water table. The lake was popular with hospital staff; weekends would find

them and countless other city dwellers out ther'
and camping. But in 1985 the water level start'
years it was totally dry. The lake's demise '
expansion of local agriculture; the huge circl
sandy desert that are visible from aircraft pa
irrigation boreholes remains the most plausible exp..
paradise lost.

A few trees appeared alongside the road to Riyadh and an occasional herd
of goats. At sunset we looked for our last campsite. The off-road sand was
the softest we had encountered in the whole journey and despite our recently
honed desert driving skills, three of the vehicles became bogged down and
had to be dug out. We pitched camp for the night, crunched on our sand-
stormed chicken and bread and turned in.

At daybreak, we set off on the final leg to Riyadh but one minor mishap
reminded us again of our vulnerability. To regain the main road, we had to
cross a flat plain. The surface was good so we raced – until Sean Sieck's car
hit a small hillock he hadn't spotted. His roof rack shot forward, crashing
onto the bonnet with enough force to cause a dent and startle the daylights
out of the driver and passengers. Fortunately the engine emerged

The author axle-deep in soft Saudi sand.

d. We abandoned the bent roof rack, divided the load between us
ceeded with a good deal more caution.

irty miles from Riyadh, a military encampment at a place called al-
arj marked the start – at least travelling in our direction – of good road.
From there it was properly surfaced and straight as far as the eye could see.
With light hearts, we raced on at top speed, an excited Duffy McDonald
sitting next to me yelling, "Pedal on the metal! Pedal on the metal, Bill!" By
late afternoon, we were home.

After enjoying an experience of a lifetime, it was only natural that
whenever we got together over a glass or two we would take delight in
reliving it. Sure enough, in a few months we started to wonder if we could
do it again, maybe going to another region in the kingdom. But times
changed and politics took a hand. King Khalid died in 1982; he was
succeeded by Fah'd and Sheikh Mohammed Abdo Yamani quietly
disappeared from the Saudi government. As usual there were no
announcements in the Saudi press and the only clue we had came from a
London broadsheet which reported in early 1983 that

...in addition to those already announced two more changes are taking place
in the Saudi Arabian government, coming on the heels of last week's
unprecedented dismissal of the Information Minister [Sheikh Yamani], and are
designed to reimpose King Fah'd's authority during a simmering quarrel with
[the Crown Prince] Prince Abdullah – these moves are seen as part of a process
by which Fah'd is consolidating his authority...

Alas, no more passports from Sheikh Yamani – we could only wonder
and wish him well.

Fifteen

O<small>N</small> 20 N<small>OVEMBER</small> 1979, <small>WHILE</small> Queen Elizabeth and the Duke of Edinburgh celebrated their thirty-second wedding anniversary in England with a reception at Buckingham Palace, Islamic Sunni dissidents were seizing the Grand Mosque in Mecca. The effects of the dissidents' actions reverberate to this day; some say it led to the formation of what was to become the terrorist organisation known as al-Qaeda.

That year – 1979 – was a turbulent one full of events that would have far-reaching consequences. The mighty Soviet army invaded Afghanistan, at the request of the Afghan government, to fight (and after ten years to ignominiously lose) against the Mujahideen; Ayatollah Khomeini assumed leadership of the newly proclaimed Islamic Republic of Iran after fifteen years in exile; Margaret Thatcher became the first British woman prime minister; Saddam Hussein became the president of Iraq; Idi Amin, the dictator of Uganda, was deposed; and Rhodesia became Zimbabwe.

I had just begun my second year at the King Faisal Specialist Hospital when the House of Saud was shaken, panicked and paralysed by an uprising in the holy city of Mecca. The first thing the authorities did was to cut all radio, television and telephone links and close the kingdom's borders.

At the hospital, for more than twenty-four hours we were unaware that anything unusual had happened in Mecca. News gradually leaked out and a friend who had smuggled in a short-wave radio was able to pass on what he had heard on the BBC World Service – not that the BBC really knew what was going on either. The kingdom was maintaining its usual wall of silence to the outside world and hoping to resolve the situation before it hit the world media. Some of the hospital staff were greatly disturbed. Knowing how the general population loathed the Royal Family, there were fears of a bloody revolution. Some staff even went as far as to pack their cars with supplies and laid plans to escape across the desert to neighbouring countries. I personally felt little anxiety knowing that the Sauds had the national security well buttoned up and in any event, an oil thirsty Uncle Sam would not countenance having his gas-guzzling citizens deprived of their life force.

The world's media were not particularly interested. The Shah getting kicked out of Iran and Ayatollah Khomeini stepping into his shoes was of much greater moment to the West than a religious squabble in Mecca. Moreover, at that period the Muslim population in Western countries was nowhere near today's level.

To this day the story is not clear but it is evident that the roots of the religious rebellion lay in the dissatisfaction of many ultra-religious Saudis with the liberalisation of the kingdom and the friendship of the Sauds with the United States. These dissidents demanded a return to the old ways of Islam, an end to the education of women, the abolition of television and the expulsion of non-Muslims from the Holy Land.

The date was crucial; it was the first day of the Hejira year 1400. According to the Hadith,* this was the very year and the very day of the coming of the Mahdi, who would himself be a descendant of the Prophet and would become the new leader of Islam. The Mahdi would rule until the end of the world.

On that fateful day, the Imam of the Grand Mosque was preparing to lead dawn prayers for 100,000 worshippers who had gathered for the first prayer of the new Islamic year. He was interrupted by insurgents who produced weapons from under their robes. Estimates of numbers of insurgents vary between two hundred and five hundred.

How did the weapons get in? At that time, renovations of the Grand Mosque were being undertaken by a construction company called Saudi bin Laden and it is likely that weapons and food were smuggled in on construction vehicles. It is also thought that weapons were concealed in the coffins of Muslims who had just died and were being taken into the holiest of shrines to receive their final and most sacred blessing.

First the insurgents chained the gates shut and then, outrageously, a policeman was killed by a trigger-happy, nervous dissident. The worshippers were taken hostage but the majority released. Several more policemen were

* The Hadith are anecdotes about Muhammad and other founders of Islam. They are considered important source material about religious practice, law, and historical traditions.

killed. A hundred security officers tried to take the mosque but were repulsed with heavy casualties. Next the Saudi army and National Guard tried unsuccessfully to take the shrine but failed, despite being joined by Pakistani forces based at the nearby military base of Tabuk.

A serious problem for the authorities was that the Koran explicitly forbids the use of force within the sacred confines of the Grand Mosque. The Ulema, the council of religious scholars, was consulted. After prolonged discussion and pressure from the Royal Family, the Ulema gave religious approval, issued the authority, a *fatwa*, to allow arms to be carried into the holy site and the dissidents to be attacked. In return, the Ulema extracted a promise from the Sauds that they would mend their ways.

Several frontal attacks failed; from the vantage of minarets the insurgents picked off members of the security forces at will and, when helicopters lowered troops on ropes into the main courtyard in the centre of the mosque, it turned into a suicide mission.

The seizure was led by Juhaiman ibn Muhammad ibn Saif al-Utaibi, a member of a powerful Sunni tribe, with connections to the National Guard. His grandfather had fought with ibn Saud during the formation of the kingdom. Using the Grand Mosque's loudspeakers, Juhaiman broadcast a declaration that his brother-in-law, Muhammad bin abd Allah al-Qatani – who was indeed a descendant of the Prophet – was the new Mahdi. He also declared that the ruling Saud dynasty had lost its legitimacy because it was corrupt and had destroyed Saudi culture by an aggressive policy of westernisation.

It took two weeks for the Saudi authorities to gain control of the Grand Mosque. The insurgents took refuge in the labyrinth of a thousand rooms in the basement. Eventually French assault troops were brought in and flushed out the last of the extremists.

Because it is forbidden for non-Muslims to enter Mecca, the French forces were given instant conversion to Islam. How they brought the siege to an end is unclear. Some reports said that they flooded the basement and used electric shocks. Other reports suggested they drilled holes in the floor of the mosque through which they dropped grenades. The most likely method was the use of a non-lethal toxic gas.

The dissidents' leader, Juhaiman, was captured along with sixty-three others. Muhammad the erstwhile Mahdi was killed. He had declared,

"I cannot die, I am the Mahdi and I do not fear anything," but a grenade blew away the lower half of his body – the upper half fell into the hands of the security forces who displayed the grisly remains, the head, arms and torso, for propaganda.

The dissidents were mostly Sunni Saudis of the strict Wahhabi sect plus zealots from the Islamic Brotherhood in Egypt: this combination formed the nidus of al-Qaeda (the base) as it is known today. There were many *jihadi* or holy warriors from other nations, converts from the United States and England and surprisingly a number of women extremists.

An interested observer was the twenty-two-year-old Osama bin Laden. He was horrified that the authorities had desecrated Islam's holiest shrine by allowing it to be attacked by tanks, artillery and assault forces. He believed that the Saudi forces should have starved out the rebels.

Immediately after the siege ended, Osama bin Laden went to Afghanistan to join in the fight against the Soviet invaders and to formalise the movement of Islamic fundamentalist *jihadi* known to the world as al-Qaeda. Now, thirty years on, al-Qaeda is arguably stronger than ever. Its influence on young, impressionable Muslim minds is even more powerful. Despite massive military opposition and the strident claims of leaders that the West is winning, al-Qaeda shows no signs of knuckling under. There is no possibility of a political settlement. Al-Qaeda and the *jihadi* believe that they are on a holy mission... which they are winning. Winners don't need to negotiate.

Juhaiman and the sixty-three dissident prisoners were sentenced to death without trial. They were divided into groups and sent to four cities in the kingdom where they were beheaded in public squares. Films of the beheadings were broadcast again and again on Saudi television. For weeks, the daily Saudi TV news was prefaced by re-runs of the gruesome spectacle.

In the aftermath, the blame game began. Despite the insurgents' anti-Western pronouncements, Ayatollah Khomeini declared that the siege was the work of criminal American imperialism and international Zionism. His words inflamed the all-too-easily inflamed mobs in cities of the Islamic world. Anti-American demonstrations were enthusiastically joined, flags and effigies torched and the American embassies in Islamabad and Tripoli overrun and burned.

The Saud family had been shaken by the event. It would have been unthinkable to take military action without the support of the religious scholars. The payback was that they should behave in a way befitting Wahhabism. This also meant more investment in religious schools and greater powers for the religious establishment. The Sauds acceded to the demands, at least until the dust settled.

WERE WESTERNERS AT THE KING FAISAL Specialist Hospital affected? The country was already run on puritanical principles, but even so, there was considerable tightening of the rules. Now the faintest suggestion of laxity or liberalism was suppressed and the *muttawa* went about their business with even brighter gleams in their eyes. We felt that it would be wise to keep our heads below the parapet until the rabid anti-Western mood subsided.

But there was somewhere we could feel free – the desert. Within a radius of a hundred and fifty miles, there were plenty of campsites where we could escape the surveillance of the ever-vigilant hospital security guards.

The summer months were far too hot but in the winter, early spring and late autumn, desert camping was delightful. The nights were cool, even freezing in January, and the sky clear with the heavens carpeted with a thousand times more stars than you would see on even the clearest, non light-polluted night in Europe. When the moon was full, it was huge and the desert became as bright as day. The moon's craters were easily visible to the naked eye and it appeared to be so close you could touch it. The grandeur of the desert – its rolling dunes, mountainous ridges and nights of breath-taking splendour – gave you an intense feeling, not just of nature but of the presence of the supernatural. It was no wonder that Islam had found such fertile ground in those desert dwellers of fifteen hundred years ago.

To escape the miserable, killjoy and negative Saudi attitude to Christmas, we Westerners – with one or two trusted Arabs – would take to the desert. Christmas was obviously not a public holiday in Saudi Arabia but if Christmas Day happened to fall on a weekend (Thursday or Friday in the Saudi calendar) well and good; otherwise we selected the weekend closest to 25 December on which to celebrate.

Organisation and initiative were essential. For weeks in advance, the ladies would discuss the catering and the men the wine list. Festive fare was not a problem. Just before Christmas in ultra-conservative Riyadh, poultry

Foil-wrapped Christmas dinner about to be buried in the Saudi desert.

appeared in abundance in the supermarkets which were themselves ever vigilant for a profit.

Four-wheel drives would be packed the day before and the larger birds, the turkeys, pre-cooked for a couple of hours. On the day, we would set off early in order to find a campsite by two in the afternoon. Once we'd found a suitable *wadi*, a dried river bed, we set about unloading the cars. There were always plenty of willing hands with a couple of dozen adults and children in the party, each with their appointed tasks. The absolute priority was, of course, to get the cooking of the poultry under way.

Cooking a traditional Christmas dinner in the desert with no oven presented a challenge, but our Danish friends Sean and Ulla Sieck, who had worked as doctors in New Zealand, had the solution: make an oven in the sand, traditional Maori style – a *hangi*.

To lay the *hangi*, we dug a large rectangular pit about three feet deep, poured in sacks of charcoal, lit it and fanned it. When the flames had burned down, we lowered onto the hot coals the pre-cooked turkeys, the duck and the capons, well-wrapped in several layers of tin foil, and suspended on unravelled wire coat hangers. Then we shovelled the sand back in and left the poultry to cook. Cooking began at about three in the afternoon but the birds would not be ready for several hours.

Meanwhile, there was a Christmas tree to be set up and illuminations organised. One of our Syrian doctor friends had learned the technique of making holiday 'luminaries' when she worked in San Diego. You start with a brown paper bag half-filled with sand and in it plant a candle. When it's lit, the candle produces a pleasing glow, its light diffused through the brown paper. We set three dozen of these luminaries around the walls of the *wadi* and arranged a further dozen to form an avenue leading to Santa's chair. Night fell early and the effect of the hooded candles beneath myriad twinkling stars in the jet-black sky, with a cool evening desert breeze, was simply magical. Our illuminations far outshone those of London's West End.

Of course we had to have a Father Christmas, and I was it, complete with an authentic outfit smuggled into the country as I don't know what. While the adults sipped Ulla's *glögg* or *glühwein* (it never sounds as exotic when you call it plain mulled wine), I disappeared behind a dune to get dressed in the Santa Claus outfit. Half an hour later I reappeared balanced precariously on the tailgate of my highly decorated white Range-Rover driven by Sean (wearing, for some obscure reason, a straw boater), loudly clanging a camel bell and YO-HO-HO-ing like crazy. "My reindeer don't

Greater love hath no man than to play Santa for his small friends.

*The author and Sean Sieck, master of Maori cooking, in
the midst of an avenue of paper bag luminaries.*

like sand," Santa offered as a reason for his unusual mount, leaving aside
the fact that local hunters would probably have had Rudolph *et al* down,
skinned and roasted in a flash.

At eight o'clock in pitch darkness, except for our own illuminations and
that of the camp fire, we exhumed the turkeys, duck and chicken. Our
appetites, sharpened by an aperitif or two, were ravenous; the smell, flavour
and texture of the birds cooked slowly in their own juices was heavenly. We
all agreed that we had never tasted better.

Then – a miracle in the desert of Saudi Arabia – pork sausages and a
baked ham appeared. We even had roasted chestnuts and a homemade
Christmas pudding with a sprig of holly flamed with Sid. Later, and perhaps
for the very first time, the Saudi escarpment echoed to the Christmas carols
of infidels.

On Boxing Day, on our way home we passed a Bedouin lady sitting astride a donkey being led through the desert by her husband, a seasonal rather 'biblical' picture if ever there was one; we felt it augured well.

The only anxiety we had about the whole affair was whether Saudis would appear uninvited and join our celebrations. Fortunately this never happened at Christmas; however, on other occasions our campfires attracted locals.

Once, while setting up camp on the escarpment, we heard shots throughout the afternoon. In the evening, after we had eaten dinner, a group of Saudis joined us. After the usual "Salaam aleikoums" came the question we expected, "Hal indak Johnny Walker?" (Do you have whisky?) We said we didn't and offered the ubiquitous 'Bebsi' (the letter 'p' is next to impossible for native Arabic speakers and Coca-Cola was banned on account of some Zionist connection) which they accepted. Our newly acquired hunter friends started cooking the day's kill, a couple of dozen scrawny desert pigeons, on our bonfire. Their culinary technique was simplicity itself: chuck the birds on the fire and when the feathers are burned off the bird is cooked. I have it on good authority that the tastiest and crunchiest bit is the head.

THE DESERT COMMANDED RESPECT; there were rules that had to be followed if disasters were to be avoided. It was easy to get lost and separated from companions. In those days, thirty years ago, there were no mobile phones.

One Friday morning, a recently arrived Swedish consultant radiologist knocked on my door. I was packing to go on leave that night. He was excited, he had bought a good second-hand four-wheel drive; he was gung-ho for the desert and wanted advice.

"My spare tyre doesn't have a lot of tread, does that matter... I don't have a shovel, do I need one?"

I invited him in and explained that the desert is a dangerous place. "You mustn't go there on your own, always in the company of another and preferably two cars. Your tyres must be in good order; you need to deflate your tyres when the going is soft so you need a pump to pump them up again when the going gets stony. You must take plenty of water; you should let somebody at home know where you are going and if you become stuck, do not leave your car. To attract attention, burning a tyre will send a plume of black smoke high in the desert air to mark your spot and, yes, you need a shovel."

Finally I told him that he should go with an experienced desert driver who could make sure he came to no harm and would teach him the craft of driving on the various surfaces he would encounter in the desert.

When I returned from leave two weeks later I learned, to my horror, that he had ignored all my advice. He had gone into the desert taking a young man, a radiography technician, with him but driving alone. After a few days his car was found; it was deeply embedded in soft sand. Both doctor and technician were dead, their bodies found several hundred yards from his marooned car. They had separated and gone in different directions.

SIX MONTHS AFTER I JOINED THE KING Faisal Hospital, the Queen and Duke of Edinburgh were the guests of King Khalid in Riyadh. To show courtesy to a female head of state was a problem. The solution, to enable Her Majesty to attend functions, which inevitably were all male affairs, was to declare her an honorary man for the duration of her visit.

There was no such problem two years later in 1981 when the British prime minister, Margaret Thatcher, paid a visit; all the Saudis avowed that such action would not be necessary – she already had balls.

FROM TIME TO TIME I WOULD BE ASKED to visit a patient at home or in another hospital. The request would originate from relatives, and whether the hospital administration would agree to my going would depend on how much wasta was involved. The hospital was ostensibly only for Saudi citizens and there was tacit understanding that by 'Saudi citizens' one really meant that members of the enormous, infinitely extended family of ibn Saud took precedence.

Once I was asked to consult on a Yemeni. I didn't know who had made the request but the instruction came from the chief administrator of the hospital. I was given the man's name and told that he was an inpatient in a hospital in Riyadh named Al-Nasreen hospital – curious title, I thought, meaning as it does the Christian hospital.

Al-Nasreen hospital was only a mile from the King Faisal hospital. It was an old building; old, that is, for Riyadh where buildings of mud brick might crumble after two or three decades. It was of two storeys, rectangular, with a central dusty courtyard where a couple of oleander bushes were losing the struggle for life. At least a score of patients were lined up outside a door that was marked, in English, 'Outpatients Weights Here'. Some were bandaged, some in grubby plaster casts, some appearing to be holding on to life by the merest thread, but all looking desperately poor.

Needless to say, half a dozen goats were picking over a pile of rubbish in one corner. This rubbish provided additional nourishment to the usual goat diet of discarded cardboard cartons: it contained old blood-stained dressings but, I was relieved to see, no amputated limbs. Some months later, Al-Nasreen hospital burned to the ground, no doubt by its demise saving scores of lives.

I entered the hospital; it was gloomy and smelt of antiseptics and faeces. A long dark corridor faced me. At its entrance stood an enormous Sudanese nurse, glistening black, a foot taller than me and built like a battleship. She had her arms folded above her remarkably large chest. I told her who I was and asked to see the patient, Yassin al Saleh. She literally flashed me a smile with a mouth full of glinting gold teeth; she nodded, and without a word directed me, by swivelling her eyes, down the long dark corridor.

The walls of the corridor supported dismantled bedsteads and, here and there, heavily stained mattresses. I reached the end and entered a three-bedded ward. At the far end, immediately ahead of me, sitting cross-legged on his bed, was Yassin al Saleh. He looked terrified as he gazed at me with the deepest yellow eyes I had ever seen.

In the middle bed was a scraggy old man, sitting like Yassin, cross-legged on his bed. He was furiously picking his nose and flicking the bogeys around the room. In the first bed next to the door lay a corpse, apparently dead for some time, with swarms of flies buzzing around his sightless open eyes.

I examined Yassin. He had a hard, craggy, liver and many enlarged, stone-hard, lymph nodes in his neck. I had little doubt he had untreatable terminal cancer but *wasta* demanded he be given a definitive tissue diagnosis.

Yassin was transferred to the King Faisal Specialist Hospital. A lymph node biopsy showed secondary cancer that was so anaplastic, so undifferentiated, that it was impossible to say in which organ it had originated. Scans showed widespread involvement in the abdomen. After talking to the pathologist, and examining the microscopy, we knew that nothing could be done for Yassin who, poor chap, was only thirty-two. I went to his room. Relatives surrounded him, but I didn't need to be anxious about breaking the bad news. His family had turned his bed to face Mecca, the direction for the dying.

Yassin died two days later. A post-mortem examination would have been of only academic interest. In any case, post-mortem examinations in Saudi Arabia were almost non-existent, except in forensic cases. Once a person died, the book was closed. To interfere with a corpse was anathema to Saudi Muslims.

Western doctors hold a different view. As a student, I had regarded the many hours I spent in the autopsy room as time very well used. Although unpleasant, post-mortem examinations provided me with the sort of learning you don't get from a textbook. At the King Faisal Specialist Hospital, if we had doubts about the final diagnosis in a Saudi, we would take numerous biopsies from the deceased using needles that left almost no evidence of interference with the corpse. It was not simply an exercise in medical vanity to confirm our diagnoses; the biopsies might reveal a different diagnosis and we might learn from it.

MY NEXT DOMICILIARY VISIT WAS different, about as different as it was possible to get. One evening, I was escorted to the Riyadh palace of King Khalid. The king had a gastroenterological problem.

I was quite used to opulence: at the King Faisal Specialist Hospital, even the walls were carpeted and the library ceiling coated in gold leaf. But here the adjectives magnificent, vast, opulent were inadequate. Surrounded by guards sporting arms, daggers and dripping with bandoliers of ammunition, we passed through enormous golden gates hanging from pillars of the finest white Carrara marble. I was taken to an anteroom and given the customary glass of freshly squeezed orange juice. Ten minutes later, I met the king.

His Majesty sat at the end of a long room with his queen to his left. Between them, on a small table, was a telephone of an unusual green colour, probably *eau de Nil*, possibly duck-egg blue with a tinge of green. Then I hurriedly caught myself in mid-thought. "What on earth am I doing, standing here, before one of the most powerful men on the planet, debating with myself the colour of his telephone?"

Along each wall were ranged what I took to be the royal children, all teenagers, princesses on the left and princes on the right. Their attention was focused on a big screen on which a television film was being projected. I recognised the lazy drawl of James Garner in *The Rockford Files*. It was subtitled in Arabic. The episode was nearly over and I was asked to wait. When it finished the queen, princes and princesses got up and left. I was motioned to approach the king. He smiled; he had a charming smile.

I bowed from the neck and said, "*Salaam aleikoum, taal amrac*" (Peace be upon you, long life). The '*taal amrac*' bit cracked him up and he laughed. I was confused because whenever I had been around important royals in the hospital, '*taal amracs*' flew left right and centre. Wishing 'long life' to your royal betters at the end of every sentence was *de rigueur*.

The king chuckled and indicated that I should sit near him. He did not speak English; no matter, there was a bevy of royal palace doctors eager to make their presence felt and falling over each other to interpret.

"What is His Majesty's problem?" I asked.

"When he gets up in the morning, His Majesty immediately has to use the bathroom and then later during the morning he has to use it again, maybe five, even six times."

"Do you mean to pass stool or urine?"

"Stool, of course."

"For how long has this been going on?" I enquired.

"Many years."

"How many years?"

"Maybe twelve, maybe fifteen."

"Has he seen other doctors about this problem?"

"Yes, many."

"And what have they said?"

"Alas, they have made no diagnosis."

"Has His Majesty had stool examinations, blood tests, small bowel studies, x-rays, sigmoidoscopy and rectal biopsies?"

"Many, many times; in London, in Germany, in France and in America at the Mayo Clinic and in Houston; but nothing abnormal was ever found."

I asked if I could inspect the clinical notes and examine His Majesty. His Majesty raised his eyebrows (hmm, he had understood my request – in English) and said, "*La, halhayn, badain*" (Not now, later).

There was an interruption; a retainer appeared with a falcon perched on his wrist. The bird did not look at all well, his feathers drooped and if a bird

Saudi with hooded falcon on its 'wakar', or perch.

can have a hang-dog expression, he had it. The falcon's clinical problem took precedence.

The king had an abiding interest in falconry and certainly knew his birds. A long discussion followed. It was terminated when the bird had profuse diarrhoea... fascinated, I couldn't help but observe (to myself) that the bird's stool was exactly the same blue/green colour as that of His Majesty's telephone. Fortunately I was not asked to give an opinion on the bird, even though it obviously had a gastroenterological problem.

His Majesty wanted to know what I thought of his condition.

To me the diagnosis seemed clear. If His Majesty had had these symptoms for up to fifteen years, and had been thoroughly investigated at so many centres of excellence with no abnormal findings, there remained, by exclusion, only the diagnosis of a functional disorder of the bowel.

In fact he had a variant of the irritable bowel syndrome known as the 'Morning Rush.' I explained the situation through what appeared to be the most intelligent of the eager interpreters. I further explained that I had brought some medication with me from England that I thought would benefit His Majesty. He should take just one capsule at night when he went to bed and one capsule in the morning when he got up. The medication was safe and acted simply by slowing the muscular activity of the bowel wall.

The king told one of the doctors to accompany me back to the hospital to get the medicine I was recommending as he would like to start it that night.

The consultation over, King Khalid rose. He was taller than I had imagined. He was dressed in the most elegant of elegant robes edged in gold. He moved slowly and gingerly using a stick; he had undergone hip replacement surgery a couple of years before. The king turned to me and smiled an enchanting smile; I was entranced. He spoke in the most gentle voice imaginable. The palace doctor standing next to me translated, "His Majesty thanks you for your visit and your expert opinion. He hopes to meet you again soon."

The medication was loperamide – just released on prescription in the United Kingdom. A couple of years later it was judged to be so safe it could be sold over the counter for the symptomatic relief of diarrhoea. The most common proprietary name is Imodium.

It worked a treat. No longer did King Khalid have to abruptly leave council meetings several times in a morning, made all the more troublesome by the none-too-successful hip surgery.

A week later I was told to go to Jeddah to see His Majesty there. The king had recalled that I had asked to examine him and he wanted me to come to Jeddah to do so.

The flight from Riyadh to Jeddah took less than an hour. Numerous glasses of freshly squeezed orange juice and Saudi champagne were pressed on me – the Saudi official who escorted me when I boarded the aircraft had announced that I was to be treated specially, "as he is the king's doctor."

In Jeddah, a young, elegantly dressed Saudi greeted me. He reeked of perfume and took me by the hand to a waiting Rolls-Royce. The king's palace in Jeddah was even more impressive than the one in Riyadh. I waited an hour alone in a room the size of a tennis court. It had sumptuous gold drapings, elegant chandeliers and glass tables on gold-plated legs, a style we irreverently at the King Faisal Specialist Hospital called Lebanese Louis. I refused numerous glasses of juice, Saudi champagne and cups of coffee.

I was taken to the king, bowed and greeted him as before with, "*Salaam aleikloum, taal amarac,*" which again amused him no end. He motioned me to sit next to him. He had just a few words of English, my Arabic was rudimentary but we seemed to have a rather jolly conversation with our limited abilities and an interpreter.

He told me how pleased he was with the treatment I had prescribed. I expressed my gratification at the good outcome and told him again how safe the medicine is, that he had a perfectly benign disorder, and he could continue the treatment indefinitely.

The king talked generally about Saudi Arabia. Did I enjoy the climate? Was I happy living in his country? Was I happy at the hospital? He told me that one of the most interesting events of his life had been when, as a young man, he took a train journey from Liverpool to London after sailing to Liverpool in a ship from Jeddah. He then mentioned that I could examine him but that first he needed to pray and have a siesta. Would I mind waiting? "Not at all, Your Majesty."

I was taken off for lunch in a vast dining room where, seated alone at a huge resplendent glass table, I was waited on by three servants. They gave me more juice, very nice rice and meat dishes and offered me a dessert called *Umm Ali* (Mother of Ali), which resembles bread and butter pudding with the addition of pistachio nuts, cinnamon, almonds and cardamom. It was two hours before I was taken to the king in his bedroom. I examined his abdomen and found it normal apart from a scar of gastric surgery which had not been mentioned at the original consultation. But no matter, His Majesty was better.

After the examination of his abdomen, I told King Khalid that I thought he had nothing to worry about with his bowel, it was simply a disorder of function. He then said, through the interpreter, "You know Fah'd has stomach problems. I think you should see him. He's here in Jeddah at the moment. I'll tell him you will see him before you return to Riyadh."

So I said my farewells to this most delightful and gentle man and was taken to Crown Prince Fah'd's palace. Evidently I was expected but after two hours received a message to say that the crown prince was involved in important state business. He would not be able to see me that day but would come to see me the next time he was in the capital.

I flew back to Riyadh that night, reflecting on one of the most extraordinary days of my life.

THE NEXT SENIOR ROYAL I ENCOUNTERED was King Khalid's wife. The queen had a long history of indigestion, very suggestive of a duodenal ulcer. Sure enough, at endoscopy she had a chronic duodenal ulcer. I took photographs of the ulcer. To my surprise, at the end of the procedure one of the palace physicians demanded that I give him the roll of 35mm film on which I had taken pictures of the royal ulcer. Quite what he expected me to do with the photos I don't know. I doubt that the popular exclamation mark magazines, like today's *Hello!* and *OK!*, would give tuppence for a picture of an ulcer no matter which royal duodenum it came from.

The queen responded well to treatment and when I reviewed her case at the king's palace, I was asked to go to the crown prince's palace, this time to see his son, Abdul Aziz.

Abdul Aziz was a delightful eight year old. He had abdominal pain every day which came on about half an hour before a car would arrive to take him to school. It was so bad it sometimes prevented him from going to school; however, the pain would subside within minutes of the car being sent away.

I examined him; he was a perfectly healthy boy. I explained that he had a mild school phobia, that there was no disease and that all that was necessary was for his nurse to try to discover what it was at school that was making him unhappy. Relief all round. I was thanked. I got up to leave. As I turned my left knee knocked against the occasional table on which rested a large glass of freshly squeezed orange juice that had been brought for me. The glass tumbled over, the orange juice spread in a large patch on the white deep pile shag carpet. To my relief, everybody smiled.

Being Fah'd's favourite son, Abdul Aziz received $300 million from his dad on his sixteenth birthday. There was a story that soon after Abdul Aziz was born, a soothsayer had told Fah'd that he and his son must never be separated, otherwise something dreadful would happen to Abdul Aziz.

The last time I saw King Khalid was in the Royal Suite at the King Faisal Specialist Hospital. His Majesty had been admitted with drowsiness and was close to coma. Various scans and neurological tests had not shown the cause. However, one astute physician, our senior psychiatrist, Dr Jim Willis, observed that the king had developed an acne-like rash affecting his face and suggested that he might be suffering from bromism. He was: his blood levels of bromide were high. The big question, how come the king had a condition which could only be caused by the ingestion of bromide-containing substances?

Bromism was very common before the sale in over-the-counter bromide containing sedatives and medications, such as tonics and Bromo-Seltzer, was banned. British Army soldiers in the First World War claimed they had been given bromides to calm them down and suppress sexual urges which might take their minds off dying in droves for king and country. American soldiers claimed that they also had been given the stuff and, naturally, sued the government after the war.

Bromism affects the nervous system in many different ways. No specific treatment is required. In most cases, the body eliminates bromide and good health returns.

Careful investigation at the palace revealed that one of his physicians had been giving the king sedatives containing bromide to help him sleep. These were stopped; history does not relate the fate of the physician.

When I saw the king, he was well on the road to recovery. He told me that he was still taking the medication I had given him for his diarrhoea and remained pleased with it.

King Khalid died suddenly of a massive heart attack at his palace in Taif at ten in the morning on 13 June 1982. He was sixty-nine years old. He had undergone open-heart surgery in the United States in 1976. His body was immediately flown to Riyadh where he was buried less than seven hours after he died.

With sadness I watched the proceedings which were broadcast on Saudi national television: there was none of the pomp one would see with a European monarch. When the Saudia aircraft taxied to a standstill on the apron at Riyadh airport, it was surrounded by a seething mob of men. The body, wrapped in a seamless white shroud, lying on a wooden bier and covered with a carpet, was unloaded with some difficulty through the aircraft passenger door which was slightly too narrow to accommodate the bier without tilting. As the bier was being carried down the steep aircraft steps, it again tilted, this time alarmingly and causing great consternation.

The police had enormous difficulty in forcing a way through the crowd, so many pressed forward to attempt to touch the body as it passed. The bier was loaded onto an ambulance. There was no procession. The ambulance drove to the Grand Mosque in the central square in Riyadh. After funeral prayers were recited, the remains of King Khalid were taken to the Oud cemetery, some five kilometres away, and buried in the family cemetery alongside his brother Faisal: the simple grave was marked only with a stone.

Sixteen

WHEN I WAS IN SAUDI ARABIA, IT WAS in many ways an isolated country, especially for doctors who were remote from the world of international medicine. The hospital administration recognised this and encouraged consultants to take time off to attend approved clinical meetings.

We needed no encouragement; leave outside the kingdom was always welcome. It could sometimes be extended by tacking on a public holiday such as the Prophet's birthday or the Hejira New Year. Travel was first class; daily expenses, hotel bills and course fees were paid. Naturally, when scanning the medical journals for suitable meetings, one was as much influenced by the attractiveness of the location as the clinical content of the meeting.

So it was that I found myself at a meeting of the American Society of Gastroenterology in New Orleans in February 1979, which conveniently coincided with Mardi Gras. I checked into the Inn on Bourbon Street with excitement undiminished by the long haul from Riyadh via New York. The hotel was about two hundred years old; a large colonial style red brick building with ferns in every nook and cranny. An ornate wrought iron balcony, painted dark green, encircled the rectangular structure. Alas, a large notice at the check-in desk announced that the Mardi Gras parades had been cancelled: the City Police Department would be on strike that day. What a disappointment! No jazz bands marching down the streets and no gay pride parades. Nonetheless New Orleans was to prove extremely interesting.

On my way to breakfast on the first morning, I encountered a mountain of a man at the entrance to the dining room. Huge and enormously fat with glistening jet black skin, he was wearing a light brown Stetson with a brim eight inches wide; his vast belly overhung his belt to which were attached a truncheon, a pistol in its holster and handcuffs. He wore a blue uniform shirt bedecked with the US flag on both upper sleeves, epaulettes with stripes of gold braid and badges of a military nature embroidered on the breast pockets. His tight-fitting black trousers accentuated his thighs – the size of gateposts. I thought he was a cop and asked him if there was a problem. "No, sah, I works heah," he replied – he was the doorman.

It was to get better. Next morning, as I was eating – for the first time in my life – hominy grits with maple syrup, I was joined by a bizarre character. He was about thirty-five, skinny, had formidable halitosis, rotten teeth, a goatee beard and a wild look. He said, "You're a doctor, I see."

I agreed that I was. I could scarcely deny it; I was sporting a badge announcing that I was a doctor and that I was attending a medical meeting.

"I'm a very interesting case," he announced.

"Is that so," I said.

"Yes, I have insulin dependent diabetes."

"Oh," I muttered; sounds like a cheap consultation, I thought.

But he went on. "Yes, and what's more, for five years I have suffered from erectile failure, but a week ago I came to New Orleans and had a penile pump fitted. It's fantastic. Would you like to see it work?"

"Well…" I demurred, wondering if his delight extended to whipping off his pants and giving a demonstration to the breakfasting crowd. But no, he thrust a hand into his trouser pocket, made pumping movements, and before my popping eyes a huge bulge appeared in the front midline of his trousers. "Wow, that's impressive!" There was a faint hissing noise and the bulge subsided.

"I haven't tried it out yet, but I kept the old feller up for an hour last night."

"Well done," I said. Some lady might be in for a treat provided she could get past his rotten teeth and smelly breath.

"And another thing…"

"Yes?" I held my breath to avoid the halitotic gusts.

"I can forge signatures so well you can't tell them from the originals."

"Really?"

"Yes, it's easy but you need an egg."

"Go on." I glanced at my watch. The conference started in fifteen minutes but this random speaker was in full flow.

"What you do is this. You boil the egg until you are absolutely sure it's hard – at least ten minutes – let it cool, remove the shell and then carefully peel off the membrane covering the hardened white. Then you take the egg between your fingers and thumb and carefully, with a little pressure, slowly roll it over the signature. The egg picks up a thin layer of ink and then you have a mirror image of the signature on the egg. Roll the egg where you want the signature, and bingo, a perfect forgery."

I thanked him and told him I would try it out when I got home. I did: it works but I haven't yet found a suitable occasion to use it.

Walking through New Orleans from the Inn on Bourbon to the conference at the Hilton, about a mile away, was much more entertaining than downtown Riyadh. On one occasion, a young man collapsed on the pavement ahead of me. Passers-by merely walked around his prone form. They're accustomed to it, I supposed. More than once I was accosted in the mornings by ladies interested in my happiness: "Hey fellah! Would you lak a good tahm in Noo Orrlins?" As I strolled along one fine morning, I witnessed a blue-and-white police car, with screaming siren, hit the sidewalk just in front of a snappily dressed guy. The cops shot out at lightning speed, slammed him face forwards against the side of the cruiser, yanked back his arms and handcuffed him. I was disappointed that a lollipop-chewing Telly Savalas didn't appear.

And of course there was the jazz... traditional New Orleans jazz is the only sort for me. In the past half century, Preservation Hall has become the Mecca of New Orleans jazz. The hall is a simple, dusty little warehouse room in a block in the French Quarter, just around the corner from Bourbon Street. Three benches provide seating, otherwise the audience stands crammed shoulder to shoulder.

When I was there, an ancient, diminutive, stick-like lady wearing a red beret and more wrinkled than any prune was playing piano with dancing fingers beneath a sign which read, 'Requests: Traditional – $2: All others – $5: Saints – $10'. A neighbour told me in a hushed, reverent voice that she was the celebrated 'Sweet Emma' Barrett. The trumpet player looked about eighty and had cheeks which inflated like a bullfrog's when he played his horn; years and years of playing had blown apart the fibres of his buccinators, the muscles of his cheeks.

Bullfrog cheeks were on display everywhere there were bands playing: in the streets, in Jackson Square and even in a cemetery I visited one afternoon. That was part of an organised tour. These days all corpses have to be entombed above ground in stone sepulchres. New Orleans is prone to flooding, particularly in the hurricane season. Occasionally – before the city passed its ordinance – the departed, buried by sorrowing relatives who thought they had said their last farewells, had been known to pop up again.

It so happened that my tour coincided with a funeral. A large crowd was gathered, a five-piece jazz band played blues and dirges before the coffin was consigned to its resting place. But the instant the interment was over, the band broke into *The Saints* and the crowd swung into a ragged, syncopated march to the cemetery gates led by a vastly obese man. He was shaped like a globe with short stubby arms and equally short plump legs. He held aloft a tiny pink parasol which wobbled as, with the daintiness possessed by some very fat people, he pranced from foot to foot. Behind him the mourners sang lustily. Everybody knew the words of the New Orleans national anthem.

For the rest of the official tourist experience I sampled O'Brien's bar (tastiest prawn gumbo in town), rode on an old streetcar (named Desire), splashed down the Mississippi on a stern-wheeler paddle boat and visited Jackson Square where, for twenty minutes and the price of five dollars, I felt like a plantation owner out of *Gone with the Wind* as I rode in a horse-drawn carriage with a driver dressed in full livery including a shiny top hat, white gloves and flashing white teeth.

For the ghoulish, there were cemetery tours at night; for my part, I preferred to commune with the spirits I could find in a mint julep.

To return to Riyadh, I retraced my steps from New Orleans to New York where I joined a Saudia flight for the rest of the journey. A couple of hours outbound came the message over the aircraft's intercom, "If there is a doctor on board, please make yourself known to the stewardess." My instinct, as always was to sink down into my seat, close my eyes and hope that there would be a keen young doctor eager for glory. Sometimes there was. But this time no such luck, so I made myself 'known' and was taken by a beautiful Lebanese hostess to the rear of the aircraft where I was greeted by a bizarre sight – a stewardess lying across four seats. She looked ill, she moaned, her belly was bared and a colleague was sponging her abdomen with warm water from a red plastic bowl.

"What happened?" I asked her buddies who were crowding around her making solicitous noises.

"This came on after she went to the toilet and vomited several times."

I asked if she had pain in her abdomen. She didn't. I asked if she had eaten anything unusual. She hadn't, but she certainly had drunk unusually the night before. The chief steward confided in me that all the crew had been invited to a party by a very rich Saudi in his New York apartment and it emerged that she had consumed an amount of brandy which would see off a couple of sailors on shore leave. Her abdomen was soft, her tongue dry and her breath still conveyed the fumes of last night's excesses. Poor girl, she had a really nasty hangover. I reassured her (and her colleagues) that though she felt that death was imminent and would be a relief, a simple cure was at hand, the passage of time and several glasses of water – tomorrow she would be fine.

As I turned to go back to my seat, another attractive Lebanese hostess said to me, "But what about the eye?"

"Eye? What eye?" I said turning back and bending down to lift one of the patient's eyelids.

"No no," said this new attendant, "my eye. It has been itching and is red. Please look."

The previous flight I had taken on Saudia had also included a medical diversion. That time, sitting next to the aisle and an hour before landing in Dharan on our way to Riyadh, I saw a pair of male legs jerking on the floor ahead of me; the remainder of the body was also involved in a major epileptic fit. I attended to him but there was little to do except turn him on his side and protect his tongue. He came round remarkably quickly and was able to tell me that he was a known epileptic and took anticonvulsant medication. Before we reached Dharan, I told the steward that he should be offloaded there and taken to hospital. If he was having repeated fits, the situation could become dangerous.

When we took off for Riyadh an hour later, to my amazement there he was again, fitting in the aisle. When it subsided, I asked the steward what had happened with the doctor in Dhahran airport. "He told the doctor that he had to get to Riyadh for important business meetings so the doctor gave him a couple of paracetamol tablets and said he would be okay to travel."

IN 1981, I WENT TO HAWAII TO THE Pan-Pacific Congress on Liver Diseases and presented a paper on my experiences in treating bleeding oesophageal

varices and liver diseases in Saudi Arabia. This was a triumph for me –
getting to Hawaii, that is, not the presentation of the paper. There was at
the King Faisal Specialist Hospital an informal competition to see who could
get the furthest away for study leave. I won that year. The time difference
between Hawaii and Riyadh is twelve hours; you can't get further away
than that and remain on the planet.

I spent a couple of days on the Big Island, Hawaii. I had a look at
Waikiki Beach. It was big, populated by big, brown, well-oiled people and
surrounded by skyscrapers which had their feet in the sand. The sea was
flat; there were no young men with rippling muscles 'hanging five'.

I went to the USS *Arizona* memorial in Pearl Harbor and stood on the
ship's bridge. It remained above water when the *Arizona* was sunk by
Japanese torpedo planes on 7 December 1941. I stood for a few minutes and
reflected on the 1,177 sailors permanently entombed in the sunken hull; what
a waste of young lives. And what an ignoble act by a nation proud of its
tradition of honour. My thoughts were interrupted by noisy chattering and
the clicking of camera shutters; quite a crowd had assembled in a semicircle
around me as I mused. I looked at them: each and every one was Japanese.

The conference was being held at the Kaanapali Beach Hotel on the
island of Maui. It was a magnificent hotel, set in forty acres of landscaped
grounds with rocky features made of glass fibre, pools on which artificial
swans were anchored (they tried real ones but they kept flying away) and
everywhere ancient Chinese artefacts: fierce warriors scattered around the
halls and many Ming vases... I could of course spot that those were fake.

Fifteen minutes after I got to my room, there was a knock on the door. I
opened it to a smiling Hawaiian girl in a grass skirt. Mesmerised, I caught
only a few words, but I thought she said, "Would you like a lay, sir?" Before
I could react, she leaned forward as if to embrace me. Alas, she simply put
something around my neck, turned on her shapely heel and disappeared
down the corridor, leaving me with my lei, just a long daisy chain of flowers,
and possibly some errant thoughts.

If the meeting was interesting, Hawaii was more interesting. At the end
of the congress, I flew to the eastern tip of Maui where I stayed at the Hana
Ranch Hotel overlooking what the American author James Michener
described as the most perfect beach in the world. It was beautiful and must
have seemed so to the great British explorer, Captain James Cook, when he

sailed past it in 1798. No doubt standing at his side on the bridge was his sailing master, a certain William Bligh, who ten years later achieved fame for himself (and a couple of centuries later for Messrs Charles Laughton, Trevor Howard and Anthony Hopkins) as master of HMS *Bounty*. The following year, on St Valentine's Day, Captain Cook was clubbed to death by natives on the Big Island, Hawaii.

It was early evening when I checked in at the Hana Ranch Hotel. The weather was cool and pleasant, there were brown cows grazing in nearby meadows surrounded by tall, thick hedges. It looked for all the world like a pastoral scene typical of my home county, Devon.

A flag fluttered high above the hotel. At first glance, it looked like the stars and stripes, but then I looked closer... it had eight horizontal stripes in red, white and blue but where I expected to see stars occupying the upper left corner I found instead the British flag, what everyone calls the Union Jack. I enquired and learned that the Union flag was in memory of when the islands were a British protectorate (until 1843 they were the Sandwich Islands, so named by Captain Cook for his sponsor, the Earl of Sandwich) and each horizontal stripe represented one of the eight islands which form Hawaii. That was the official version. However, the story I prefer is that during the 1812 war between Britain and the US, the king of Hawaii was concerned that either side might bombard his vessels. So, to bamboozle each of the combatants, he designed a flag which would at a distance fox the Americans and, viewed through their telescopes, confuse the British.

I spent the following morning on James Michener's perfect beach below the hotel. It was crescentic; the sand was fine black volcanic, the waves were formidable and I was the only soul there. I tried the surf but after being thrown around like a rag doll and having my face scraped on the gritty bottom, I gave up. So I sat beneath the dipping palms with happy fiddler crabs clicking around me and read the local guide book. I discovered that Charles Lindbergh, the first man to fly solo non-stop across the Atlantic in 1927, had spent his last days on Maui, in Hana to be precise. He was buried nearby; I had to see his grave. I already had a rented car and set off after lunch. It was some ten miles to the churchyard in which he had been interred eight years before.

Driving through peaceful, delightful countryside (oh-so-green after dusty, drab, brown Saudi Arabia) a signpost directed me down a sun-dappled leafy lane which suddenly opened to reveal a simple old church. Its walls were of white limestone coral, the upper third of the walls were clad in green clapboard supporting a slanting grey slate roof with a rudimentary square steeple.

The church faced the sea and in front was a small graveyard. Lindbergh's grave lay close to the cliff edge overlooking the Pacific. The church was open but empty. I was quite alone. The only noise was that of the breakers below. The utter tranquillity of the place moved me. I felt the same spirituality I had experienced gazing in solitude from the edge of a high escarpment in the remote Saudi desert. Allah, God, or whatever he is called seemed close at hand.

I spent an hour musing and just sitting quietly on the cliff edge. Lindbergh had chosen his final resting place with care. In a reflective mood, I drove back to the hotel as the shadows lengthened. I rested in my room. Still feeling emotionally charged, I had to phone somebody I knew. I called a girl, Maria, in Riyadh. I had met Maria a couple of weeks before I left for Hawaii. Connections were not easy in those days but eventually I got through; it was six in the morning there, but my call was not unwelcome.

I showered, changed and went to the bar; it was empty apart from a Hawaiian beauty polishing glasses behind the counter. She looked up, smiled and asked, "What would you like, sir?"

"I'd like to try something typically Hawaiian," I replied.

She laughed and throwing wide her brown bare arms said, "I'm typically Hawaiian!"

WHEN I RETURNED TO RIYADH, CHANGES had occurred. There had been a *coup d'état* in the hospital; there had been a *coup de cœur* for me. My personal coup was caused by that girl Maria. She was a young Irish secretary and ran the department of paediatrics. I had met her at a party not long before my trip to the Sandwich Islands. Within days we met again; my feelings for her grew. I wondered if she returned them.

One evening as I said good night to Maria, she thrust a packet into my hands and said, "Don't open this until you are safely home." I didn't; I obeyed her then, as I have done for the past almost thirty years.

The packet contained six rashers of the best Irish bacon. What better demonstration of love in Saudi Arabia?

Medical Affairs secretaries, 1982. 'That girl' Maria is seated, second row left, on the arm of a chair. Jean Parks Sasson is seated on the floor, front row right.

As I cooked my breakfast next morning, occasionally bursting into *I just met a girl named Maria*, the delightful smell of frying bacon permeated the house. Thoughts of Maria perfused my brain; she had found a niche in my mind and a corner in my heart. It was a week later that I flew to Hawaii via San Francisco.

Looking back at my stay in Hawaii, I had been like some callow teenager mooning over Maria. She was there all the time. Even while I watched elderly hula dancers in a show put on by the hotel, she was there, prancing around somewhere in the frontal lobes of my brain. As I picked over kalau pig and ate poi, she was there. The pig cooked underground was delicious but didn't distract my thoughts; not even the poi – a purple, gag-inducing paste with the consistency (and flavour) of glue – could do that.

Happily, back at the hospital I was frequently called upon to consult on paediatric gastroenterological problems. This meant visiting the paediatric department and of course passing the time of day with the enchanting secretary. It wasn't long before the consultants and residents took notice. They were delighted. Over six years Maria had become their mother, sister, counsellor and friend. She had a sparkling personality, a ready smile and a stunning figure. I was undoubtedly smitten, badly smitten and – Hallelujah! *Alhamdulillah*! – it soon became evident that my interest was reciprocated.

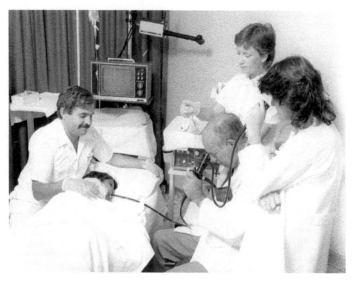

The author endoscoping a child in the paediatric department.

We had a bizarre courtship, but the vigilantes added spice to the proceedings. I would pick her up on the road outside the hospital accommodation and when we returned from visiting friends she would hide under a blanket in the back of the car. If she were to visit me in my house, we needed all sorts of subterfuge to outwit the security services but now, on reflection and with hindsight – they probably knew our every move.

LIKE MOST *COUPS D'ÉTAT*, THE ONE AT the hospital was dramatic. The American executive director had gone to the US on leave. A Saudi, with powerful backing, stepped into his shoes and the former executive director was never seen again at the King Faisal Specialist Hospital.

The Saudi, Dr Nizar Feteih, was already a member of the medical staff; he was a consultant cardiologist who had trained in the United States. I met him when I did my locum in April 1978. Then he was jolly, cheerful and friendly, enjoyed a party and took a glass or two of wine… in short he was one of the boys.

But when he assumed both mantles of executive and medical directors, he changed. Power went to his head; he became the absolute monarch of the King Faisal Specialist Hospital. Bearded, aggressive and loud with a fanatical gleam in his dark eyes, Feteih swished around the hospital corridors in his Arab robes, exuding an air of authority unless a senior member of the Royal

Family appeared when he became fawning and obsequious; like most bullies, he scorned those below him in the pecking order.

Dr Feteih was sure he had total independent power and all the trappings that went with it. Robert Louis Stevenson's *Strange case of Dr Jekyll and Mr Hyde* comes to mind. In the book, Stevenson's Mr Hyde appears at intervals. In contrast, King Faisal Specialist Hospital's very own Mr Hyde, once he appeared, was there permanently. He enthusiastically embraced his power and he enthusiastically abused it. Much favoured by King Khalid, he felt – and for the next two or three years it was true – that he could do as he pleased. He developed such overt megalomania it became pathological.

Within the confines of the immense institution of the King Faisal Specialist Hospital, which had a payroll at the time of more than six thousand, he formed a dictatorship. He organised the hospital security services as his own intelligence and enforcement agency. If he had made them wear brown shirts, jackboots and arm bands, it would not have been out of place. He instituted telephone-tapping, armed his guards with night vision binoculars and had them perch on roof tops to maintain round-the-clock surveillance of his fiefdom.

Life for nearly everybody at the hospital was getting uncomfortable. It had become a seething mass of intrigue, a Byzantine confusion of devious and underhand activity. If you were in Nizar Feteih's favour, your path would be strewn with petals; if not, a most trivial request, say for a new dustpan for the house, would be denied. Like all despots, he had to know everything. No decision was too small for him – he could not delegate; even the delivery boy in the post room had to be approved by him.

The discomfort for Maria and me was particularly acute. As we already wanted to marry, we went ahead. We hoped that legitimising our association would make our lives at the hospital more secure. We married at the American Evangelical Church in Bahrain. About twenty colleagues and their families made up the wedding party and joined us at the wedding breakfast at one of Bahrain's best hotels.

We honeymooned in Malaysia. I had fond memories of Penang, had heard that a new university was opening there and that a medical school was planned. What more attractive prospect than a new venture in a place I loved? Maria was keen; I had already taken her on holiday to Penang and to the Cameron Highlands the year before.

Wedding day, Bahrain 1982.

I wrote ahead to the dean, sent my *curriculum vitae* and expressed interest in a post as a gastroenterologist and a teacher in the medical school. I told him we would be passing through Penang and he invited us to visit him at the university campus.

The new university campus was on familiar grounds, Minden Barracks, home of the 10th Gurkha Rifles when I was there ten years before. The medical school had yet to open and a new general hospital under construction at Kota Bharu would be used for clinical teaching. I would initially be appointed as a consultant there.

This seemed scarcely a practical arrangement. Kota Bharu is in the north-east tip of Malaysia more than two hundred miles from Penang. But we said we would take a look and were given a letter of introduction to the medical administrator of the province of Kelantan.

After five restful days in Penang with little more arduous to do than decide where to dine and watch the spectacular thunder storms, we set off for Kota Bharu. The road soon deteriorated, becoming slow and tortuous; worse, it ran along the Malaysian side of the Thai border. Communist terrorists were still a problem; they concealed themselves across the border in the Thai jungle. Every fifty miles there were military posts, but fifty miles is a very long way on a lonely road with the ever-present fear of being surrounded by grinning gun-toting terrorists in our minds. "Oh yes," one helpful contact had told us, "terrorists attack private cars, rob and sometimes kill their victims." It took more than seven hours to reach our destination.

We had made reservations at what was described as a luxury holiday beach resort and moved into a comfortable bungalow – comfortable, that is, until we went to bed and looked up. Armies of the largest ants we had ever seen were marching across the ceiling, skirting the skylight in the centre and proceeding to the corner diagonally opposite. Then, to our horror, a malevolent Chinese face appeared, looking down at us through the skylight… in a flash, he disappeared.

The journey and Kota Bharu had bad vibes for us. It came to mind that thirty years earlier, the Japanese had begun their invasion of the Malaysian peninsula at Kota Bharu: this was where Japanese soldiers mounted bicycles and astounded the Allies that on such primitive transport they were able to advance so swiftly down the peninsula to Singapore. The Allies thought they would take weeks hacking their way through the Malaysian jungles; instead they pedalled along roads and rubber tappers' paths and then attacked Singapore from the tip of the Malaysian Peninsula, surprising everyone.

Next morning, we met the medical administrator who took us to see the hospital. The construction had started only a few weeks earlier. The foundations had been laid but the building was only a skeleton of steel girders. There was no completion date and the monsoon season would soon arrive and interrupt work.

It was clear to us that thoughts of a post in Penang in the near future would have to be abandoned. The medical school wouldn't open for months, maybe years; the hospital would take years to build and the two hundred mile journey between the two was fraught with danger.

We drove down the East Coast looking for places to stay. After a couple of nights at low cost, low facilities, low comfort hotels, we were delighted late one morning to come across a Club Méditerranée at Kuantan. We hadn't known of its existence but we thought that if anybody knows how to enjoy themselves, it's surely the French. They had a couple of vacancies; we checked in and were directed to a pleasant wooden apartment with a balcony overlooking the sea.

To our surprise, we saw that the twin beds were positioned at opposite ends of a long room, there was only one chair, only one glass and no lock on the door. When we asked for a second glass and chair, without as much as a 'sorry' we were told that it was policy to have the apartments furnished this way and that there was no need to lock the door, "*C'est normale.*"

We went for lunch and found the place in an uproar. It was full of Australians, big Aussies with even bigger Aussie wives. They were all tight and engaged in a log-sawing competition – which the women won. It turned out that the club was popular with Australian tourists and the French, knowing the quickest way to Australian hearts, provided free beer by the gallon at midday.

Ourselves, we couldn't get a drink; we didn't have the necessary plastic interlocking beads. You could buy them at reception.... but the bead-seller had gone for lunch. There was no way the bar would accept cash. I complained and the French manager looked at me as if I was some '*rosbif*' who had emerged from under a stone. "*Evidemment monsieur,*" he said, "you `ave nevaar stayed at a Club Med! Thees his the way we do eet `ere."

I agreed I had never stayed at one of his clubs and added that I was unlikely to do so again. He was offended; he sniffed... as only a Frenchman can sniff when he's offended.

But we stayed for another couple of days; it was a nice spot and the *entente* eventually became more *cordiale*, a factor that weighed in France's favour many, many years later.

We had entertainment laid on every noon when our fellow guests slurped huge jugs of ale for a couple of hours while engaging in sporting activities. The women always won; they were bigger, stronger, better muscled and held their beer well. I shudder to think of England's chances if they competed in an Ashes series.

We returned to Penang via the cool hill station of the Cameron Highlands and spent another couple of days lounging on the beach, swimming and riding hired jet-skis like a couple of teenagers on the loose.

But our time in paradise was up – it was time to go back to Riyadh; back to uncertainty and anxiety but back to good friends.

What awaited us in the Kingdom of Saudi Arabia?

Seventeen

WHEN WE FLEW INTO RIYADH AFTER our honeymoon, the first question we asked was, "Who's been sacked?" Fortunately, not us... not yet at any rate.

It turned out that Dr Feteih had gone after a paediatric resident. He had come across the doctor talking to his – Feteih's – secretary, Jane Richards, in her office which was next to his. It was quite innocent; the young doctor was simply asking for clarification of a recently issued administrative order.

Feteih had already staked his claim on Jane. He was furious and sacked the resident on the spot. Within twenty-four hours, the doctor was out of the country; happily he is now a successful paediatric cardiologist in the United States. Ironically, Jane was herself shipped out a few weeks later when she fell out of favour.

Nizar Feteih's megalomania had blossomed. His goons took it upon themselves to design their own uniforms: dark three-piece suits, white shirts, ties and shoes polished to a mirror finish. Their haircuts were short, their bearing military and they strutted the hospital corridors exuding power. The highlight of their day was when they appeared before Dr Feteih and presented their reports of the previous twenty-four hours' surveillance and all its infringements. Like hounds straining at the leash, panting, waiting on his commands.

Part of his vanity expressed itself in his malignant libido. Like so many Saudi stallions, our medical director felt compelled, even duty-bound, to favour every Western woman who took his fancy. In his fiefdom, he held the *droit de seigneur*. His possessiveness was total and he would be insanely jealous if he felt that any of his many mistresses was cheating on him. He had a bevy of compliant secretaries; but not only secretaries – he had an affair with the gorgeous wife of a young American consultant physician.

Medical staff and residents of King Faisal Specialist Hospital, 1978. Dr Feteih, at the time a consultant cardiologist, is fourth from the right in the back row.

Her humiliated husband sent her back to the US and followed as soon as he could at the end of his contract.

Jane Richards was succeeded by Jean Parks as the head of the secretaries. Jean was an American, a southern belle if ever there was one with her pretty face, dainty figure and long fair hair curling to her waist. When Jean walked the long hospital corridor, it became a Marx Brothers set as mens' heads turned; some stumbled into walls or bumped into each other with mouths agape.

Jean was the sort of woman one might think that Feteih needed to conquer. But she was a tough cookie under that sugar coating. Feteih preferred young, naïve, pliant women who he could control. Jean had a boyfriend who was quite a character, an Anglo-Italian businessman called Peter Sasson who was working in Riyadh. Jean and Peter had known each other for years; they married; Jean Parks became Jean Sasson and a few years later was to make her mark on the world stage as a celebrated author and expert on Middle Eastern affairs.

Around this time, Maria had an urgent call from home. The condition of her brother, Leo, who was known to have aplastic anaemia, had suddenly deteriorated and he was gravely ill. Aplastic anaemia is a form of anaemia caused by failure of the bone marrow to make blood cells. Leo was in the Hammersmith Hospital in London, one of the leading specialist medical centres in the world. Previous tests had shown that Maria and her brother were tissue compatible. Her brother desperately needed a marrow transplant from his donor sister. Without it, death would be certain – and not far off.

To everyone's amazement, and jaw-dropping horror, Dr Feteih refused to allow Maria to take emergency leave. It took all the powers of persuasion of Jean and numerous consultants to make him relent. The marrow transplant worked.

Meanwhile, Feteih's current number one mistress, Susan Price, was receiving exceptional favours. She had a house on her own while all the other single women shared. A team of hospital gardeners attended to its grounds and security personnel drove her to her daily relaxation, horseback riding. She had a dog despite animals being forbidden in hospital accommodation.

Such was her influence – and arrogance – that she was heard to boast one day as she walked down the crowded hospital main corridor, "I can get anyone sacked if I have a mind to do it." Word quickly spread among the staff, male and female, and she found herself shunned.

The atmosphere in the hospital had become intolerable for Maria and she resigned her post as secretary to the department of paediatrics. Because she was now my wife, she came under my 'sponsorship' – that's how things are done in Saudi Arabia. One benefit was that with Feteih's approval to travel no longer needed, Maria was able to return to London without fuss when Leo needed further marrow transplants. Maria's marrow was to give her brother an additional seven years of normal life but he died eventually of a common end-stage complication of the disease, acute leukaemia.

Despite having married, life was not getting simpler for us; if anything, it was getting more and more difficult. But why was this so? What was the explanation?

When she worked in the department of paediatrics, Maria was well-liked and invited to practically all the social functions, formal and informal, that the department hosted. It later emerged that, long before we married, Maria had been asked by Jane Richards to take her to parties organised by the young paediatric doctors. No one knew that Jane was at that time number one in Feteih's string of mistresses. This was an explosive situation, a recipe for disaster. Despite casting his favours in all directions, he was nonetheless enraged because he thought that Maria was leading his woman, his very own property, astray.

Nothing could have been further from the truth. Parties by the Middle Eastern paediatric doctors did not include the ingredients or feverish B-class movie activities so vividly imagined in his jealous rage.

This was the root cause of all our problems; why he had it in for Maria and – by association – for me. Suddenly I began to experience, even more vividly, a recurrence of the, "Why am I here?" – The sensation which haunted me in my first weeks at the King Faisal Hospital. It would spring on me many times a day. Was I paranoid? No, I was neither neurotic nor psychotic. It was real. Nizar Feteih was indeed persecuting me.

New and attractive housing for senior doctors had become available and as one of the senior consultants, I applied to move into it. My application was flatly rejected: no reason given. I watched in dismay, anger and confusion, as colleagues and consultants junior to me took up residence in the new houses. A further syllable had appeared in the writing on the wall.

ONE FRIDAY EVENING, TOWARDS THE END of November, we had friends around to play a few rubbers of bridge. First we had dinner and drank some wine. It was a pleasant evening.

Next morning at the hospital I was faced for the third or fourth time with a patient who had been wrongly assigned to my gastroenterology clinic. He had a pain in the leg due to sciatic nerve compression. I was irritated; recently this had been happening every week. I had complained repeatedly to deaf ears.

The Lebanese interpreter couldn't care less. I lost my temper and shouted; she disappeared.

The next thing I knew, Feteih's head of security, an American called Ed Burke, appeared in my consulting room. "Doctor, were you drinking alcohol last night?" he asked.

Taken by surprise, I said, "Yes, as a matter of fact I had a glass or two of wine."

"I'm afraid I need you to give me a blood sample," said Burke.

In hindsight, I should have refused, but being uncertain about what was going on, and also being a civilised person, I cooperated. My colleague and good friend, Dr Sean Sieck, was called from a neighbouring consulting room to take the blood sample.

When the sample had been taken, I was driven to the security department and held there waiting for Nizar Feteih's orders. While waiting, I asked Ed Burke, "How do I appear to you? Do I look drunk?"

"You look like a perfectly sober, dignified, English physician," he replied, and left me with my thoughts. I wasn't too distressed. I thought I would simply forfeit my job. I had felt for some time that I could be much happier out of this nightmare place.

After half an hour, Burke returned. "We've been instructed to hand you over to the police," he said. I couldn't believe my ears; I was shocked; I'd heard tales of Saudi police methods and their awful jails.

"I want to see a lawyer," I said. None was available for me. "Does Feteih have the authority to send me to jail?" I demanded. The reply was a shrug of the shoulders.

Three security guards were deployed to see that I made it to jail. One of them was a shaven-headed, bull-necked brute called Bernie Kerik. At the jail, there were no formalities, no forms were filled in and no identification made. My belt, shoelaces and spectacles were taken from me. I was taken by the elbow and shown through a barred door into a cell.

The door clanged behind me. I was dumbfounded. Amazement, incredulity, fear, anger and confusion coursed through my brain; one minute a senior consultant physician in a prestigious hospital, the next in jail with assorted low-life and other unfortunates.

The cell was a rectangular room about twenty feet by forty feet. There were eighteen other occupants. There were no chairs, no beds and no table. The peeling walls were covered in Arabic graffiti. In one corner were the toilet facilities: a dripping tap and a squat-style lavatory bowl with slots for the feet. The bowl was filthy, covered in old dried and recent liquid faeces. The place stank.

Although mid-day, the cell was almost in darkness. It had one small barred window high up and close to the ceiling. A couple of bare, low-wattage light bulbs provided night-time illumination but were extinguished before ten. There was a central ceiling fan but it was still. Thankfully it was the end of November, a cool part of the year. That room, crowded with unwashed men and disgusting toilet facilities, would have been insufferable in the heat of a Saudi summer.

To my relief, an hour after my arrival I was taken out of the cell. I thought that higher authorities had countermanded Feteih's draconian action. My relief was short-lived. I was taken to the Riyadh Central Hospital for another blood alcohol test and then returned to the jail.

I later learned that the level of alcohol in the sample taken at the King Faisal Specialist Hospital was less than half the level at which one is permitted to drive in England. The second test at the Central Hospital showed a level of zero.

BACK IN THE CELL, WE SAT ON THE STONE floor around the room with our backs to the wall. My fellow prisoners were mostly Arabs but there were five Filipinos. All were amazed to see a Britisher among them, just as amazed as I was amazed to be there.

The Filipinos had been caught gambling – an extremely serious offence in the Kingdom of the Holy Shrines guarded by that upholder of virtue, King Fah'd. It was no longer mentioned that, just a decade or so before, Fah'd had managed to lose one million dollars in a single dusk-to-dawn Scotch-fuelled session gambling in a Monte Carlo night club. Or that there were many photographs of him emerging in the early hours from casinos on the Côte d'Azur impeccably suited with a hostess on each arm.

The Filipinos had been arrested in a flat on the third floor of a block. The police, acting on a tip-off, broke in with guns drawn. One gambler tried to escape by shinning down a drain pipe; it gave way and he crashed to the ground and broke a leg. The leg was in plaster but the fracture had been badly set and was giving him a lot of pain. His friends had been arrested at gunpoint. The five had been shackled together before they were thrown into this cell to await sentence. The sores on their ankles caused by the shackles were freely suppurating but there was no medical care.

Those weren't the only wounds in that cell. One Jordanian, an alleged forger, showed me the cigarette burns which had been inflicted to encourage a confession from him.

Three Palestinians said they were there because they had witnessed a car accident which involved a Saudi. They had committed no offence and were simply witnesses. They were being detained so that they would be instantly available to give evidence when the case came before the police court, maybe in a few days, maybe in a few weeks, whatever. Innocents confined to jail – but as the Saudis are wont to say, "*Ali wali*, they are only Palestinians."

Most of the others were there for visa violations, although one poor chap was being held on a charge of theft and was increasingly fearful that his sentence might involve losing a hand in Chop Chop Square.

"Has anyone spoken to a lawyer?" I asked. My question was met with a blank look. Such defence as would be mounted would be provided by the Saudi court. A Sharia judge, sitting alone, would pass sentence.

Evening came; the calls to prayer could be heard from the mosques surrounding the jail. The Muslim prisoners performed their pre-prayer ablutions, lined up and went through the ritual while we non-Muslims looked on. Then food arrived. It was the only meal of the day and was the same every day: scrawny boiled chicken, rice and a few vegetables. The lot was spread on sheets of newspaper in the middle of the cell floor; everybody sat around and, of course, ate with their right hands. I wasn't hungry but I was touched when my fellow inmates made room for me to join them and insisted that I had something.

The next morning I was interviewed by a young Saudi police officer. His English was not brilliant, but clearly what he was after was an admission that I was making wine and selling it, even to Muslims. I admitted that I made wine. We had several cases in the house. He asked why so much if I was not selling it. I told him that Christmas was coming and that we would be entertaining.

He seized on this, "So, you give wine to others, do you?"

"Yes, of course, when we entertain at home."

"Do you ever give wine to other peoples?"

"Yes, when we visit close friends."

"And you sell it to them?"

"No, never; I have never sold wine."

"Why not, you make plenty money selling wine?"

I repeated, "I have never sold wine. I don't need to: the hospital pays me well." This seemed to satisfy him so it was back to the cell to rejoin my fellow inmates.

I HAD AMPLE TIME TO REFLECT AND PLENTY of time to worry. I knew that what had been done to me would be considered outrageous by my colleagues, by most Saudis and by the world at large. In fact, I later learned that my colleague and close friend, Dr Nicholas Woodhouse, was so incensed when he heard what had happened that he immediately went to the police station, accompanied by an Arabic-speaking surgeon who could translate for him, and asked to see the officer-in-charge. He said to the senior police officer, "This man has treated your king, show him respect."

Nick also contacted a Saudi friend, Ibrahim Obaid, who was a government minister, and indignantly told him the story. Ibrahim shared his indignation, declared Feteih's behaviour scandalous and said he would take it further. Although I never learned exactly what part Ibrahim played, Nick told me later that it was crucial in securing my release.

Wryly, as I sat on the stone floor, I thought of the last patient I had seen before I had been carted off. He was a senior Saudi customs officer who worked at the airport. He had an intestinal infection with amoebae causing diarrhoea and severe inflammation of his colon.

I had prescribed a medication that didn't mix with alcohol. Half-joking, as I wrote his prescription, I told him to avoid all alcohol during the ten-day course of treatment. "How can I do that?" he asked. "Tonight I'm going to Bangkok for a week. I always drink there, you know, with the girls; very nice girls and very clean girls. Can I leave treatment until I get back?"

"It's better you take the treatment now," I told him. "If you leave it a week, it will probably still work but in the meantime the inflammation will get worse. It's up to you."

The unforgiving cell floor made it difficult to accept that this upholder of Saudi morals, this customs officer who daily searched incoming passengers' baggage hoping to find alcohol or photographs of scantily clad girls, this exemplar of Islam would, at that very instant, himself be drinking alcohol and whoring in Bangkok.

Then I was thinking of Feteih and the extreme punishment he had exacted. I knew he drank, I knew he smoked marijuana; sometimes its characteristic smell wafted behind him as he walked with his *thobe* billowing down the hospital corridor. What I didn't know then was that he was also taking Valium tablets by the handful. Looking back, it becomes obvious that his obsession with his power, his jealousy and the disinhibiting effects of marijuana and Valium, was an explosive mixture of terrible portent. Another factor, of which I was also unaware, was that several of his mistresses had been treated for gonorrhoea the previous month. If he was himself suffering from a dose of the clap, that would further contribute to his evil humour.

I reflected on the number of Saudis, and in particular Saudis of the Royal Family, whose alcoholic liver disease I had treated – even Sharia judges. Years later a Jordanian friend was to say to me, "They say there is nothing perfect in this world but there is – it is Saudi hypocrisy. That is perfection." He was right; his opinion was spot-on.

But as I continued to ruminate, I thought with horror of the British workers, convicted of alcohol trafficking soon after I arrived in Saudi five years before. They were still languishing in Riyadh's feared Central Jail; perhaps that would be my fate.

Saudi logic was equally problematical. I recalled the case of the British expat who was jailed when an infant was killed after it fell off the balcony of a block of flats in Jeddah. The expat's crime was that he had parked his car, quite legitimately, in an allotted parking space three floors below, and the infant landed on it. Saudi logic... if this foreigner had not been in their country, the infant would not have landed on his car.

The days passed slowly; distractions were few. Maria could visit for a few minutes very occasionally but I was not allowed out of the cell and she had to stand on the other side of the barred door. To encourage me, Maria said, "Darling, in years to come you will look back on this as an interesting episode in our lives. Think of all the great men, like Gandhi and Churchill, who have spent time in jail." She reassured me, "All your friends are working hard to get you out" and handed me some food that she had brought and a huge bar of chocolate that I shared with my new friends.

It was well nigh impossible to sleep on the stone floor with eighteen others making a variety of nocturnal noises, the least offensive of which was gentle snoring. The Jordanian alleged forger slept next to me. He spoke English and was pleasant and friendly.

One night a visitor gave him a bag full of *falafel*. This is a very popular snack in the Middle East: the main ingredients are mashed chick peas with onion, garlic, herbs and flour squashed together into an egg shape and then deep fried. He proffered the bag. I declined: I'd tried *falafel* before. He consumed the lot. I knew there would be trouble – chick peas are flatogenic in the extreme. Sure enough, the rumbles began in half an hour and then, at fifteen minute intervals through the night, silently released gusts of garlic-rich flatus drifted my way. If this was one of Maria's 'interesting episodes', give me boring any day.

One night at three I was woken by a guard shouting my name, "Doctor Lark!" He ordered me to come to the cell door. On the other side of the bars stood a well-dressed Saudi wearing a white *thobe* and *goutra* and a diaphanous black cloak edged in gold. He was clearly a man of importance. He asked me in impeccable English if I was well and if I was being treated properly. I said I had no complaints about the way the police were treating me. He nodded and left.

Next day I had a visit from my close and steadfast friend, Dr John Froude, the Irish colleague who I had assisted at his wife's home delivery. He had come to collect my keys so that my desk at work could be emptied. When he asked for them at the prison reception desk, he was given a large box in which there must have been a hundred sets of keys. So I was allowed out of the cell and, after scratching around for several minutes, was able to identify my keys. John took the opportunity to whisper encouragingly, "Take heart, Bill, things are on the move outside, people are working hard on your behalf and I have had a word with an official in the Ministry of Interior for you."

ON THE SIXTH DAY, I WAS HANDCUFFED and shackled and driven to the notorious Malaz Central Prison. We entered through enormous iron doors and proceeded for miles along corridors lined with cells to a large crowded hall. Groups of prisoners were noisily quarrelling while others lay sleeping on the cement floor and the smell... a melange of unwashed bodies, inadequate lavatory facilities, stale food, human sweat and fear – I swear I could smell fear.

Fear mounted in my own stomach as I saw a prisoner sitting on the floor, legs astride a pillar and ankles chained around the other side. He was weeping; a banana had been tossed to him and its blackening skin lay on the floor beside him. As I stood, slack-jawed, gazing around, a line of four men passed before me. They were loosely handcuffed, chained together around their midriffs with shackled ankles connected by more chains. In order to move about, they had developed a swinging rhythm. They shuffled past, arms and legs moving in unison like pistons, feet sliding along the ground in perfect time.

In another room I queued with twenty others to have my photograph and fingerprints taken. Then I was led to a cell with a wooden bed, a basin and a bucket and, to my horror, told this would be mine. Mine! For how long? Years and years? Horrifying thoughts tumbled through my brain.

But then, suddenly, a police officer appeared and spoke rapidly in Arabic to my escort. Out we went through many exit gates. At one, a pathetic skin-and-bones creature, dressed in rags with scrawny, filthy arms and long black talons tugged at my sleeve and whispered in unaccented English, "Please take me with you." A guard brushed him aside. I remember to this day the empty look of hopeless desperation in that poor fellow's eyes.

Outside the jail, I was put in a police car, handcuffed, shackled, unwashed, unshaven…

The experience had shaken me; the prospect of years in that hellhole was terrifying. My brain repeated over and over, "What if I'm thrown into that awful place I had just come from? Could I survive?"

Back at the police station, my old cell, an alien place, strangely felt like home and my fellow inmates like family. I was uncuffed and unshackled. I felt like weeping but I didn't. I knew I had to muster my courage and trust in my good friends outside working like fury to get my release.

But it was the unknown that was my pressing anxiety. What was going on? Were my pals succeeding? Was Feteih arresting my mates? Not knowing, and having no way of getting to know, was destabilising me; I had to pull myself together. I determined to demonstrate to all, particularly to Maria, that I was made of stern stuff.

Later Maria told me that on the day I was taken to jail, she had been visited by one of the hospital senior security staff, Sid Shorthouse, with a group of underlings. He told her that something had happened to me, that I had been taken out of my clinic and was on my way to jail. He and his staff had been ordered by Dr Feteih to search our house. That was quite illegal and should only have been undertaken with a properly issued legal search warrant. But the all-powerful security *gauleiters* went ahead, found wine and took it.

It was unspoken but commonly known that practically all Westerners were making alcohol. Without wine to take to your host – or if you were the host yourself, wine for the guests – dinner invitations would dry up. Likewise it was generally accepted that if the authorities wanted to get rid of an individual, and had nothing else to go on, they would search his home expecting to find wine and use that as the excuse to fire him.

After the wine was discovered, Maria was left alone in a state of shock in an empty house not knowing what to do. Before long there was a hammering on the door and when she opened it she found our good friend, Dr Don McDonald, chief of obstetrics, on the doorstep. She tried, unsuccessfully, to close the door on him, just as she did to each of the subsequent procession of colleagues and their wives that day... she warned them all that they were putting their jobs on the line by demonstrating where their sympathies lay. But they were steadfast; Maria's confidence was restored by their support and this gave her extra courage. It stood her in good stead when the next day she was taken to the hospital security department to be interviewed by Ed Burke. She told him that she had made the wine.

Some days later, she was warned by hospital security that she would be collected and taken to the police station where I was being held for interview. When the security men arrived to collect her, Maria was relieved to see reliable and courageous Don at the door, ready to accompany and support her. She told the investigating officer the same story – that she alone had made the wine. He told her that she would be sent to jail, but she persisted – she had it fixed in her mind that she would take my place and, being seventeen years younger, would be better able to survive the ordeal.

Maria and Don were told to sit on a bench outside the office. Feeling sure that she was about to be led away, she began to take off her jewellery and give it to Don. He whispered to her, "Maria, you can't do Bill any good if you are both in jail. Bill will certainly be released very soon, because David Barkham and John Froude have been working together to get the Minister of Health, Dr Ghazi al-Gosaibi, to sign a letter requesting Bill's release. They are taking it to the Mayor of Riyadh this morning. Please rethink this."

At that very moment, she spotted me down the hall being led back to the cell after my visit to the Central Prison. I was shuffling along, handcuffed and shackled... Maria tried to get my attention to give me hope but I was

Unshaven, unshowered, unbroken... the author reunited with his wife in the medical village after his ordeal in jail.

too dazed to recognise her. To her dismay, she saw no flicker of recognition in my blank gaze.

None of us knew that, at the precise moment I was being shown my cell in the Central Prison, the letter ordering my release had arrived.

The investigating officer took Maria back into his office, pulled her chair close to his and in a quiet, very kind and patient voice said, "If two people commit murder, two people go to jail for that murder. If two people make wine, two people go to jail for making wine. Your husband has already confessed to making the wine. You cannot help him. He is already in jail. Now I want you to tell me that you didn't make the wine and never, ever, change your story, no matter what happens, because that is what I am going to put in my report." Under his breath she heard him add, "I don't know why Dr Feteih is making such a fuss when everybody knows that Westerners drink alcohol."

Back home, it was evident to Maria that whatever happened, we would be leaving the hospital and the country. We were extremely fortunate to have her sister, Anne, who had been a senior nurse at the King Faisal Specialist Hospital, and brother-in-law, Roger, an ex-RAF pilot and now a flying instructor for the Royal Saudi Air Force, in Riyadh. They came and packed our belongings. Maria handled the shipping arrangements, closed bank accounts and collected my terminal pay.

AFTER A WEEK OF STRESS AND DISCOMFORT, I was released from jail. You can believe it or not, but I felt a pang in my heart as I left my fellow prisoners... they clapped me as I waved farewell to them.

Word had spread around the medical village of my imminent arrival and friends had packed into our small home to welcome me. This was a heart-warming moment, a moment I will always cherish. It is a common experience that expatriate friendships made in Saudi Arabia stand the test of time.

Though joyfully reunited with Maria, I was not allowed to remain at home. I was permitted to pick up toiletries and clothes and taken to the security department of the hospital where I was locked in a room with a barred window, a bed, a wash basin, shower and toilet – the King Faisal Specialist Hospital evidently had everything, even its own jail.

When I looked in the mirror, something I hadn't done for a week, I was shocked by the apparition staring back: unshaven, dirty and haggard. At a time like that, you truly appreciate what luxury a shave and a prolonged shower can be. I donned pyjamas and slept soundly.

Eighteen

BEFORE DAWN NEXT MORNING, 3 DECEMBER 1983, I was awoken, given a cup of coffee, told to dress and then bundled in silence into a big, shiny black limousine with darkened windows and running motor by no fewer than three security guards. Clearly I was considered dangerous. As we drove through the hospital grounds, I had my last glimpse of the institution where I had spent an interesting, and mostly happy, five years.

"Where are we going?" I asked one of the two guards flanking me on the back seat. He didn't reply. I tried the other, and he didn't reply either. Was I being smuggled out like a political prisoner? Was I being taken after all to Chop Chop Square? Ridiculous: I must be on my way to the airport, and I was… strange though how such paranoia could take control; perhaps not so surprising given my recent experiences.

At the airport, we bypassed the security search and went directly to the first-class check-in desk where to my immense pleasure I found Maria waiting with John Froude and David Barkham. Quickly detaching myself from my guards, I embraced Maria and – risking a return to jail for such a public expression of affection with a member of the opposite sex – I kissed her. There was barely time to say goodbye and thank you to John, David, the Siecks and many others before an agitated guard took me by the arm and marched me to the door of the aircraft where my guardians melted away. Five long minutes later, to my relief, Maria sank into the seat beside me. In twenty minutes we were airborne and I confess that it wasn't only Maria who shed a tear of relief as we saw Riyadh drop away beneath.

But the story was far from over. Nizar Feteih had overstepped his limits and what he did to me proved to be the first step in his downfall. Naturally he didn't go without putting up a fight.

His mistake was not to realise that such an outrageous act would provoke my friends into action. Many of my consultant colleagues had powerful Saudi friends who had been their patients; they had direct access to power and their *wasta* was to prove stronger than his.

The evening after I went to jail, the Minister of Health, Dr al-Gosaibi, entertained a group of consultants. It so happened that Dr al-Gosaibi had been a patient of mine and we were alumni: he had obtained a PhD in law at University College London. I was told that when he welcomed my colleagues, he joked about the minimal level of alcohol in my blood. Actions to effect my release were discussed.

Other officials at ministerial level were approached by different colleagues. After a week, under pressure from on high, Feteih withdrew his charges. But he was furious and lashed out impetuously.

He had Dr Michael Kingston, chairman of the department of medicine, arrested, taken to jail and subjected to interrogation amounting to torture. The interrogation lasted a day and a night. Dr Kingston was constantly exposed to bright lights and noise but later claimed he cracked only when the volume was turned up on wailing Arabic music. Feteih had hoped to silence this whistle-blower – the chairman of the biggest department in the hospital – but he failed.

He was at the same time pursuing another distinguished physician, Dr David Barkham, also a whistle-blower who had entered the fray on my behalf. David was a courageous physician who already had experience of a megalomaniac despot. Between 1971 and 1972, he had been Idi Amin's physician but upset Amin by voicing objections to the expulsion of the Asian community from Uganda. In a speech, which David chanced to hear on his car radio, Amin denounced him as insane because he had 'gonorrhoea of the brain'. David wisely took this as a signal that his time was up and fled the country with his family.

Now David knew full well that another ogre, Feteih, was after his blood. He must have sensed more than a little *déjà vu* about it because like Idi Amin, Feteih had declared David insane and put it about that he was going to have him locked up in a lunatic asylum. The net was rapidly closing on David. His house was being watched and Feteih's goons were ready to pounce.

Help came from an unexpected direction. Jean Sasson had been able to quit her job and distance herself from the goings-on at the King Faisal

Help from an unexpected direction: Jean Sasson and her husband Peter.

Specialist Hospital after her marriage. Despite all Feteih's evil actions, she retained some loyalty to her ex-boss. But when she learned that Feteih was planning to throw David into a Saudi insane asylum, she was spurred into action.

At once Jean phoned an American doctor, an old friend of hers, a pathologist called Dr Ted Bailey. Ted was aware of what was going on with David but didn't know that his seizure was imminent. Down the phone, she spoke in a commanding voice which brooked no dissent, "Ted, David Barkham is in deep trouble. Don't ask questions; get hold of him immediately! Bring him to our villa in Riyadh. Peter and I will look after him. It may be difficult because David's not at home, but don't delay, don't waste a second, go look for him right now."

Ted began a frantic search of the hospital housing complexes and finally found David at a dinner party. He dragged him out, protesting, in front of the bemused guests and bundled him – still protesting – into his car. "There's no time to explain, David, I've got to get you out of here, Nizar's bully boys are searching for you!" He made his way across Riyadh with reckless speed,

Old times: the late David Barkham shares a Saudi memory with Ulla Sieck.

lucky not to be stopped before he was able to deliver his bemused human cargo to safety.

The fate David might have endured had Feteih managed to get his hands on him doesn't bear thinking about. Feteih's word would have been law in a Saudi mental hospital; the non-Saudi Middle Eastern doctors would obey his every syllable. There is no doubt David would have been drugged against his will and incarcerated in isolation in truly terrible conditions. But thanks to Peter and Jean Sasson and Dr al-Gosaibi, he escaped this awful fate.

Feteih searched and searched. His frustrated rage was boundless; he never for one second dreamed that his former head secretary was sheltering his prey. David meanwhile made the best of his situation. His sanctuary at the luxurious Sasson villa was not too onerous with its chilled pool, squash court and servants. But he fretted. There was no way he could return to his house, leave alone to work. He knew his time at the King Faisal Specialist Hospital was over and he had to get out of Saudi Arabia. Fortunately his family was in London at the time.

Jean contacted Dr al-Ghosaibi, the sympathetic Minister of Health, who arranged David's departure. This was not straightforward: in a country that so strictly controls the comings and goings of foreigners, it was difficult to arrange an exit visa and airline reservation in total secrecy. On the day of David's departure, the minister sent a huge convoy to the Sasson villa to smuggle him to Riyadh airport where, just before take-off, he was shepherded on board an aircraft and flown to London and safety.

One would think the authority of a minister would trump that of a hospital director, but in the Byzantine corridors of Saudi power, nothing is that simple. For months there had been an ongoing power struggle between the Minister of Health and Nizar Feteih. Coincidentally, around this time, the minister lost his post. Rumour had it that he had published a poem that in some way criticised King Fah'd. Of course Feteih took Dr al-Gosaibi's dismissal as a personal victory and further confirmation of his own power.

For a second time, he underestimated his adversary. Before he left office, Dr al-Gosaibi had initiated the setting up of a Royal Commission to investigate Dr Feteih.

In London, we knew about the commission and we escapees, including David Barkham and Don McDonald, who had left ten days after us, assembled in the house of Nicholas Woodhouse's Aunt Esh in leafy Chiswick. Aunt Esh was a legend. She knew exactly how to hit the spot. Lively, intelligent, cheerful and in her eighth decade, she had discovered that a really good slug of whisky self-prescribed *q.i.d. et h.s.* (*quarter in die et hora somni* = four times a day and at bedtime) helped enormously with the nuisance of old age.

Over several days, huddled together in her West London home, the cabal wrote a detailed account of Feteih's wicked and scandalous behaviour which Nicholas hand-carried to Riyadh and delivered in person to the Royal Commission.

How much weight our report carried will never be known, but ironically in Feteih we had an ally; he was his own worst enemy. Maybe he was still coasting along under the effects of the tranquillisers he gobbled, continuing to believe that he still wielded immense power. He was antagonistic to the Royal Commission. When witnesses were called, he would stand outside the room where the hearings were being held and menace those about to go in to give evidence. He even put it about that one particular member of the commission was gay – that's just about as insulting as you can get in Saudi Arabia.

Riyadh police investigated Feteih's security corps. Ed Burke, Sid Shorthouse and six members of the hospital security staff, including Bernie Kerik, were summarily fired and deported.

It took time but eventually the Commission concluded that the complaints about Dr Nizar Feteih's behaviour were well-founded and that he was not fit to remain as the hospital director. He was relieved of his office.

And what was his fate? From being head of the most prestigious hospital in the Kingdom of Saudi Arabia, he was appointed to be the personal physician to the wife of King Fah'd, who was chronically sick. He would be required to dance attendance upon her, figuratively sit at the foot of her bed, to attend to her every whim, and accompany her around the world touring medical centres of excellence. When she died, he was appointed medical officer to the Saudi national football team.

TWENTY-ONE YEARS LATER, ALMOST TO THE day I heard the cell door clang shut behind me in the Saudi jail, I received a call out of the blue from the *Washington Post*. It was a reporter who introduced himself as John Mintz and said, "I'm calling you about somebody you were involved with a long time ago."

I was intrigued. "Go on," I said.

"It's about a man called Bernie Kerik who was a security guard at the King Faisal Specialist Hospital when you worked there. Do you remember him?" I did and as Mr Mintz talked and sketched in the background, my memory became clear.

President George W Bush had nominated Bernie Kerik for the post of head of Homeland Security, he informed me. "We think it's a bad choice. We're looking into Kerik's background and we think you can help us by telling us of your experiences of the hospital security services."

Mr Mintz told me that he had already talked to one of the hospital managers, John Paul Jones, and John Froude; he outlined their stories and I agreed that what they had told him fitted with the story I remembered. I said, "Kerik was part of the private Gestapo of the medical director, Dr Nizar Feteih. He was one of his enforcers and, yes, I had heard that he was involved in telephone tapping and illegal surveillance." I confirmed that I had indeed been thrown in jail on a trumped up charge, and that's roughly what appeared in his article in the 8 December 2004 edition of the

Washington Post. A day or two later, I began hearing from incredulous former colleagues. They too had known Kerik at the hospital, and were amazed that so great a thug could be nominated for such an extremely important national position.

It had come about because, after being booted out of Saudi Arabia by the Royal Commission, Bernie Kerik had done remarkably well for himself. He had risen from New York mayor Rudy Giuliani's bodyguard and chauffeur to the city's commissioner of police. The Bush administration had detached Bernie to Iraq for several months to organise the Iraqi civilian police. Mayor Giuliani had made him head of a New York correctional centre – a large prison. In the aftermath of the 9/11 terrorist attack in New York, he and Giuliani had been named America's 'Top Cop' and 'Top Mayor'.

Giuliani was to regret his patronage of Bernie. It displayed a deplorable lack of judgement – something which was gleefully seized upon by his political opponents. It played a part in Giuliani's withdrawal from the US presidential campaign in January 2008, leaving the Vietnam War hero John McCain and the entertaining Sarah Palin to carry the torch for the Republican party against Barack Obama.

I read many articles about Bernie on line. Photographs were splashed all over the American and international press.

The *Washington Post*'s crusade ended when irregularities concerning an illegal immigrant Kerik employed as a housekeeper-nanny came to light and he withdrew from the nomination. Subsequently he was convicted of tax evasion and sentenced to jail. While on bail, he again ran foul of the law and was put behind bars with no possibility of bail. Newspapers reported that he was incarcerated in a 'secure environment'; one can only speculate on the capers his fellow inmates might get up to if they could lay their hands on New York's 'Top Cop'.

WE RETURNED JUST ONCE TO SAUDI ARABIA when, a year after our departure, we were living in Sharjah and flew from Dubai to London transiting through Jeddah. The Saudi airport authorities were suspicious, not because of my criminal past – in fact I had never been charged – but because they thought it extraordinary, unheard of, that anybody should choose to fly via Saudi Arabia to go anywhere in the Western world.

The answer was simple: we were using up Saudia first-class tickets, relics of our stay in the 'magical' kingdom. After we explained this to the curious airport authorities, we were shown to the VIP lounge to await our connection.

At that time, the King Abdul Aziz airport at Jeddah was brand new. It was huge, built to cope with the tens of thousands of pilgrims coming to perform the annual Hajj, and it was luxuriously appointed from the chandeliers overhead to the marble underfoot. The floor of the VIP lounge was covered in a deep white pile carpet with what appeared to be a most unusual design of short black lines, like thousands of exclamation marks thrown haphazardly on the carpet. On closer inspection, we discovered they were indeed random. They were cigarette burns.

AS FOR DR NIZAR FETEIH, HE PAID heavily for his dalliances, particularly at the hands of Susan Price, his number one mistress. She was pregnant when she left Saudi Arabia at the time of Feteih's demotion. Years later, when Feteih visited the United States, she had him nabbed and a paternity order served on him. He paid her five million dollars to keep mum.

But money was the least of his worries, as we learned when John Froude stayed with us for a few days in our home in Provence. On a flight, while escorting a royal patient, Feteih suffered a major epileptic fit – a serious problem, completely out of the blue. "He'd never had one before and of course it indicated a serious disorder affecting his brain," John said. The aircraft, over Cairo at the time, diverted to Jeddah where he was admitted to the King Faisal Specialist Hospital – virtually an offspring of the one in Riyadh.

John continued. "At the time I was working in that hospital as the infectious diseases consultant. One evening I passed by the x-ray department to look at the films of one of my patients and my eye fell on a list of CT scans taken that day. One name, Nizar Feteih, stood out. I asked to see his scan films. The radiologist slotted them into the viewing screen for me, 'Very nasty,' he said, 'it's a glioma (malignant brain tumour).' 'No doubt?' I asked. 'No doubt,' he confirmed."

The very next day, John was called to consult on the case. One of Feteih's sons was a doctor. He asked whether it could be a tuberculoma (a tuberculous mass in the brain). John replied, "Definitely not." But they agreed between themselves that to placate the family a course of anti-tuberculosis treatment would be started.

John said he saw Feteih many times in his final days. "Initially I wasn't sure whether Feteih remembered me. We chatted, mostly about Feteih's business interests. He had become a diamond expert and was proud of his trading skills. Later I sensed that he knew exactly who I was but we never talked about those awful Riyadh days."

John met Feteih's family when they visited and it became clear that they adored him. But the progress of the tumour was inexorable. Twenty-five years after he threw me in jail, Nizar Feteih died of his brain tumour. He was sixty-two years old.

I had heard about his illness a few weeks before the end; I confess to a moment of grim satisfaction and even to a flight of fancy that I might send a 'Get well soon' card from Bill Larkworthy, but his was a fate I would not wish on my worst enemy – a definition he most certainly fitted.

When I heard that Feteih had died, my feelings were flat: no sorrow, no elation, empty, just nothing...

Part Three

Dubai: my pearl in the Gulf

It was a miracle of rare device,
a sunny pleasure dome with caves of ice

– Xanadu – Kubla Khan
Samuel Taylor Coleridge

Clinic boss's birthday: cake in form of a can of Amstel beer, presented by his Australian nurse, Jenny Hosking.

Nineteen

The year after we left Saudi Arabia, 1984, was not a year of momentous events for the world at large. George Orwell's book, *Nineteen-Eighty Four*, had been published thirty-five years earlier. In it he foresaw an authoritarian state which manipulated peoples' lives to the last detail; the 'thought police' and 'Big Brother is watching you' were vital aspects of his concept of all-pervasive government surveillance. Had it come about? Maybe not in the actual year of 1984, but today for sure, a quarter of a century further on, if we take a look at our lives, Orwell's nightmare has indeed arrived.

The ruthless manipulation of the truth by spin doctors; the ubiquitous presence of video surveillance cameras; the creeping paralysis of political correctness and the interference by bureaucracy at every minute of a citizen's life, all indicate that we have moved much closer to the Orwellian concept of totalitarianism. It seems ironic today that it was described as 'science fiction' when it was published sixty years ago.

But for one celebrity, 1984 began with a bang: on 27 January, Michael Jackson's hair caught fire while he was filming a Coca-Cola commercial. That was three decades almost to the day since George Orwell had died of a fatal haemorrhage in University College Hospital after a three-year battle with pulmonary tuberculosis, and three decades minus four years since I had entered UCH to study clinical medicine – a curious concatenation of events in my mind.

This was the sort of reflection my brain had time for in the first half of 1984 as Maria and I rested and licked our wounds. It took several weeks to recover from the trauma of our departure from Saudi Arabia; it would take years to come to terms with the victimisation and persecution by one man.

For six months, we visited relatives and took holidays. Our friend David

Barkham, who had lost his job batting for us, generously offered us sanctuary in his beautiful and spacious home in London. The whole family made us very welcome and, to be honest, we felt most comfortable in the company of those who had a detailed understanding of the stressful time we had just come through. It was there that we rehabilitated ourselves.

London is a wonderful city; one can never tire of it. But the winter weather was so drab and so tedious that we started craving sunshine. So we headed south, to Morocco.

We found Morocco a delightful halfway house between the Middle East and Europe. The people were friendly, the food interesting, the climate agreeable, the wine passable and most of all, Islam was not intrusive... except on one occasion when Maria was taking photographs in the souk in Marrakesh and a young man with a long, woolly beard and a fanatical gleam in his eyes berated her. Shouting and waving his arms, he appeared to be verging on physical violence. It seemed prudent not to stick around and find out for certain.

We rented a small, rather battered, car not noticing that two tyres were bald, and undertook a circular tour from Casablanca through the Atlas Mountains and back along the coast to our starting point. Both tyres blew in the mountains where we couldn't buy new ones and instead had to settle for inserting inner tubes and proceeding with caution until we reached a sizeable town. Driving on suspect tyres, on hairpin bends and narrow roads with precipitous drops made us less appreciative of the magnificent scenery, but we made it.

Spring had arrived by the time we returned to London. It was time to start thinking about work. But even the daffodils, cherry blossom and pleasant weather in London could not persuade us that England was where we wanted to be. Having spent so many years overseas with the Royal Air Force and then in Arabia, the prospects of working in Britain were not appealing. Moreover, I knew that my hopes of getting a good gastroenterology post in Britain were unrealistic.

Many years previously, while I was still in the RAF, I had considered working in the National Health Service (NHS). I applied for a couple of jobs but the competition for the popular consultant posts, in which I was interested, was intense. Not having climbed the NHS ladder was against me; I was not in the club, not one of 'them'. Appointments seemed preordained in the sense that it was a racing certainty a senior registrar from a teaching hospital, with his professor's backing, would be the odds-on favourite for any sought-after consultant post.

And besides, there was still sand in my shoes. The Middle East is not everyone's cup of tea, but for me it remained attractive. There were opportunities, oil prices were booming and I knew others places in the Gulf were more liberal and much easier to live in than Saudi Arabia.

AN ADVERTISEMENT IN THE *British Medical Journal* caught my eye. It was for a post in Kuwait, in the university medical college. At the same time, a locum post at the Kuwait Oil Company's Ahmadi Hospital was advertised. That post was for six weeks from the beginning of July, the hottest time of the year. I applied for both, thinking that it would be sensible to take a look at Kuwait before making any commitments, and landed the locum post.

The Kuwait Oil Company had constructed Ahmadi as a town for its employees and their families. The hospital it built was well-equipped and associated with the university. Maria and I flew to Kuwait, landing in the early hours. I joined a long, slow queue of British workers; Maria, with her Irish passport, sailed through immigration control – at that time the 'troubles' in Ireland were making news and all Irish passport holders were singled out for special treatment.

The country we were entering was a constitutional monarchy, an emirate ruled by an emir or prince, situated at the head of the Gulf, bordered on the south by Saudi Arabia and on the north and west by Iraq. The Sabah tribe became the rulers of what is now Kuwait in the middle of the eighteenth century. In 1775, they sought the protection of the British against the Ottoman Turks who were colonising the whole region. Kuwait remained a British protectorate until it gained full independence in 1961 at which stage Iraq asserted ancient sovereign rights and threatened invasion. British military forces returned and the Iraqi threat dissolved but as later events showed, the Iraqis never forgot their claim.

Originally the few inhabitants scratched a miserable living as traders, pearl divers and fishermen. This was to change dramatically with the discovery of vast quantities of oil in 1937. Exploitation by British Petroleum and Gulf Oil did not take off until after the Second World War. With the nationalisation of the oil industry in 1976, tiny Kuwait became one of the super-rich Arab oil states and, holding twenty per cent of the world's oil reserves, a formidable economic power in the world's markets.

The six weeks we spent in Kuwait included the fasting month of Ramadan. Most families who could leave Kuwait had done so and the place seemed practically empty. It was also climatically the most arduous part of the year – very hot, very humid and extremely dusty. A searing wind off the interior would blast sand from the desert early in the mornings and keep it whirling around in a dense fog until late afternoon. The sun was obscured, the sky was an ugly dirty orange, and lights were needed indoors all day long apart from an hour or so around noon. A fine dusting of sand got everywhere; it covered furniture in the house and clothes in the wardrobe; it got into the shower, sandwiches in the kitchen and every bodily orifice.

I was given a house in a compound and a car, a huge American vehicle that swished and rolled along like a tug boat in a storm. It had excellent airconditioning, vital for survival in hot, steamy, sandy Kuwait but starting it was a trial: when the airconditioning kicked in it created a mini sand-storm. I learned to start the brute, leap out and leave the doors closed until the interior was clear. It was truly a beast and a thirsty one at that but I could fill its tank as often as I liked at the Ahmadi petrol station – for free.

This was all very well but there was nowhere to go. You could drive into Kuwait City but that was just a vast commercial oasis over which, in sandstorms, the three huge balls of the Kuwait Towers appeared to float unsupported in the air. There was a beach close to the hospital but after being driven from it a couple of times by the black, choking oily fumes of the nearby refinery when the wind changed direction, we decided to give that a miss. The water in the swimming pool in the compound was turbid, strewn with leaves, and the walls were coated with a glutinous, dirty mixture of sand and sun screen creams.

But the hospital was busy; it had an open-doors policy to all comers. Twice a week I held rounds for students at the Kuwait Medical College. They were keen as mustard, hard workers and had only good words to say about their education. Many of them were in fact from Pakistan; Kuwait's population, on its own, seemed at that time scarcely large enough to support a medical school. The medical college was well organised but new; the year before, in 1983, the first batch of students graduated as doctors.

Although the medical college and its facilities were attractive, Kuwait itself held no lure. It was not for us, so we returned to England via a couple of weeks in southern Spain.

IN ENGLAND A MESSAGE AWAITED ME from my old RAF friend, Graham Pinn, who was leaving his post as consultant physician to a private hospital in Sharjah in the United Arab Emirates – would I be interested in taking over? I called him; he told me about Sharjah, the hospital, the salary and the benefits. The hospital was new and many of the consultant staff, like Graham and I, were ex-military medical specialists.

Sharjah was attractive and much more liberal than Saudi Arabia. It had been ruled by the Qassimi family since the beginning of the eighteenth century and had a long association with Britain. An obvious part of that legacy was that Sharjah was cricket-crazy. A local businessman had built a stadium with a capacity of 27,000 to hold international matches between the major cricket playing countries in the northern off-season. They were called Off-Shore Test Matches.

The emirate had changed in the two decades since I had passed through on my RAF inspection tour. It had restaurants, pubs, live entertainment and cinemas – even a Christian church. Alcohol was available in restaurants and bars and non-Muslims could buy wines, spirits and beers from two large local outlets discreetly hidden in the industrial area. A liquor licence was necessary and, with a sponsor's permission, would be supplied by Sharjah police. It was a small red leather-bound book proclaiming that as I and all Christians were alcoholics, we were licensed to buy the stuff. There was a space to record each month's purchases. The allowance was for about £140 but thirty per cent tax was added that went into the ruler's pocket.

Sharjah's creek – actually a tidal basin, like all the 'creeks' on that side of the Gulf – swarmed with activity; dhows came and went, trading across the Gulf. It was hot and humid for the six summer months but the remainder of the year was delightful. Very occasionally there were sandstorms but none like those we had experienced in Kuwait.

With my old friend's recommendation, the job was mine. The hospital, Al Zahra, had a hundred beds and I would head the department of medicine. The work was mostly run-of-the-mill medical problems: hypertension, heart attacks, pneumonia, kidney and liver problems with a fair sprinkling of ulcers, occasional intestinal infections and a few cancers of various sorts. The population served was largely expatriate and in the pre-cancer age group; the expatriates were mostly young and working overseas to save to make a better life when they returned to their home countries.

We had a few local Emirati patients. One in particular sticks in my memory. He was fifty-five, very rich and getting richer by the day. Lacking direction in life, other than making oodles of dough, he had taken seriously to the bottle. He split his time between a palatial villa in Sharjah and a marble palace in Granada, Spain. He was admitted under my care for drying out so often that he developed a routine. He would appear at the hospital reception desk, demand his usual bed and that I be called. He always brought with him a large, rather tattered, canvas hold-all which he insisted should be placed under his bed. The hold-all was stuffed full of five hundred dirham notes, each worth about £90, so he was carrying possibly the equivalent to half a million sterling.

After a few days of treatment, when the shakes had stopped and there were no more spiders running around the walls, he would pay his bill, thank the staff and be off again for a few weeks. Counselling had no effect, "Doctor, I like very much drinking, me and my friends we have good times."

After he hadn't appeared for a few weeks, I made enquiries. I learned that he had ended one merry evening with his pals in Granada by tumbling down the marble staircase of his palace, banging his head and never regaining consciousness. A great pity because he was such a nice chap; alcoholics generally are. So often the PAFO syndrome (pissed-and-fell-over) ends their lives prematurely.

SHARJAH HAD A FAIR BIT OF COLOURFUL history spread out over its territory from the Gulf across the Hajjar mountains to the Indian Ocean. Carbon dating showed parts of the area had been inhabited for four thousand years. For most of that time, it was a land forgotten; its people were desperately poor. That changed in the eighteenth century when local tribes spotted an economic opportunity with quick returns. It coinciding with an increase in the amount of sea traffic in the Gulf as the British in India and the Portuguese in the Far East stepped up their commercial activity. They took up piracy.

The most active tribe was the Qassimi but they had competition from the Busaids, a tribe from around the corner in the Oman.

In the late eighteenth century, the British signed an agreement with the

Busaids to keep out the French who were nosing around. This upset the Qassimi who then felt justified in thinking that the British East India Company ships were fair game and attacked and plundered them whenever they could. The area became notorious as the Pirate Coast.

It was clear something had to be done. The Royal Navy launched several campaigns against the Qassimi but without lasting effect until, in 1819, a large fleet was dispatched from Bombay. By 1820, it had destroyed every Qassimi ship and occupied all the forts on the Pirate Coast, even Qassimi hideouts in Persia, on the other side of the Gulf.

Following their success, the British imposed a General Treaty of Peace on nine Arab sheikhdoms in the area and installed a garrison. But tribes continued to hack at each other's throats, so the British imposed another treaty, known as the Maritime Truce, by force. The *modus operandi* was one that the warring tribes understood but, naturally, it was resented when the treaty was enlarged to include a clause banning slavery, a trade much favoured by the Bani Yas, the rulers of Abu Dhabi.

In 1853, the Maritime Truce was upgraded to a 'Treaty of Peace in Perpetuity' under which the British became responsible for arbitrating between all the rival sheikhs in the area. It was this final truce that gave this part of the Gulf the name of the Trucial States, a name which lasted for 120 years.

In the 1890s, the British formalised their agreements with the sheikhs and rulers throughout the Gulf, protecting them from the Ottomans (at the same time halting the growing interest of the French and Russians in the region) and banning them from dealings with foreign powers, except with permission from the British. An important spin-off was that when ibn Saud was busy cobbling together Saudi Arabia, just after the end of the 1914-18 war, he kept his hands off the Trucial States. Much as he would have liked them, he didn't know how strongly the British, with their superior armed forces, would react.

Peace reigned for well over a century. In truth, the British weren't greatly interested in the Trucial States as long as the lines of communication with India were secure. Oil had yet to be discovered; the area was poor and even poorer when the Japanese crucified the pearl industry by growing the little gems artificially.

The discovery of vast quantities of oil in the Gulf in the 1930s changed everything. From being a dusty, arid, impoverished region, it became a dusty, arid, rich region – one of the richest in the world. Abu Dhabi had the largest share of the new wealth; other emirates discovered varying amounts of hydrocarbons as exploration continued.

While working at Al Zahra Hospital in Sharjah, I frequently visited neighbouring Dubai. It soon became apparent to me that Dubai had a buzz that Sharjah lacked. Sharjah prided itself on being the culture centre of the Gulf. Dubai traditionally had its eyes directed more toward commerce. It was developing rapidly, its population was growing almost exponentially and new business ventures were opening daily.

Wandering around the centre of Dubai, I saw many private clinics; a few were good, but none were British in style. There was one private hospital in Dubai, and I took a look at it under the pretext I might consider applying for a position. The director was pleased to show me around but it was a poorly run establishment. Opening one door, the entrance to the doctors' lounge, released a dense cloud of tobacco smoke through which could be seen half a dozen scruffy, tieless, unshaven members of the medical staff in dirty white coats drinking coffee. When the director opened another door, this time to the dental department, we found the dentist asleep in the dental chair. In the laboratory, I peeked into a metal refrigerator cabinet marked 'Blood Transfusion' and saw one dusty bag of blood lying on the bottom. There were just two patients in the hospital.

I looked at some private clinics. A few were well-organised but others were quite amazing. One clinic boasted an x-ray apparatus but it didn't function – a technician would stand the patient in front of the machine and make clicking noises. The doctor kept just one chest x-ray film in his desk which he displayed to different patients.

In another, there was an expensive piece of equipment in the laboratory. I complimented the technician and asked, "How many tests are performed on the average day?"

"None on that piece, sir," he said.

"None?"

"Actually, sir," he said, looking around furtively, "nobody knows how to use it."

Another clinic had a great reputation because the doctor was not expensive and every patient got an injection.

Two things became clear to me: one, that Dubai was in sore need of a good quality clinic and two, that burgeoning Dubai was the place to set up – not Sharjah.

I met a European businessman who I will call Miro Vladic – not his real name – for reasons that will become apparent. Miro had come into Al Zahra Hospital as a patient and we got chatting about the prospects of opening a clinic in Dubai. He was enthusiastic; he knew the ropes – rather complicated ropes as far as starting a new business goes. In the UAE, a local partner is required and the local partner owns fifty-one per cent of the business. My European friend could find a local partner, he could arrange the finance, he would find a location. He would manage the clinic and my input would cover the medical aspects.

I resigned my post at the hospital in Sharjah. Maria found a villa to rent in Dubai. Miro organised the clinic premises but there was an enormous amount of bureaucratic red tape to deal with. The premises had to be inspected and the staff recruited had to be interviewed by the Department of Health. I was graded as a medical specialist and another doctor, a Scot named Dr Helen Michie-Brown, became our specialist obstetrician. We soon attracted a lady paediatrician. We set up our own pathology

A place of our own: Dubai London Clinic, Dubai.

laboratory with a UK-trained laboratory technician and an x-ray unit with a radiographer and part-time radiologist. To establish our British credentials, I persuaded the British Embassy in Dubai to let me have a framed copy of Annigoni's portrait of the Queen to hang on the wall of my office. We christened the clinic the Dubai London Clinic... my original intention being to recruit only London-trained staff.

A month before we left Sharjah, it was announced, out of the blue, that Sharjah had gone 'dry'. Alcohol was banned and bars in hotels were closed. It was rumoured that the ruler had issued the decree because one of his sons had been killed in an accident involving alcohol.

As part of the winding up process when we left Sharjah, I had to return my Sharjah booze licence to the police. The officer I gave it to laughed and asked, "Are you moving to Dubai because Sharjah has banned alcohol?" No, but that's how rumours start.

The clinic was opened by the British Consul General for Dubai in January 1986.

Twenty

There was a story – I heard it from so many lips it must be true – that sums up the difference in attitudes between Dubai and Sharjah. One day in the middle of the twentieth century, the ruler of Sharjah called on the ruler of Dubai and told him he had come to him because he needed his advice. After a few cups of coffee, he came to the point. The British Agent had been to see him and had told him that because Sharjah has such good port facilities, the British government wanted to expand its commercial interests in Sharjah.

Thoughtfully, the ruler of Dubai stroked his beard and, after a minute, said, "That is indeed good news. You will prosper, trade will flourish – but I should warn you."

"Warn me?" queried the ruler of Sharjah.

"Yes, it will spell the end of the Sharjah we all know, love and respect. The British will come in, they will want their alcohol, their pubs, their churches, their recreations and it will mean the end of the traditional peaceful Islamic way of life in Sharjah."

"I will think about it," said the ruler of Sharjah. He gathered the folds of his cloak around him and departed in pensive mood.

The next day, when the British Agent called on him, the ruler of Sharjah told him that he was sorry but he could not agree to the commercial development of Sharjah.

A few days later, the British Agent went to see the ruler of Dubai and said, "Because Dubai has such good port facilities…"

"Say no more," interrupted the ruler of Dubai, "come in; sit down; have a coffee, let's talk about it."

The first thing the ruler of Dubai, Sheikh Rashid bin Saeed al-Maktoum, did was to dredge the waters of Dubai Creek to open it to seagoing vessels.

This soon increased Dubai's trade, so much that Sheikh Rashid built another harbour, what is now Port Rashid, a deep-water harbour with thirty-five berths for ocean-going vessels. Business increased even more, he built yet another deep water port at Jebel Ali which could accommodate more than sixty large vessels and had the brilliant idea of creating a duty-free zone around it for manufacturing and entrepot trade.

He built Dubai Drydocks, second only to Singapore's in size, to service the hundreds of huge oil-tankers from all over the world using the Gulf. He built an airport and to kick-start the various airlines' business, he bought hundreds of seats. He built a large administration centre, the tallest free-standing building in the Middle East, the Dubai World Trade Centre.

Business boomed, Dubai became a global business hub and the distribution centre for the whole of the Middle East. Manufacturing industries were established in the Jebel Ali duty-free zone; all manner of goods were manufactured – I remember while holidaying on Fraser Island off the coast of Queensland, Australia in 1992 I bought a packet of potato crisps, made in Dubai – Dubai flourished.

The burgeoning economy needed workers, and in they came. To keep the expatriates happy, Sheikh Rashid encouraged the building of churches, clubs, pubs, bars, hotels, sailing clubs, marinas, sports clubs.... He made it a rule that Emiratis in traditional dress were not to drink in pubs, and for the most part pubs turned their business away or created special 'taxi bars' away from the public eye – a small example of the adaptability that makes Dubai tick. In short, Sheikh Rashid was the visionary who turned a small Gulf trading port into a major Middle East cosmopolitan city with worldwide aspirations.

Dubai's native population, though adept at small-scale business, risked being swamped and overwhelmed by the vast influx of fortune seekers who drove the population from a modest 20,000 to an incredible one and a half million by the beginning of the twenty-first century. Fortunately for the Emiratis, Sheikh Rashid decreed many years earlier that any business venture in Dubai had to have a local citizen sponsor who, regardless of whether he invested or not, would own fifty-one per cent of the company. This law applied to every venture except in the free zones. And it worked, though not without some unintended consequences which began to appear much later, with an impact on my practice.

A TYPICAL STORY IS THAT OF SAEED Mohammed al-Jindi. I met Saeed in the clinic. Unusually tall for a local, clean-shaven, highly articulate and always dressed in a freshly laundered thobe, he was one of the thousands of Emiratis who benefited from Sheikh Rashid's foresight.

Saeed is now very rich. He owns a palatial villa overlooking the blue waters of the Persian Gulf bordering on Jumeirah Beach, the most popular of Dubai's beaches. Jumeirah is Arabic for Friday and that beach is where the locals used to go to relax on the Islamic weekend.

He wasn't always rich; he came from an ordinary family in Dubai. He didn't have much education but he was born at the right time. While in his mid-twenties, he had worked for the British administration, running errands and doing odd jobs.

Saeed liked the British in those days. They were civil servants, businessmen, army and air force officers with a sprinkling of wives and families and a respect for the host nation's culture. "Not like some of today's Britishers," he said, by which I gathered he was not impressed with the Costa del Party mentality and behaviour that seemed to be taking over. "Still," Saeed shrugged, "they spend their money in Dubai, and that's good for us. They're like long-stay tourists."

When they pulled out of the UAE in 1971, the British military sold off vehicles that were not worth the cost of transporting elsewhere. Saeed told me that he had scraped together a little money and for next to nothing he had been able to buy an old Bedford army truck. It was in good shape: well maintained by British Army mechanics.

With that vehicle, he had started his transport business. The square fronted, olive green truck became his livelihood and it became his home. The cab was his lounge, his dining room and his bedroom. When the nights were very hot, he slept under his truck which he parked next to the Gulf to catch the slightest cooling breeze off the water.

There was little competition in those days and Saeed's transport business flourished. He carried goods to and from the dhows moored in the Creek. He would carry barrels of water to villas without a well, jerry cans of fuel to those with their own generators, sacks of grain to feed camels and sheep by the dozen when the Eid al Adha celebration of sacrifice came around at the end of the Islamic year.

After a year one truck was not enough; he could afford another and hired a driver. He flourished. He was intelligent, quick-witted and had an abundance of the entrepreneurial spirit that formed the bedrock of Dubai's explosive development. He saved and over a few years acquired franchises from among the many international companies that were falling over each other to grab a chunk of the new wealth of the region.

Dubai's success became his success. Dubai had a buzz about it, like neighbouring Sharjah had once enjoyed and which Abu Dhabi, looking on from just down the coast like a rich and somewhat disapproving aunt, could only envy. Neither could match Dubai for panache and a 'can do' approach, which resulted in some imaginative solutions to what others considered insurmountable problems.

On one occasion, the Dubai international tennis competition (always held in the cooler month of February) coincided with Ramadan. There was consternation. Players could not be seen on world-wide television taking drinks between games during the hours of fasting – not that the rest of the world gave a fig. Impasse... until Dubai declared that, for the period of the competition, the area encompassing the tennis courts and stands was non-Muslim.

As for Saeed, in less than a decade he went from owning a couple of ex-British Army trucks to being the sponsor of several international companies in Dubai. His story is by no means unique; every successful expatriate venture in Dubai has an Emirati finger in the pie.

There are good sponsors, generally those who leave companies to run their own affairs, help them when necessary and take their dues. And there are bad sponsors who want larger and larger slices of the profits. For the rich, acquiring more money in no way diminishes their desire for even more.

THE SPONSOR THAT MIRO VLADIC, THE manager of the clinic, found for us was a local doctor. It seemed a good match, but after a few months it became evident that his personality was too timid to deal with government bureaucracy based on Anglo-Indian civil service traditions and spiced with Gulf Arab wiles. Somehow Miro was able to change our sponsor, don't ask me how; I thought it wasn't possible but I guess an adequate transfusion of *fuloos* (money) was involved.

We anticipated that the new sponsor found by Miro would wield clout; he had the magic name of Maktoum, a member, though peripheral, of the ruling family. Our sheikh was quite different. He was very intelligent; he had a mercurial nature, a puckish sense of humour and was very short – with all the assertiveness of short men. Symbolically he built himself a palace clad in black slate and boasted that he did so because he was the black sheep of the Maktoum family (a boast not unfounded, according to those in the know).

The Black Palace was constructed in an un-Arabic cuboid style. It was festooned with radio aerials, the hallmark of a ham-radio enthusiast. When I looked at it at dusk, as the daylight dwindled and darkness fell, it took on the appearance of a Transylvanian castle from which, at any moment, a cloud of bats might appear led by our sheikh in his flapping *thobe*.

The décor inside was equally exuberant and reminded me of the foyer of the Tooting Odeon cinema, which I had visited when I worked at St George's Hospital in London: wall-to-wall plush red carpets and plenty of highly polished chromium. In his basement, he had a firing range which he delighted in showing off. His arsenal held enough weapons, from Kalashnikov semi-automatic rifles to elephant guns, to arm an insurrection, and there was no shortage of ammunition – he made his own.

In the year before I left Dubai, our sheikh acquired the most eccentric of his pastimes, to the terror of his servants and the disquiet of his neighbours – a collection of crocodiles. Naturally word quickly spread in Dubai and such a fertile source generated stories like wildfire; of servants who had offended him being thrown to the reptiles but rescued in the nick of time; of crocs escaping and waddling down the road – but the truth was that they were well fenced in and so well fed that they spent their lives in a quiet stupor.

THE CLINIC WAS LICENSED IN MY NAME; my postgraduate qualifications helped that along. We were inspected and had all the basic necessities demanded by the department of health. We had recruited nursing, laboratory, x-ray and secretarial staff, and I had been to England to buy endoscopes. At the beginning there were three specialist doctors, myself, a consultant obstetrician and paediatrician. Expansion was rapid; we registered about four hundred new patients a month.

One of my early patients was a man named Abdul Walid Henry Smith. He was tall, smartly dressed in a well-cut business suit and very English. I don't remember his medical problem but I remember I couldn't resist asking him if he had converted to Islam. "Why, yes," he replied.

"How is it?" I asked.

"Good, very good," he said, and correctly forecasting the cloud of questions forming in my mind, told me about it.

He had been working very successfully in Bahrain, business was good and he had a lovely family life with his wife and three small children. One day out of the blue his wife announced that she had fallen in love with another man and wanted a divorce. "She told me that the man she wanted to marry was an Indian doctor. She also said that she would be taking our son with her, that I could keep our two daughters and the reason she wanted our son was because her intended had only one testicle," he said. For obvious reasons that detail stuck with me; you don't have to be a doctor to know that one testicle is perfectly adequate for all purposes.

Abdul Walid Smith continued, "I took advice; I converted to Islam and divorced her quickly. I kept all the children. It was easy, there was no opposition and she was badly in the wrong when she admitted she was having this affair in a Muslim country. I moved to Dubai. She left Bahrain and went, wherever – I don't know or care – with her one-balled Indian doctor."

"So how is it?" I asked again.

"Fine," he said, "business has never been better. I go to the mosque on Fridays, I make a lot of contacts, I am treated very well and I am happy with my life in Dubai."

"How do you find the religion? I imagine you were a Christian before."

"Yes," he acknowledged, "I was indeed a Christian and you know what, your average Muslim practises his religion in what could be regarded as a really Christian way: 'Love thy neighbour as thyself, do no harm, look after weaker members of society and all that sort of thing."

That was essentially how the expatriate Muslim communities like the Afghanis conducted themselves. Dubai had a substantial Afghan population. Most were traders and the majority suffered from dyspepsia and ulcers. I established a reputation as a medical wizard with such problems and soon I was seeing several Afghanis most days, endoscoping many and treating their ulcers.

My success came about because I started treating ulcer patients with antibiotics a couple of years before it was generally accepted that infection plays a crucial part in causing ulcers. Previously it was thought that an excess of acid was the main cause: 'No acid – no ulcer'. The reason so many ulcers returned after treatment then became apparent. It was because a bacterium, called helicobacter pylori, had colonised the stomach. Infection with *helicobacter* causes inflammation which leads to an increase in acid secretion but the cunning bacterium protects itself from the onslaught of the acid by secreting an enzyme which allows the formation of a sort of protective overcoat. Thus the acid attacks the stomach and duodenum while the helicobacter continues its nefarious work.

I became interested in the part played by bacteria in gastrointestinal diseases while I was at Nocton Hall with the RAF. There was a Ministry of Agriculture research laboratory near Lincoln and I did some work with a veterinary pathologist who was also studying intestinal infections. His interest was in a group of organisms that caused disease in pigs, disease which resembled Crohn's disease, an inflammation of the intestine in humans. These bacteria belonged to a group called *campylobacter*, to which *helicobacter* also belonged. One particular bug, *campylobacter bulbosus*, was found only under the foreskins of bulls – follow that wherever your fancy takes you.

In Australia, a young doctor called Barry Marshall struck lucky and cultured *campylobacter pylori* (later renamed *helicobacter* because it has a helical shape). It swims along in the gastric mucus spinning its many tails, buries itself in the stomach lining and causes inflammation. Dr Marshall swallowed cultures of *helicobacter*; this gave him a bellyache and made his breath very smelly. He had a pal endoscope him, his stomach was inflamed and biopsies showed the bacteria adhering to the lining. He then took a course of an antibiotic, his symptoms went rapidly away and his breath became sweet.

The medical establishment gave him the thumbs down, saying the equivalent of, "Harrumph, poppycock, what's this young bloke talking about, doesn't he friggin' well know that bacteria can't live in the extremely acid environment in the stomach!" But, as we knew later, this bug can because of its own defence mechanism. He was right, and years later he picked up the Nobel Prize, belatedly in my view, for his work.

A year or two after the clinic opened, simple tests for *helicobacter* became available; they were easy and could be carried out in minutes on the premises. Nearly all my Afghanis were positive, as were patients I saw from Qatar, Somalia, the Sudan and Ethiopia. Treatment was with an ulcer healing drug and an antibiotic cocktail taken for ten days. Results were excellent, rapid, dramatic and permanent.

On one occasion, as I was reviewing an Afghani who had finished a course of treatment, his companion, who could speak passable English, asked, "Why my friend have thees problem?"

"It's because he had an infection with a germ in his stomach," I told him.

He turned to his friend and explained what I had said; they argued for a minute, I understood not a word and then he looked at me, smiled shrewdly and said, "I know how eet happen."

"Yes?" I encouraged.

"He eat head of rotten dead sheep he find on hillside at home. His family say, 'No! No!' but all same he eats – even crows leaving it alone."

Another Afghani, a very successful businessman highly regarded in the Afghan community, said to me at the conclusion of a visit, "Doctor Lark, you have nice clinik, you should make same Kabul, I will pay for it, you be boss doctor."

I thanked him and said, "But Kabul is very dangerous, there is no money there, everybody is too poor to come to a clinic like this."

He looked at me in astonishment, "No, no, no, is no danger in Kabul and there is plenty moneys."

"Plenty moneys?" I asked, raising an eyebrow.

"Yes, plenty moneys, we have moneys from Amerikee, Britannee, Canadee and all over."

That was more than twenty years ago. I guess there is even more 'plenty moneys' in Kabul these days.

WITHIN A COUPLE OF MONTHS OF OPENING the clinic, we had a call from an international Japanese electronics company in Dubai. One of their staff, a young Englishman in his twenties, had been admitted to the psychiatric wing of the Rashid Hospital. He was newly diagnosed as schizophrenic: would I escort him to London?

I visited him in the secure acute psychiatric ward. I was impressed: the psychiatric department was clean, well-organised, the atmosphere calm, the doctors and nurses efficient and kind and the patients walking the corridors and sitting in the lounges were in no apparent distress. My patient was pleasant and cooperative but his doctor told me that he would become extremely agitated, but never violent, several times a day.

Arrangements were made with British Airways. Twelve seats were taken out to accommodate him on a curtained-off litter. A nurse and I would sit with him. He was sedated at the hospital but required a further shot soon after we were airborne. During the flight, whenever he started to surface and become agitated, I would top up his sedation. At Heathrow, the other passengers deplaned and we waited for a private ambulance. Meanwhile, a couple of police officers, one male, one female, boarded the aircraft with sniffer dogs. The dogs rushed around the cabin sniffing frantically everywhere. They seemed extraordinarily excited. I asked the police lady if they were looking for 'a fix'. She went to great lengths to explain that the dogs were not addicts... I remain to be convinced.

A twenty-mile drive took us to the psychiatric hospital. In contrast to the modern, efficient unit in Dubai, this example of the British National Health Service was old, dirty and run down. It had probably started out as a workhouse. Disturbed patients wandered the corridors muttering and occasionally shouting out. So much for the UAE being 'backward'. Fortunately our patient was admitted to a private room.

The next morning I took the tube to Heathrow for my return flight. The Japanese company had arranged to fly me back to Dubai first class. I luxuriated in my surroundings as I sipped my welcome-on-board glass of champagne. Two hours after take-off, a hostess brought me the menu. Lunch would be four courses with a choice of two main dishes, chicken supreme or camel curry... camel curry? Presumably the World's Favourite Airline was ingratiating itself with rich Arab first class passengers. Naturally I chose the chicken supreme... and, naturally, was served camel curry.

I summoned the hostess. "Awfully sorry, sir," she said, "we've run out of chicken supreme."

I asked her if she'd ever eaten camel curry. "Actually no, sir," she said.

"Well I have, and I don't recommend you try," I said. She apologised, took back my tray and said she would see what she could do.

Then the meal got entertaining. The chief steward, evidently a chappie very much in touch with his feminine side, minced up to me. "You know, sir," he hissed, "if you have special dietary requirements, all you have to do is inform British Airways the day before you fly and we would then be able to attend to all your wishes."

So now I was the villain of this pantomime! I must admit to a certain degree of genuine irritation but decided to be a sport and play my role. I replied, "I don't have special dietary needs ('Oh yes you do; oh no I don't'). Camel curry is foul and I don't expect to be given it on a British Airways flight, even if you are flying to the Middle East."

That rather brought the curtain down. He reddened, flounced off and minutes later the hostess reappeared, smiling and bearing a large tray of cheeses, fruit and an assortment of small bottles of wine. More than mollified, I passed the remainder of the flight smoothly in a savoury haze with jazz flowing through the headphones.

IN THE YEAR FOLLOWING THE OPENING OF the clinic, there was a revolution in Sharjah. It wasn't really a revolution, more a bit of a coup and an unsuccessful coup at that. The ruler of Sharjah, Sheikh Sultan bin Muhammad al-Qassimi, was away in England on a private visit when his brother, Sheikh Abdul Aziz bin Muhammad al-Qassimi, declared that he would be taking over because his brother was mishandling the country's finances. Abdul Aziz had the upper hand. For starters, he was head of the Amiri Guard, Sharjah's only military force. He was also chairman of the Chamber of Commerce – scarcely an aggressive organisation – but he had counted the dough in the coffers and came up with a deficit of $1.3 billion US.

We saw no patients from Sharjah that day. There was a curfew. Excitement spread like a bush fire in Dubai; word was that tanks were rumbling around the deserted streets and that Sharjah police were out in force to shoot looters! Abdul Aziz had barricaded himself in the royal palace, surrounded by three thousand of his loyal troops in sand-bagged emplacements.

Part of the problem seemed to be that Sheikh Sultan was more interested in his books than his people. But Dubai supported him. He hurried back from London and took refuge in one of the palaces in Dubai.

Abu Dhabi was in favour of Sheikh Abdul Aziz; he and Sheikh Zayed of Abu Dhabi were pals from way back and Abdul Aziz had recently married an important member of Zayed's family.

However, after days of round-the-clock meetings, the UAE Supreme Council (the rulers of all seven emirates) voted in favour of Sheikh Sultan. The coup was over; Abdul Aziz had reigned for six days. As a reward for stepping aside, he was made heir apparent. His Highness Dr Sheikh Sultan resumed his seat and his cultural and scholarly activities... His Highness Doctor Sheikh? He had a PhD in history from Exeter University.

ONE OF MY DUTIES IN THE CLINIC WAS TO examine commercial pilots to assess their medical fitness. On the basis of my air force career, I had been accepted by the British Civil Aviation Authority. I examined pilots from the Dubai Air Wing who flew the royal family, pilots from Emirates airline, air traffic controllers and holders of private pilot's licences.

A transient group was half a dozen Canadian pilots who normally flew in and out of the millions of lakes at home and had been brought to Dubai when a tour company set up seaplane tours of Dubai. The seaplanes used the tranquil waters of Dubai Creek and, from personal experience, I can vouch that the trip was stunning. Flying at a leisurely speed, a few hundred feet above Dubai, enabled you to appreciate just how rapidly the place was developing.

Unfortunately the company folded after only a few months, but not before I had made the acqaintance of one particular pilot, who came from Vancouver. He told me a story as I examined him. One day as he was leaving for work at home in Vancouver, he saw his neighbour, a turbaned Sikh, energetically shaking the dust out of a small carpet. As he passed him on the steps he gaily asked, "What's the matter, won't it start?" His neighbour obviously didn't see the funny side, because he pressed charges of racism and took the pilot to court. This cost him $200, but when you consider that $200 Canadian wouldn't buy much more than a good dinner for two in Vancouver, at least the judge seems to have appreciated the joke.

Another pilot I examined flew micro-light aircraft. He lived in the emirate of Ras al Khaimah. Three sons of the ruling family of Ras al Khaimah had taken a fancy to flying these flimsy aircraft but, of course, hadn't gone to the bother of getting properly trained – after all the planes are small, don't fly high and are slow.

What happened? In no time, there were three crashes (one son died) and the wreckage of the three micro-lights was strewn across the beach. The pilot, with permission, acquired all the wrecks, cannibalised them and then had his own aircraft, with spares – at no cost.

About this time I was asked to examine a group of about thirty Filipinos who worked on the oil rigs in the Gulf. Their company was keen that I did a thorough examination to make sure they were fit as they worked in such challenging conditions, isolated and exposed to the searing heat and humidity of the Gulf summer weather.

They were a cheerful bunch; I enjoyed them. To my surprise, I found that most of them had curious mobile lumps beneath the skin of their penises and a few had small rings inserted in the underside of the shafts, at the tip.

Curious, I asked one what the lump was. He looked a bit embarrassed but said, "Well doc, you know it gets very boring out on those rigs. We do this to pass the time."

"But what are these lumps?" I asked.

"Sapphires," he said.

"To please the ladies?" I speculated.

"Well," he replied, "I really don't know if they notice them."

"And how do you insert them?" I persisted.

"Oh, it's done properly," he announced as if it were a standard hospital procedure. "The medic injects with local, makes a slit and pops in the sapphire."

You live and learn.

Twenty One

MY MOST CELEBRATED PATIENT IN Dubai was Sir Wilfred Thesiger, the legendary British desert explorer who twice crossed the Empty Quarter on camel and on foot – this after winning the Distinguished Service Order (DSO) for gallantry in the Second World War while serving with the SAS in the North African desert – explored remote areas of Arabia, the Middle East, the subcontinent and Africa. He was remarkable among other things for his uncompromising attitude: he always adopted the ways of the peoples he lived and travelled among, gaining insights few have matched before or since.

He came to me via Ian Fairservice, the managing partner of a publishing company in Dubai which was publishing several of his travel books. Sir Wilfred was in his early eighties; tall, distinguished, grey-haired with a prominent Roman nose on which nestled (like with Cromwell) a wart. His whole visage was hawk-like and his eyes alert with an unmistakeable twinkle.

In taking his history, it emerged that some years before he had been seen by a surgeon and diagnosed as having cancer of the colon which would need an operation involving removal of half his colon. "So I said to the surgeon," he told me, "please go ahead, I would much rather be a semi-colon than a full-stop."

At the conclusion of the visit, Sir Wilfred mentioned that he had a very painful foot. I examined it; he had a simple corn. I told him to hop onto my couch and with a scalpel I trimmed and shaved the corn down to the soft skin. I'd watched with fascination as my mother did this many times for my grandmother when I was a small boy. She didn't have a scalpel, she wielded a cut-throat razor.

Job done, he jumped off the couch, put on his sock and shoe, stamped his foot on the floor and exclaimed, "Ah, perfect!" – the exact words used by my granny each time. He looked at me and said, "I really didn't know how I was going to manage but tomorrow I will be able to take that walk in the desert with Charles." I looked at him. "Yes," he said, "We have a meeting with Sheikh Zayed tomorrow morning in Abu Dhabi and afterwards Prince Charles and I will go for a long walk in the desert."

One evening after dinner with Sir Wilfred, I introduced him to a dentist friend of mine. Knowing that Sir Wilfred took it upon himself to look after the medical needs of his travelling companions on his interminable desert treks, the dentist asked, "What about problems with their teeth, did you take care of them?"

Sir Wilfred smiled and said, "Ah yes, I always carried a pair of pliers. My treatment was radical – just pull it out. I would sit on the ground with the patient lying on his back, I would hold his head firmly between my thighs, grab the tooth with the pliers and yank it hard – it always worked, and of course the Bedu wouldn't let out a squeak because he had an audience of his pals."

Sir Wilfred died in August 2003 at the age of ninety-three; his *chef d'oeuvre*, *Arabian Sands*, remains a classic of travel writing and is a treat awaiting anyone who hasn't read it yet. Once, when asked what he regarded as the most valuable thing in life, he replied, "Friendship; all that really matters is relationships with people. In the desert, you learn that. If you don't have good relationships, then you die."

SOCIAL LIFE IN DUBAI WAS HECTIC; COMPANIES vied with each other to put on the most generous spreads. Caviar (abundant, came from the other side of the Gulf) and champagne were often served as a starter. Western culture, such as it was, came in the form of theatre shows sponsored by British Airways – usually the Whitehall farce sort of play entailing a glimpse of a bare bottom or fallen knickers. Rather posh balls were held in the cool season, the most popular being the Irish Ball with its inevitable green theme, including uninviting green drinks. The Poppy Ball in November was a must for those who wanted to be seen among Dubai's high society.

Western expats relaxed at beach clubs at weekends. There were many scattered along the coast. Most were attached to hotels but the one we joined was to start just simply as a pool, a strip of sand on Jumeirah Beach and a small restaurant. It was run by three Lebanese brothers who managed to develop the club at breakneck speed, adding squash and tennis courts, health centre, gym, three theme restaurants and residential blocks. One attraction was the 'monthly accumulater draw'. The club started a pot which members were eligible to win, if they were present on the night of the draw. The pot accumulated month by month if there were no winners and would frequently reach a substantial amount. I never won; the odds weren't long, they were impossible. I knew that when I witnessed one of the draws.

One evening, with a friend, I sat in the bar at the club, had a meal, a couple of beers and we chatted. We noticed a family group, clearly friends or relatives of the owners, sitting next to the small dance floor. After an hour they were joined by an elderly chap who appeared to be the father, maybe the 'Godfather' of the family group. With a canned roll of drums, the draw was announced and the master of ceremonies invited the young and strikingly attractive daughter or even granddaughter of the Godfather to make the draw. She did – and guess what? To everyone's surprise and amazement, especially that of the MC and the daughter, Pappa's number came up – the family shrieked with joy and... he walked off with 20,000 dirhams (more than $5,000). Of course we joined in the applause at his good fortune; we really had no use for the money either...

FOR MANY LIFE IN DUBAI WAS ARTIFICIAL, far removed from the lives they led at home. House servants were cheap; most families had live-in servants from Sri Lanka, India or the Philippines. Supermarkets abounded and goods were no more expensive than in England. There was British-style schooling for children. Fathers were earning well, mothers had time on their hands. A new culture emerged, that of the Jumeirah Jane.

Jumeirah Janes were easy to recognise; they had white Japanese four-wheel drive cars (their own: hubby had the Porsche) and they wore sunglasses perched on the top of their coiffed hair. They were well made-up, wore designer clothes and designer jewellery, had perfect fingernails and exuded an air of girlie bonhomie as they perched and chattered like starlings around outdoor café tables sipping their designer coffees.

I frequently saw Jumeirah Janes in the clinic. Many were simply unfulfilled and bored; their complaints were largely psychosomatic. I felt I should tell them to get rid of their servants and washing machines and busy themselves with housework – that would be the right treatment for most.

But there were some whose problems, although psychosomatic, were more serious – their well-paid, equally bored husbands had fallen for the charms of a Filipina bar girl, or worse the wife of a workmate, or even worse the housemaid. Short of banging their heads together and telling them to make the most of their good fortune there wasn't much I could do… just like with those blokes who came to see me with a nasty dose after a weekend of fun in Bangkok. When I told them that normal relations were off for a while, they would always wail, "But what can I tell my wife?" I could never think of a convincing suggestion.

Some Jumeirah Janes became enthralled by what one could call the Dubai Alternative Medicine Industry: miracle workers with bottles of scents or foot massage with the preposterous title of reflexology; herbalists with exotic remedies (must be safe, it's 'natural'… but so are deadly nightshade and curare 'natural'). Clinics sprang up all over the place, many promising the delights of Ayurvedic medicine, others Chinese medicine (has to be right because the Chinese have been doing it for three thousand years).

One noted practitioner in the alternative field was known as Dr Jon. He was from Eastern Europe and had a remarkably successful practice – it might have been his thick accent that did the trick for him. He was short, tubby, teddy-bear like, amiable and likeable but totally batty. From time to time I gave lectures to general practitioners in Dubai and whenever I spotted him in the audience, my heart sank. When, after the lecture, the chairman invited questions, Dr Jon held the floor for as long as he could and asked questions unrelated to the topic under discussion. For instance, if I gave a lecture on thyroid disease, he would stand up at the end and, under the guise of asking a question, spout about some new herbal remedy from Timbuctoo or ask me if I had used magnetism for the treatment of heart disease.

He didn't just practice acupuncture, he didn't just do electrical acupuncture (you squirt a little electricity down the needle, it adds a tickle), he did electrical/musical acupuncture; that is, he also squirted music down his needles – please don't ask me how, or whether classical or modern.

A journalist from the local paper, *The Gulf News*, aware of my dedication to conventional medicine and occasional asides about complementary characters, invited me to attend Dr Jon's clinic to meet a visiting famous Indian guru who had amazing healing powers and could see into the future with crystal clarity. I remember thinking at the time that she was up to no good, that journalist; she was hoping to work up a story. But I agreed and on the appointed morning, arrived ten minutes ahead of the guru. Dr Jon showed me a video of the guru in his guru uniform, the standard issue Ghandi-like outfit draped over one shoulder. In the video, he was seen striding through a smoky, incense-rich temple plucking precious gems from the air with his bare hands and tossing them to worshippers. I made no comment; Dr Jon and the reporter declared, in awed tones, that the guru was working miracles.

Dr Jon then handed me an extraordinarily thick black leather bound book. It was a book entirely devoted to disease diagnosis by tongue inspection. On each right-hand page was a picture of an open mouth with dangling uvula and the tongue protruded in a fashion forbidden to me when I was a boy. On the facing page, the text gave a detailed description of the disease which could be confidently diagnosed solely on the appearance of the tongue. In my time I've looked at thousands of tongues, for sure there are appearances which are diagnostic – but not the hundreds illustrated in that tome.

Half an hour later the message came through, "We are sorry, something unforeseen has come up and the guru won't be able to come."

"Vot a shame," said the apologetic little Dr Jon; totally missing the irony of the situation. The reporter looked crestfallen. I said to her, "Well there's your headline... 'The soothsayer who couldn't see into the future'." I smiled; she glowered: somehow I knew I'd be seeing her again, whenever.

But the subcontinent didn't have a monopoly on alternative medicine. Chinese medicine was so popular in Dubai that when a Chinese doctor approached me and asked to join the clinic, I took him seriously. Dr Cheng's curriculum vitae was as exhaustive and as incomprehensible as Chinese medicine itself; he had been trained at university schools of Chinese medicine and had degrees and diplomas as long as your arm – but, most important to me, he had already successfully appeared before the Dubai Department of Health committee. The clinic would not have to go through miles of red tape to get him accredited.

Although the Jumeirah Janes and others extolled Chinese medicine, Dr Cheng never made the grade. His practice didn't develop despite his knowing all the meridians, the Yin and the Yang business, having all the proper needles, cups for blistering and cigar-shaped objects for heating specific points. He applied funny poultices made of herbs, he applied pungent oils, he administered quaint medications like snake bile which was a glutinous yellow liquid, and came in glass ampoules. He rubbed and pulled people about but he didn't cut the mustard… maybe when he stuck needles in people's ears to stop them smoking, he reeked so strongly of tobacco himself that people wondered.

Not surprisingly homeopathy flourished in Dubai. I quickly learned to hold my tongue when, at a cocktail party, a fellow guest would say, "I believe in homeopathy, what do you think of it?" If I responded negatively, I was immediately branded as prejudiced; if I responded by asking "What is homeopathy?" I was met with a puzzled and pitying look that said 'everybody knows about homeopathy, it's safe, it cures and it's part of holistic medicine'. Holistic: that's an irritating word if ever there was one; ugly as well. It's as if it's a concept recently invented – 'treat the whole man, not just the illness' has been around since Hippocrates. When I was a student, if I referred to "the duodenal ulcer in bed twelve" I would be roundly rebuked: I should know my patients' names, I should know all about them, I should be concerned with the whole person.

As it happens, I know a bit about homeopathy… quite a bit, actually. It was invented by Samuel Hahnemann in 1810. Note the word 'invented': it was not a discovery. Hahnemann was a German physician who, after dosing himself with an extract of cinchona bark (contains quinine) used for treating malaria, developed symptoms which he thought were identical to those of malaria. But I guess no fever, no shakes (rigors), and no headaches… all typical of the many cases of malaria I had seen. From this highly questionable observation, he concluded that effective drugs must produce symptoms in people that are similar to the diseases they will be expected to treat; this was the principle of the 'Law of Similars'.

He further postulated that the doses needed to produce the symptoms of the disease would be too strong and he therefore diluted the agents he used to such a level that what was regarded as therapeutic by a homeopath was indistinguishable from tap water on chemical analysis.

Hahnemann was immediately successful – very successful; but why?

At that time, conventional medicine was still in its dark ages. Doctors purged, bled, applied leeches, blistered their patients, stuck on poultices, blew tobacco smoke up their bottoms and gave them enemas of coffee.

Conventional medicine at Hahnemann's time was not only ineffective, it was brutal and downright dangerous; doctors killed patients in their hundreds. Hahnemann gave no treatment; his medications with fancy names were simply water with a smart label. Mother Nature is wonderful: she cured where a natural cure was possible and no meddlesome physicians interfered.

Homeopathy reared its head at the clinic one morning when a young lady doctor appeared. She told me she was considering working in Dubai, having just moved there with her husband and new baby. She knew about the clinic because she had worked in general practice with my GP nephew, Andrew, in England. She was pleasant, said all the right things and was well trained (University College Hospital) but when she told me that she also practised homeopathic medicine, my jaw dropped. "Don't look so surprised." she said. "It's very effective. For example, when I give my baby homeopathic gripe water, we all have a remarkably quiet night."

"So what's in this homeopathic gripe-water?" I asked. She rattled off several homeopathic names which meant nothing to me, but added, "it also has twelve per cent alcohol."

No wonder the child slept so well. I didn't ask if it was particularly grizzly in the mornings.

Many controlled trials have been carried out on homeopathic medications and arguably not shown more than a placebo effect. But as the Queen and Prince Charles subscribe to homeopathy, it follows that by royal command it is bound to work... just as touching the hem of the king's cloak cured scrofula, tuberculosis of the lymph glands of the neck, the so-called 'King's Evil', centuries ago.

I HAD ALWAYS HAD A HANKERING TO paint in oils, in particular to paint portraits. Dubai had a very active arts centre and there were some fine teachers who taught in the evenings, having full-time day jobs. One teacher was a lawyer called Nick Bashall. He worked for a Dubai bank but his passion was portrait painting.

Nick was tall; he was not too concerned about his appearance and for classes (and posh dinners) dressed as an artist should, in jeans with a ragged T-shirt and bare feet. Nick had a right wrist drop. He was naturally right-handed but a motorcycle accident had so severely damaged the nerves to his right arm that his right hand was useless for painting. So he taught himself to paint left-handed. Of course we all know that left-handed painters are the best: famous left-handers included Leonardo da Vinci, Adolf Hitler – and me.

Nick's passion ran in his family; his mother was a successful portrait painter but as I recall, he told me that his mother would never teach him or give him any advice for fear that it would impair the development of his own individual style. In fact Nick had a very interesting family background and over a glass or two of Dubai's finest *vin rouge* he told me his story.

"My father was a Wiltshire man, born and bred. He was a young army officer in the Wiltshire regiment when he met my mother in London where she was at art school. They married in England and had three of their four children there. In pursuit of adventure and to escape depressing post-war England, my father engineered a posting with the army to the colony of Southern Rhodesia, what's now Zimbabwe. Its capital is Harare, but in our time it was called Salisbury."

He told me the family was happy for many years but then in February 1960, British prime minister Harold MacMillan made his infamous 'wind of change' speech to the South African parliament. In it he said quite clearly that times had moved on, that African countries were entitled to their independence. The secondary message was an indirect indication that England was getting out of Africa altogether.

This blew a wind of change on the Bashall family. Like so many young English army families in Africa, they were faced with a choice: go back to England with the army or resign their commissions, stay put and try to make a go of it.

Nick's father chose to stay, left the army, and with another former officer bought a farm. Neither had farming experience but both relished the adventure and those were still the days when an enthusiastic young man could make his fortune in one of Mother England's colonies.

"It was tough, both men had young families and no matter how hard they worked money was very tight," said Nick. "My mother wanted to help. She took out her pastels and after practising portraiture on us kids decided she could help the finances. She packed us into the old family Ford Consul and drove to Salisbury. It was several hundred miles and she ran out of petrol on the way. She was too poor to buy more but happily knew many people, found a family to draw, got paid, bought petrol and continued on to Salisbury."

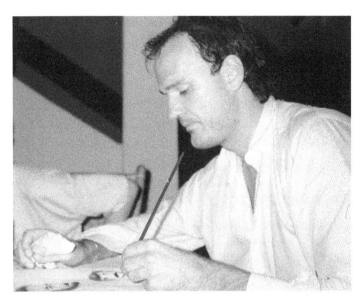

Nick Bashall: art in his blood.

In Salisbury, Nick's mother had a friend with a department store. He allowed her to take over a small area near the lift where she demonstrated her skills by drawing her children. This attracted commissions. "She spent a couple of months at it then, flush with dosh, she returned to the farm," said Nick.

"In the meantime, my father and his farming partner were forced to the reluctant conclusion that no matter how hard they tried the farm would never be able to support two large families and one had to leave."

Intrigued I asked, "How did they decide?"

"By the flip of a coin and my father lost." Rather wistfully Nick continued, "And that's how my father left the farm. Mother's infusion of cash helped and she was quite willing to repeat the adventure but the toss of a coin had fallen against my father."

When the family returned to England, Nick went to Cambridge to read law. There he gained a boxing blue – just like Sir Wilfred Thesiger, another undergraduate who had grown up in Africa, did several decades earlier, although Thesiger's was a dark blue.

When I knew him, Nick was happy in Dubai working as the Emirates Bank in-house lawyer but determined, when he'd saved enough, to throw up the law and train in a good art school.

And that's exactly what he did. Nick enrolled in a very fine art school in Mallorca. He eventually settled in London, where he is enjoying success and a growing reputation as a portrait painter but only after initial hardship. "It was a difficult field to break into, Bill," he recently told me. "At the start, times were so tough I slept on the floor of my studio."

As for me and my painting, after a few years, my interest dwindled and painting is like playing tennis: if you don't keep it up, you lose the strokes. I had, apart from being left-handed, another feature in common with a famous artist, van Gogh – I sold just one painting. Van Gogh made the equivalent of a thousand dollars for his painting, *Red Vineyard* – I made almost fifty dollars for my painting, *Dubai Creek*.

I learned a fascinating point about faces through my painting. Portraits require over-all accuracy but there is one line which, if executed correctly, gives an instant likeness, and that is the line between the lips. I was told never to paint subjects with open mouths, as an open mouth removes that line. Hogarth did a couple but he was such a good artist he could make a smiling cat look real. Take a look around the National Portrait Gallery in London. Of the hundreds of good portraits hanging, very few – less than a handful – feature subjects with open mouths. One I recall well that does is of Prince Charles in green wellington boots. His teeth glare at you from the portrait and sadly (at least to me) give an overall goofy appearance. Next time you are with a group of people, say in a waiting room or on the tube, take a look at them, study that line and I think you will be convinced that indeed it is that which gives a likeness to a portrait.

IN THE SUMMER OF 1990, MARIA AND I accepted an invitation from our good friend Dennis Stickley, a very successful businessman, to celebrate his last evening in Dubai. He had been head-hunted by a large company in Kuwait. The package offered was extremely attractive; he would be flying out for good the next day. The date was 1 August.

We kicked off the evening with a drink at the home of the Middle East Airlines manager, Hasani Ghattas. His Irish wife, Orla, was well-known for being a hypochondriac and a drama queen. When we three – Dennis, Maria and I – arrived at their villa, Hasani told us that Orla wasn't well and couldn't join us. Maria was disappointed; she enjoyed Orla's company and wasn't too pleased to be the only lady in the group but, when Hasani served

Dom Perignon accompanied by tiny sweet strawberries in crystal dishes, she perked up. We three drank and ate happily before heading off to a restaurant at the Hyatt.

We later discovered that Orla was furious; she had been sitting in her four-poster bed, dressed in one of her designer negligees, face painted, hair coiffed, perfumed and waiting for us to enter her boudoir and share champagne with her; but instead she could only lie there listening to us laughing and joking from afar. She had made an all-too-common mistake: she thought her husband would be able to read her mind, so she didn't tell him that she would expect him to bring us into her room… where she would be lying dramatically pale and languid and only just able to sip at her glass. They divorced a couple of years later.

At the hotel, Dennis ordered more Dom and said to the head waiter, "Now we want Beluga caviar, Eduardo, and don't bother giving us any of those miserly teaspoon measures, just whack a big dollop onto each plate, there's a good man!" That set the course for a memorable evening that only ended in the early hours with warm farewells as we wished Dennis good fortune in his new venture.

On 2 August, the next day, Dennis flew into Kuwait. He landed at dawn, about the same time as another 'visitor' entered the country. That was Saddam Hussein, and he brought lots of his pals with him.

I was shaving and listening to the BBC World Service when I heard of the invasion. I phoned Maria who was already at work. She was an administrator for General Motors in Dubai. She told the boss, he called headquarters in Detroit and within twenty-four hours General Motors staff with their families had been evacuated from this dangerous war zone – leaving Maria holding the keys to their houses and cars.

Local radio stations and newspapers did not break the news for forty-eight hours; they had to wait for government permission. But everybody knew what was happening – short-wave radio sales went through the roof in Dubai as residents made sure they could tune in to international broadcasts – and there was a good deal of anxiety and fear floating freely in the air. Dubai and Kuwait are roughly at opposite ends of the Persian Gulf, as the crow flies about five hundred miles apart; yet one might have thought from the numbers fleeing the country, and the rumours circulating, that Saddam and his mighty army were already speeding along Saudi Arabia's

Gulf coast and were only hours away. Panic buying cleared the shelves of duct tape because some thought we were within the range of Saddam's chemical warfare rockets and ought to seal our windows and doors.

Those prone to hysteria made comparisons with Hitler's *blitzkrieg* through Europe, but it wasn't at all like that.

Families left Dubai in droves. Dubai life continued but it was quieter than it would be when Ramadan fell in the hottest month. In the uncertainty of war, business shuddered to a halt, owners and sponsors got cold feet, stayed home, counted their assets and as well as sending their families to Europe or America, sent their dough to Switzerland.

A week after Saddam's invasion of Kuwait, I received a formal letter from the Dubai Department of Health advising me that when Dubai was invaded – when, mind you, not if – I must make myself available at the nearest government clinic.

Meanwhile, down the Gulf in Kuwait, the Iraqis were making themselves at home. Saddam's Iraq was broke. It had just concluded a long, inconclusive and costly war against Shiite Iran in which Saddam had been sponsored to the tune of $40 billion by Sunni Saudi and Sunni Kuwait, who didn't like what Iran was getting up to.

When peace was declared in the Iran/Iraq war, Saddam suggested that the Saudis and Kuwaitis might forget the loans; after all, he had been fighting on their behalf. They declined. Saddam was irritated. He cast his eyes over Kuwait, a soft target if ever there was one. He claimed ancient rights of governance from Baghdad dating back to the early days of the Ottoman rule, before the meddling British appeared on the scene. Moreover, he claimed that the Kuwaitis were filching Iraq's oil from the Rumaila Field by directional drilling. A week after he invaded, he declared Kuwait the nineteenth province of Iraq.

Saddam knew that the Kuwaitis were a pretty dozy lot and their military forces were incapable of resistance against his armoured divisions and crack Republican Guard troops. He didn't anticipate the immediate response by the Western world to join the Gulf states in a multinational military coalition, led by the United States, to oust the invaders. Israel of course wasn't invited to the party. The United Nations gave Saddam six weeks to quit Kuwait or be thrown out forcibly. He dug in for a siege.

Realising the vulnerability of strategic sites in Iraq and Kuwait to

Dennis Stickley and friend: a glass of Dom Perignon to cure most ills.

coalition air strikes, Saddam rounded up foreigners and, against all conventions of warfare, set them up as human shields.

One of them was our friend Dennis. The day after our champagne and caviar night in Dubai, and only hours after he landed in Kuwait, he went into hiding but was discovered after a few days. He was tortured; the torture consisted of having a brick placed in an armpit and being repeatedly hit hard on the upper arm... it becomes very painful. Why he was tortured was not clear to him but after a few days he was taken to a munitions dump and held there as insurance against an air strike.

In response to world outrage and United Nations resolutions, Saddam released many human shield hostages, including Dennis, in December 1990. He returned to Dubai, pale and thin; his hair had turned grey and he had worry lines where none existed before. But Saddam had not destroyed his spirit. He soon bounced back. He checked into a plush suite in the five-star Hyatt hotel, booked a private dining room and invited his old friends to another carefree celebration with Dom Perignon and Beluga caviar.

Dubai started to function again but there were scaremongers. I remember one, an ex-British Army Air Corps captain. "Saddam Hussein's Republican Guard are crack troops and there are 60,000 of them," he said with all the authority of his present position, which was propping up a bar. "He has modern Mig and Mirage fighters, plenty of attack helicopters, several fast armoured divisions and – let's face it – we're only a hop, skip and a jump away from the war zone."

Analysis of Saddam's strength after 'Stormin' Norman's shock and awe' brought the 1991 Gulf War to a conclusion in four days showed that my knowledgeable captain's assessment could not have been further from the truth. The Iraqi air force did have Migs and Mirages, but they were old and many were unserviceable. And his crack Republican Guard cracked soon after the first shots were fired. His tanks were ancient; they looked good on parade but their armour was thin and they had none of the sophisticated weaponry and targeting capabilities of the coalition forces. As for Saddam speeding down the well-paved Gulf coast highway, the reality was that his lines of supply were over-extended as soon as he crossed Kuwait and reached the Saudi border.

A WEEK AFTER THE INVASION, I HAD A CALL from the captain of one of the Royal Navy supply ships docked in Port Rashid. "Good morning doctor, I hope you can help us. We have what might be a serious problem."

"I'll do what I can." I replied. "What's the problem?"

"Well," said the captain, "we don't have a ship's cat but in the week since we have been alongside, we have been adopted by a rather good looking tabby."

"Yes," I said, puzzled as to what was coming next.

"We thought that cat was healthy but this morning one of my ratings found it frothing at the mouth and obviously sick. I'm afraid it might have rabies and could infect the crew."

I thought a while then said, "You had better bring the cat to my clinic. In the meantime, I'll make enquiries about rabies here, but I must say that I haven't ever heard that it's a problem in Dubai."

Ten minutes later, he called me back and exclaimed, "The cat's dead."

"Stick it in a box and bring it to me."

Another ten minutes passed and he called again, "When we went to pick up the dead cat it jumped up and ran away!"

"Well," I said as patiently as I could, "you must still bring it in. Get your chaps to catch it."

After ten minutes, the captain was on the phone again, "We've got it, it's in a box, we're on our way."

In the meantime, I had spoken to a local veterinary surgeon, a loud, ebullient character who had been working in Dubai for more than twenty years. "Dick," I said, "is there any rabies in Dubai?"

"Never to my knowledge," he replied.

He laughed when I recounted the story and said, "Well, when the cat arrives, you can send it to my clinic and I'll take a look at it but I can tell you, with ninety-nine per cent certainty, that cat does not have rabies."

I waited, two hours passed, no cat arrived but eventually the captain called again, "Doctor," he said in a small voice, "the cat is dead. What happened was we put it in a box on the back seat of a car. On the way to you, the driver – one of my lads – and his pal decided to stop off for a little refreshment. After an hour, they remembered the cat, went back to the car and it was lying dead in the box."

Poor cat: with ambient temperatures around forty-five to fifty degrees, and probably ten degrees higher in the box on the back seat, it must have perished of heat stroke in no time.

I reassured the captain that a vet who had been in Dubai for twenty years had never heard of a case of rabies. He promised to let me know if any of his sailors fell sick. We never did find out what, if anything, had been wrong with the cat, and as for the ship's company, I can only assume they went back to contracting ailments more traditionally associated with sailors and ports.

IN A PARTING GESTURE OF MUSLIM SOLIDARITY and Arabic brotherly love, as he retreated, Saddam poured four hundred million barrels of Kuwait's crude oil into the waters of the Gulf and set fire to the Kuwait oilfields. The only people to profit from Saddam's fond adieu were Red Adair and his merry men and the other teams of specialist oil-well firefighters.

It was over; we could breathe again. Dubai could restart its expansion and development and General Motors and other companies could resume their labours.

Twenty Two

DUBAI WORKED HARD TO CATCH UP with the rest of the world. Most of the time this translated into importing whatever it was they wanted, lock stock and barrel, from another time and space and thereby reinventing the place as something it was not so that people could pretend they were somewhere else. So the Hilton Hotel beside the Dubai World Trade Centre tower looked and felt like a Hilton anywhere in the world. It had a bar called Humphrey's dedicated to the memory of an American movie star of the 1940s and selling large volumes of beer to expatriates. I cannot tell a lie: at times it was very comfortable.

One evening as Maria and I sat there surrounded by photos of a world-weary Bogart and beautiful young Bacall, eating our fish and chips, I spotted a bloke sitting at a table nearby; his face was familiar. He looked at me, smiled and said, "Aren't you Wing Commander Larkworthy?" I admitted I was; his face became more familiar. "I used to be Corporal Policeman Johnson when I was in the air force years ago," he said. "I was stationed at Waddington near Nocton Hall and you treated my ulcer. As a matter of fact I was one of your guinea pigs."

"Really?"

"Yes, I had to chew funny gum for weeks," he said. "And do you know that got me into a lot of trouble?"

"How come?" I asked.

It seems he was on guard duty one evening when a staff car flying an air marshal's pennant rolled up to the camp entrance. Johnson snapped to attention and saluted as the car drove past – it stopped, reversed, the passenger window shot down and from inside the Air Marshal demanded to know if he was chewing gum.

"I said I was," Johnson recalled, "but explained that it was on doctor's orders. 'Never heard such bloody nonsense! Get your sergeant – on the double!' the Air Marshal shouted.

"I called the sergeant from the guardhouse and the Air Marshal ordered him to put me on a charge of 'improper conduct whilst on guard duty'. The charge couldn't be dropped, even after the station doctor had spoken on my behalf. But by the time it was heard, my station doctor had a supporting note from the hospital. The Wing Commander administration couldn't but agree that I was indeed acting under a legitimate medical order and dismissed the charge."

I asked ex-corporal Johnson what he was up to in Dubai. "Came here to seek my fortune," he told me.

"And how's it going?"

"Not well," he replied. "I came here as the manager of a European car-hire company but we're doing very badly – the problem is that we rent a lot of cars to young Emiratis, they beat the hell out of the cars, don't pay for any damages and sometimes just abandon them; they even try to sell the cars they rent. There's very little we can do about it."

I sympathised, got him a pint, chatted further and didn't see him again… but he did mention before we parted that he had never had a problem with his stomach since I treated him some twelve years before.

In those days, the late eighties and early nineties, it was likely that if you went into any pub, club or restaurant in Dubai, you would spot a friend or two. By the time we left in 2001, we could wander the streets of Dubai, go into pubs, clubs and restaurants and not glimpse a familiar face. Watering holes seemed to be an easy way of separating the working population from their earnings, so their number had increased enormously, in parallel with the population which had quadrupled from the 370,000 it was when the clinic had opened in 1986.

'It's a bubble, it's bound to burst!' Everybody said that from the day I arrived in Dubai. It was said time and time again: every year it was the same. The bubble continued to expand and the prophets of doom shook their heads. But during my fifteen years, there was no indication of an upcoming rupture. Year on year, the rate of change was accelerating, driven by the vision of Sheikh Mohammed bin Rashid al Maktoum who eventually succeeded his elder brother Maktoum as ruler. Buildings were going up everywhere; humans and their endeavours were encroaching more and more on the sands of the desert. Expansion into the Gulf waters was beginning. Millions of tons of rock quarried from the Hajar mountains were being dumped off the coast of Dubai to make the foundations for new marinas, luxury hotels and villas. There was no limit to Sheikh Mohammed's vision: when the population reached 1.6 million a couple of years after we left, he declared that, "Dubai is only one-third of the way towards its goal."

I used to walk on the beach front in the cool of the mornings before going to work. I remember looking back at Dubai and seeing building cranes from horizon to horizon – in a few years it would be said that Dubai had twenty per cent of all the cranes in the whole world – and then when I turned and looked out to sea I could see a layer of dense orange pollution extending for twenty degrees upwards from the horizon; there was no pollution and few cranes when we arrived.

The bubble didn't burst in our time, but the warning signs were there. Property developments were springing up like mushrooms. Prices were astronomical and expatriates – newly allowed to own property – were snapping up houses off-plan, before a brick had been laid, at the equivalent of half a million pounds sterling and up. Phantom properties were sold twice over before a foundation stone had been laid. Obscene profits were made fuelling the market and fuelling the cupidity. Banks were so anxious to lend they were almost pressing wads of notes into buyers' hands.

We left while Dubai was still in its heyday; before the collapse of the world's markets had such a disastrous effect on this surreal kingdom built on sand.

IN THE EARLY NINETIES, I WAS BEGINNING to have problems with my own health. Increasingly I was developing pain and stiffness in my hip joints. X-rays showed that I had severe osteoarthritic (degenerative) changes. Getting out of low chairs was difficult and sleep was impossible. Lying on an arthritic hip caused pain which would wake me; I would have to turn over to relieve the pain but then, within minutes, pain in the equally arthritic opposite hip would awaken me again. I knew the causes – pressure on an arthritic joint pushes the roughened joint surfaces together, reduces the blood supply and increases pain by stimulating the pain fibres – and now I knew the effects too.

I blamed my arthritis on squash. I had played a lot in the RAF and became an accredited coach. Normally squash courts are constructed with wooden parquet floors, which are resilient when one prances around, but the floors of the squash courts of the Amenities Centre at the King Faisal Specialist Hospital were laid with flag stones. Sometimes I would play seven or even eight times a week – a good work-out helped with the frustrations of living and working in Saudi Arabia. But the effects of years of squash on my hips had overtaken my global rate of natural degeneration by decades.

Something had to be done. I sent my films to an orthopaedic surgeon I knew in Abu Dhabi; he phoned me, "You need surgery on both hips, both need replacement." Not good news; at that time there were no surgeons or hospitals in Dubai I could entrust with such major surgery – especially on me.

My Abu Dhabi friend recommended an ex-boss of his, an orthopaedic consultant surgeon under whom he had trained. He told me how marvellous he was and that he performed his operations in a first class private hospital in London. I sent my x-ray films to him. The surgeon in London wrote back saying that there was no doubt that I needed to have both hip joints replaced. We corresponded and arranged that I should be admitted to the private hospital in London, under his care. I would have both hips operated on during the same admission.

A date for admission was set. I wrote to the surgeon to express my concern about known complications of hip joint surgery – namely, infection and pulmonary embolism. He wrote back reassuring me that I would be given antibiotic cover, to prevent infection, and daily injections of a substance called low molecular weight heparin, which would prevent thrombosis and protect me from pulmonary embolism. Pulmonary embolism is a well-recognised complication of hip surgery and occurs because of the formation of large clots in the big veins of the lower limbs or pelvis. If these clots detach they shoot along the great veins and are carried to the heart, like a tube train rushing down the tunnel. When the length of clotted blood reaches the heart it blocks the flow to the lungs leading, by no means uncommonly, to death.

To further prepare myself for the biggest procedure I had ever undergone, I went to the blood transfusion service in Dubai and arranged to have two units of my own blood taken a month apart and stored. The clinic manager and the senior laboratory technician had the same blood group as mine and they each donated blood for me to take to London.

By the time I set off for London, my disability had increased so much that I needed a wheelchair to get to the aircraft. I sat in the chair, with four units of blood in plastic bags on my lap, and was wheeled to the aircraft. In those days, 1993, one boarded aircraft in Dubai by climbing steps but this was impossible for me so I took the lift... the fork-lift, that is, normally used for loading catering supplies onto the aircraft.

I confess to having considerable anxiety; hip surgery is not minor surgery, but my friend in Abu Dhabi had reassured me that I was in excellent surgical hands and, moreover, the private hospital also had a fine reputation. All the same, with my most recent visit to the surgical suite as a patient being in 1962, I wasn't exactly relaxed.

Back in the sixties, I was young and took the excision of a pilonidal sinus, a condition known as 'Jeep Bottom,' in my stride. It was carried out in the plastic surgery wing of the RAF Hospital in Halton, Buckinghamshire. The surgeon, Air Vice-Marshal Morley, was a protegé of Sir Archibald McIndoe – famed for the pioneering work he did on severely burned and disfigured aircrew. My condition wasn't quite on that scale; rather an irritation that won't go away.

Pilonidal sinus is a condition which mostly affects hairy men, although it is not that uncommon in women. The problem occurs at the upper end of the internatal cleft, the 'builder's cleavage', the top end of the space between the buttocks. Hairs which have been shed from the back lodge there and then work their way in through the skin rather like the way an ear of barley, with its projecting hairs, will work its way up your sleeve. A lot of sitting and bouncing around on a hard surface, like for instance the seat of a jeep, or maybe in my case an endless flight to Hong Kong in a de Havilland Comet, encourages the formation of little holes, sinuses which get infected. Recurrent infection leads to abscess formation, for which the only effective treatment is surgery.

I had the best of surgeons but recuperation involved lying on my stomach for a couple of weeks. Very tedious but I was kept cheerful by my neighbours on the Officers' Ward. On one side was a retired fighter pilot having severe hand contractures dealt with. He had already undergone many operations (elsewhere) and was now wearing what is called an aeroplane splint: his shoulder was elevated to ninety degrees and his elbow flexed to ninety degrees, the whole supported on a frame. On the other side was a war-time Lancaster pilot having plastic surgery for reconstruction of the tendons of his right foot, which had been crushed when his bomber crashed. He wore a below-knee plaster.

Both were amusing characters and when, a few days after I had been allowed up for the first time, the subject of a few illicit pints at the Red Lion in Wendover came up, the vote was one hundred per cent in favour.

We let ourselves out at dusk on a late spring evening; it was downhill all the way – in more than one sense. After three weeks in hospital, the spring air was delicious, the birds were twittering in the trees and we made a clownish trio as we staggered along. On the right a character with his arm stuck in the air, on the left another with his lower leg encased in plaster and in the middle me, with an obvious large pad attached to my rear and walking bent to some forty-five degrees.

We made it, we had quite a few and then what I was dreading happened – we were offered a lift up the hill to the hospital.

The other two were very pleased; they installed themselves in the back of the car, one with his arm projecting out of one rear window, the other with his plastered leg sticking out the opposite rear window. My problem was I couldn't sit. After being eased into the front passenger seat, I had to kneel on it with my bottom facing forwards towards the windscreen while I could only gaze back at my companions laughing at my predicament. We made it and managed to creep back to our rooms without the night sister spotting us.

The old Lancaster pilot happened to be the secretary to the Hallé Orchestra, and he was visited frequently by its celebrated conductor, Sir John Barbirolli. Bored as we were, we hatched a plot with Sir John's complicity. We selected the two prettiest nurses on the ward and Sir John gave them complimentary tickets for a performance of the Hallé due to take place in a few days in the Royal Festival Hall, London.

In the meantime, we three had our photograph taken together. We each pulled the most outlandish face we could. The photo was framed, wrapped in brown paper and given to Sir John.

At the performance, it was announced in the interval that there would be a special presentation for the 'millionth member' of the audience. The ticket number was called out and, surprised but delighted, one of our nurses went to the podium to be presented with the 'prize' by Sir John Barbirolli... who told her not to open it until after the performance.

She did wait, but only until Sir John had left the podium. We learned later that the two of them simultaneously burst into gales of laughter, clutched each other helplessly, tears streaming down their faces. The amused and puzzled audience, ignorant of the nature of the prize, gazed perplexed as it filed out.

The following night when we climbed into our beds we each found a sprig of holly nestling between the sheets.

I MET MY ORTHOPAEDIC SURGEON IN London for the first time on the day before the operation. I handed over the four units of blood. He re-examined my x-rays and took a look at me. After the examination, he told me that without his ministrations I would be permanently wheelchair-bound in a matter of months. He reassured me that, as already agreed, I would be given antibiotic cover and protection against thrombosis.

The operation lasted a couple of hours and after an hour in the recovery ward I was back in my room. All was well. Next day the surgeon came to see me, expressed extreme satisfaction with his work (surgeons often do, have you noticed?) and to my surprise announced that he was going to be away for a couple of days. He had booked a skiing holiday some time ago; already his family was enjoying the slopes in France. "Nothing to worry about," he reassured me, "you'll be in good hands because my anaesthetist will be keeping an eye on you." And with that he was off. I was rather put out but the surgeon was confident.

Three days after the operation, I had a massive pulmonary embolism.

The timing was awful, couldn't have been much worse; it happened at half past two on a Sunday afternoon. My memory is as stark today as it was fifteen years ago. The duty physiotherapist was helping me out of bed for the first time since the operation, when I was seized by extreme breathlessness, a sense of constriction in my chest, a feeling of faintness and an overwhelming need to lie down.

I quickly lay on my bed and Maria called for help which arrived in the form of a garrulous Irish nurse.

"What's up, Bill?" she demanded. I couldn't speak for breathlessness. "Are you not feeling too grand, Bill? Would you like a glass of water, Bill?"

"O-x-y-g-e-n," I croaked. "D-o-c-t-or," I managed to get out.

"Well, let's sit you up, Bill," said the wretched woman. Now patients having a large pulmonary embolus need to lie down and she was forcing me up... Maria intervened, "Get a doctor!" she commanded.

There was just one problem with that. The hospital was private, not large, about 140 beds, and had only one doctor on call: a junior doctor earning pocket money by doing a weekend locum. Fortunately he was good. He quickly took an electrocardiogram; while he took it, I asked him if I had been getting the injections of low molecular weight heparin. He said he would take a look at my drug chart. He organised a portable chest x-ray.

When he returned to show me the electrocardiogram, I could hardly believe my ears when he said that I had not been getting the heparin. Then I looked at the cardiac trace and made the diagnosis for him – my own diagnosis – and it was bad! 'S1Q3T3' it shrieked at me: a wave pattern diagnostic of a serious pulmonary embolism.

The chest x-ray showed appearances compatible with a pulmonary embolus. I was given oxygen but I needed heparin to break down the embolus (clot) and I needed it to prevent further emboli flying down my veins to my heart. I needed expert attention and the junior doctor needed help. He could not locate the anaesthetist who was supposed to be looking after me. My surgeon was presumably at that moment zipping down some Alpine slope with not a care in the world.

Two-thirds of the functional capacity of my lungs had been damaged. I was desperately short of breath but even through my intense distress I could recall the statistics... they were frightening: a patient who survives the initial large pulmonary embolism – and a lot don't – has, without treatment, a fifty per cent chance of a second embolism in the next twenty-four hours and a fifty per cent chance of dying of that second embolism.

Eventually the hospital located a cardiologist. He came to see me at ten thirty, eight hours after the embolism, prescribed the heparin and had me moved to the Intensive Care Unit (ICU). I was still short of breath and had a low blood oxygen level according to the pulse oximeter – a clever little instrument which measures the degree of oxygen saturation of the blood – attached to my finger. I was actually feeling better, but the ICU soon put an end to that...

There were four beds in the unit. One was occupied by a very old and very deaf man. Why he was in intensive care is anybody's guess. Maybe it had something to do with the hospital being contracted to look after a certain number of NHS patients – and being able to charge a good deal more for a bed in the ICU than one on a ward.

Whatever the reason for his being there, the old fellow was getting his money's worth by watching the TV with the sound extraordinarily loud. When I complained, the nurse patiently explained the obvious, that this poor old chap needed the volume up because he was very deaf.

"But I'm feeling very ill," I protested... in vain, as my ears were assailed by the noise of a tribe of Commanches pursuing John Wayne with murderous intent, a thought not far from my own feelings for the custodians of this private hospital's allegedly fine reputation.

When the old chap was given a sleeping pill, the telly was switched off but my night was restless. He was an Olympic gold medal snorer and every ten minutes, the ICU phone rang. Many of the calls were social but some were about a patient who had died just a few hours before. Hearing the unsympathetic tones of the nursing staff breaking the news to enquiring relatives did nothing to buoy my spirits; the unsettling thought occurred that I might be lying in the very bed in which he had recently breathed his last... maybe he had succumbed to a post-operative pulmonary embolus?

Fortunately my condition improved. Maria stayed with me in ICU until two in the morning. Exhausted, she told the nurse where she would be, went back to my room and slept there. For the privilege, she was charged £100 while my night in the ICU ratcheted up the costs still further. And meanwhile, that blighter who had unilaterally decided not to give me the heparin protection I needed was merrily quaffing an *après ski*.

In the morning, a large, smiling, handsome West Indian staff nurse arrived to give me a wash. While she energetically chewed gum (she had an eye-riveting trick of moving it from side to side in front of her teeth without seeming to propel it) she hummed, and occasionally broke into a phrase of *Abide with me*, rated in England as one of the most popular hymns – at funeral services.

The next day when the anaesthetist – who was supposed to be looking after me – appeared, I demanded of him why I had not been given the injections of low molecular weight heparin to prevent precisely what had happened. He told me that the surgeon had decided, towards the end of the operation, that it wasn't necessary for me to have it.

"But it had been agreed that I should have it," I protested.

"You'll have to take it up with the surgeon when he returns," he said.

I suspected, and still do, that the surgeon didn't give me the treatment for fear of an increased risk of bleeding into the operation site, in which case another surgeon would have to be called in because he could not be reached. Another surgeon: his fee split – hmm.

When he did return, despite the evidence to the contrary, the surgeon refused to believe that I had suffered a pulmonary embolus and said that he thought I might have had a 'mild coronary attack'.

Four days after surgery, I developed pains in my feet. The pains were severe and continuous, so severe that I couldn't bear to have the bedclothes on my feet. Couldn't bear to have bedclothes touch my feet... where had I heard that before? Gout!

There were dusky red patches on my feet and when the disbelieving surgeon reluctantly ordered the appropriate blood test, I was indeed shown to have that condition. Gout is generally associated with port-swilling, florid-faced retired colonels in basket chairs with an elevated leg. People who do not suffer from gout may find it mirth-provoking. But believe me, there are few conditions much more painful than acute gout.

As if having it wasn't bad enough, another complication was that I couldn't take the modern anti-inflammatory drugs which are so effective in gout because they would react badly with the control of the anticoagulant treatment. Instead, I had to rely on an old-fashioned treatment using colchicine, a true herbal remedy as it is an extract of the stamens of the autumn crocus.

I had treated patients with colchicine in the distant past and knew that the correct way to administer the medication was to give frequent doses until the pain went; but that would almost inevitably cause diarrhoea.

So there I was, lying sick in bed feeling rotten with feet causing agony, a painful post-operative hip, still short of breath and to top it all had developed diarrhoea with desperate urgency. Reader, this was not funny, at least not at the time.

The only way to get to the en-suite bathroom was to stagger across the room keeping the weight off my operated leg by using crutches. I'd never in my life used crutches, but I rapidly learned. It was a very fraught couple of days until the gout settled.

Our old friend Nicholas Woodhouse had been phoning regularly from

Saudi Arabia for updates. He was due in London for a medical conference and came to the hospital to see me. Delighted to have him with us, Maria decided that it was the right moment to celebrate by opening the bottle of champagne which lay in the refrigerator in my room; it had been a gift from the hospital when I was admitted. As I was on anticoagulants, I couldn't join them but this didn't dampen their enthusiasm as they merrily clinked glasses and demolished the bottle.

Observing the private hospital from the patient's perspective was an eye-opener. It suffered from having few permanent nurses on its staff. Most of its nurses were hired from agencies. This meant there was lack of continuity of care and less than the best standards. Most of the nurses were from Ireland and the Caribbean, and they were a pretty poor lot. I had to check my medications to be sure that they had been properly dispensed, and on a couple of occasions I had been given the medication of the patient next door, "Oops," the nurse would say, "silly me."

The final straw came after I had been discharged and was having a shower at home. Maria had a look at my wound and in some astonishment announced, "Darling, it looks to me like you still have a staple in your leg." A district nurse removed it.

It would have taken a glutton for punishment to have a second hip operation performed by that surgeon in that hospital. I wasn't and I didn't. It was carried out six months later in a London teaching hospital; I sailed through, I was always given the right treatment and had no complications. The nursing staff was mostly from Ireland and the Caribbean – without exception, they were brilliant.

The arrogant surgeon who almost closed my case notes prematurely found himself on the receiving end of legal action. It was in my view a straightforward case. I wasn't seeking vast compensation but I wanted him to appreciate the gravity of what he had done and for him to reflect on his cavalier attitude. Perhaps it might help a future patient. I won; it was an open-and-shut case.

But I also learned a lesson from my first involvement with the legal profession. Lawyers can make life difficult for a reason. The case could have been settled in a few weeks but took two years – if lawyers charge by the hour there's no percentage in a quick settlement. Imagine what life would be like if doctors did the same…

READING THE MEDICAL JOURNALS WHILE passing a few weeks convalescing in our flat in Earls Court in London, I came across an interesting technique guaranteed to make the obese lose weight. It seemed to be right up my street as it employed endoscopy.

Although the concept was simple, it required some endoscopic skill. The technique consisted of introducing a balloon into the stomach, inflating it and leaving it there for six months. The balloon was shaped like a small rugby football and, when inflated, filled the stomach. Obviously patients would lose their appetites and when they did eat, they would feel full very quickly – couldn't fail!

My first patient was a man in his forties who lived in Abu Dhabi. He was very, very fat. In six months, he lost twenty kilogrammes. News got around, the local press latched on to what I was doing; soon obese folk were beating a path to my door and queuing up for the balloon.

Two patients came from far afield, Riyadh and Qatar. I agreed to insert balloons in their stomachs on the strict understanding that they would travel back to Dubai for me to follow their progress and to remove the balloons after six months, or earlier if there were problems. Understanding is one thing; doing is quite another. I never saw those patients again after I had inserted the balloons. They were uncontactable: each had given a phone number that didn't exist.

My first patient meanwhile was delighted with his twenty kilo weight loss. After six months, I removed his balloon. In three months, he had regained what he had lost. He begged to have another balloon inserted; reluctantly I agreed. This time he didn't lose weight; in fact, he managed to gain a couple of kilos.

Altogether I treated and followed more than forty patients; half were women and half were men. After an initial few days of discomfort, most told me that while they continued to quickly feel full when they ate, they had no abnormal sensations in their abdomens.

When I analysed my results two years after I started the procedure, I found that the average weight loss in the women I treated was zero, and in the twenty men less than two kilos. I gave up. Obesity isn't in the stomach, it's mostly in the brain and stomachs quickly adapt to balloons bobbing around in them.

Surgical techniques used nowadays for morbid obesity either shrink the volume of the stomach permanently or, by bypassing the stomach and much of the intestine, drastically reduce food absorption.

THE SUDDEN DEATH OF A GOOD FRIEND made us realise that some traditions, like burial and cremation, do not travel particularly well. We attended our friend's funeral service in the Dubai Anglican Church – where we sang *Abide with me* – and a touching graveside service of commitment in the non-Muslim cemetery near the Creek. I had not visited it before. It was in a poor state. Very few of the graves were tended; most were of those whose relatives had long departed Dubai. Remnants of wreaths littered the place and blue plastic supermarket bags were scattered about clinging to the walls and trees, blown there by the wind.

One corner of the cemetery was at the time reserved for Hindu cremations. I'm told that now there is an electrically-operated crematorium in Jebel Ali, near the Free Zone. But the story I heard did not suggest the usual hyper-efficiency of such establishments; perhaps the concept, like that of tending graves, is just too foreign.

Apparently the crematorium was set up for the large Hindu population of Dubai but was made available for others. It happened that the services of the facility were needed for the remains of a staff member of a company managed by a friend, Maureen Ashton. With all the formalities satisfied – a death certificate, a 'no objection' certificate from his sponsor, a certificate of approval by the municipal authorities and another from the Dubai police, cancellation of his visa and payment of the hefty crematorium fee – the cremation was allowed to proceed.

But there was no such thing as a hearse available. So Maureen, with a colleague for moral support, took the body to the crematorium in the back of her four-wheel drive. She arrived a few minutes ahead of the appointed hour only to learn that the electric oven had not reached operating temperature and would take another four hours to do so. She was asked to come back later but was told that she couldn't leave the deceased at the crematorium. Off they drove, taking the enshrouded corpse with them.

Four hours and many cups of coffee later, they returned. When they did, they found that the two of them had themselves to push the body into the furnace.

After the furnace had cooled, Maureen was given a rake to retrieve the ashes but there were still large fragments of bone. An assistant put these in what looked like a huge kitchen mixer and ground them to dust. A small sample of the ash was placed in an urn to send to the dead man's relatives in India. Maureen was left with the remainder, which filled a large cardboard box.

Books and schools don't teach you how to deal with situations like this; sometimes you just have to go with the flow – literally. Not knowing what else to do, and reasoning that the departed had never wanted to leave Dubai, Maureen and her friend tipped the residual ashes out of the box, at dead of night, over the side of the Maktoum Bridge into Dubai Creek.

Twenty Three

I NEVER CEASED TO MARVEL, WHEN I wandered into our pathology laboratory, at the wide range of tests we could do, the speed at which we could do them and the accuracy of the results. When I was a medical student, I could spend a whole morning in the biochemistry laboratory measuring the level of urea in a sample of blood – and getting it wrong. Now we could do that measurement in a few minutes and get it right every time. We could perform tests, unheard of just a few years before, using methods which were remarkably simple and accurate; we could do a complete thyroid screen; test the urine for drugs of addiction; screen for AIDS; test the function of the liver and kidneys and so on, and all very, very quickly. In most cases, the results were available on the same day – no question of coming back in a couple of weeks; we doctors and our patients wanted quick results for a quick diagnosis.

We performed blood counts in an automated apparatus: no peering down a microscope at a grid etched on a slide and counting the individual blood cells one by one – and having to start all over when your neighbour distracted you, perhaps asking if you fancied a pint that evening.

But I had qualified getting on for half a century before and a lot had happened in those five decades; formidable advances in clinical and laboratory medicine. There had been huge strides in medical imaging; the addition of computer technology resulted in the development of unbelievable scanning techniques.

Take ultrasound. The first ultrasound apparatus I encountered in my junior doctor days was primitive and had limited applications. It could be used on a newborn's head and if a cerebral haemorrhage was suspected, it could detect the shift of midline structures. And here I was in my clinic where we had our own sophisticated apparatus and our very competent radiologist,

Dr Khailash Gusani, who could among other things show babies moving in-utero, demonstrate thyroid glands, testicular masses, measure the size of prostates and display kidneys as if they were anatomical drawings.

I recalled that, up to the beginning of the seventies, to view x-ray procedures we had to wear red goggles for twenty minutes and then we peered at shadowy images on a fluorescent screen in the darkened x-ray department. I could seldom distinguish what I was supposed to see; I couldn't spot a duodenal ulcer until the x-ray doctor, the radiologist, pointed it out. But it turned out later, when endoscopy arrived and the truth was revealed, that his guess wasn't much better than mine.

Clinical medicine in my time had advanced at an exponential rate; I considered myself privileged to have witnessed it.

Medicine was in its own Dark Ages until the Age of Enlightenment came along. This movement, beginning in eighteenth century Europe, sought to establish knowledge based on enlightened 'rationality'. It was to lead Europe out of irrationality and superstition. One might say, from a modern perspective, that when conventional medicine moved out of the Dark Ages, it left behind those elements which nowadays are graced by the labels 'alternative' or 'complementary' therapies.

The Medical Age of Enlightenment began properly with the first controlled trial. It wasn't double blind but it was, nevertheless, a properly constructed clinical study. It was carried out by an Englishman who is a particular hero of mine and with whom I have a couple of things in common. Like me, he was a military doctor (but Royal Navy) and he also became a Fellow of the Royal College of Physicians of Edinburgh.

His name was James Lind and he wrote *A Treatise of the Scurvy, 1753.* Scurvy is a horrible disease; sufferers bleed into their skin, their gums become spongy and bleed, their teeth fall out, their breath becomes foul, their wounds break open and suppurate. Patients lose all energy; they become anaemic and die. Scurvy had been described by Hippocrates. Since time immemorial, scurvy has afflicted mariners at sea on long voyages and populations under siege without fresh food supplies.

These days everyone knows that scurvy is caused by a deficiency of vitamin C, but that vitamin was not identified until 1933 by a Hungarian scientist, Szent-Györgi, who was awarded the Nobel Prize four years later for his discovery.

In May 1747, James Lind was the surgeon on board HMS *Salisbury*, beating its way up the southwestern approaches to Plymouth. The *Salisbury* had been at sea for many weeks and there was the usual outbreak of scurvy on board. At that time, Lind believed scurvy was due to 'a putrefaction of the body and might be prevented by acids'. In his treatise, he wrote of those with the scurvy, 'they all in general had putrid gums, the spots and lassitude… they lay together in one place, being a proper apartment for the sick in the fore-hold; and had one diet in common to all…'

Surgeon Lind divided twelve scorbutic sailors into six pairs. To one pair he gave a quart of cider a day; a second pair 'twenty five gutts [drops] of elixir vitriol [sulphuric acid] a day upon an empty stomach'; a third pair were given a course of sea water, half a pint daily (it gave them diarrheoa); another pair 'two spoonfuls of vinegar three times a day upon an empty stomach'; the fifth pair were given an electuary (a medicine mixed with honey) of garlic, mustard seed, balsam of Peru and gum myrrh. The lucky ones, the last two, were given two oranges and a lemon every day.

The improvement in the sailors eating the citrus fruit was rapid and remarkable; one 'became at the end of six days fit four [sic] duty' and the other was 'appointed to nurse the rest of the sick and became quite healthy before we came into Plymouth, which was on the 16th June.'

Lind did not publish his treatise for six years and it took until 1795 for their Lordships of the Admiralty to accept his work. They then issued instructions that British sailors should be given citrus fruit every day. They chose limes. Why limes when they have only a quarter the content of vitamin C of lemons and lemons were easily available? It so happened that several members of the Navy Board had lime plantations in the Caribbean.

The Yankee sailors taunted the British sailors, calling them 'limeys' or more explicitly 'goddamnedlimeys' in the Anglo-American war of 1812-15. The Americans ridiculed the British sailors for sucking a lime every day, but the Brits had the last laugh when the Yanks' teeth popped out and their breath became as foetid as a bear's armpit.

What I liked about James Lind was that he had a brilliant and inquisitive mind. He showed that the steam produced by boiling sea water could be condensed to form fresh water – that has saved more than a few lives. He was working on solar power to effect the transformation but then a very efficient stove for use at sea was invented.

In 1758, Lind was appointed chief physician to the Royal Naval Hospital Haslar in Portsmouth. He soon observed that typhus (a louse-borne disease) didn't occur in the top floor of his hospital. Why then did it continue to rage through the floors below? Hygiene was the simple answer. On the top floor, patients were bathed and given clean clothes and bedding.

Typhus was a big problem at sea until Lind recommended that regularly, 'sailors should be stripped, scrubbed, shaved and issued with clean clothes and bedding.' The mind boggles at the picture conjured up of Her Majesty's Jolly Jack Tars of today being ordered to follow Lind's instructions en masse; just under ten per cent of crews on seagoing ships of the Royal Navy nowadays are women.

Back then, the strict standards of hygiene of the lime-sucking sailors gave a great advantage to the British Fleet. At Trafalgar in 1805, the French and Spaniards were not only outsmarted by Nelson; their sailors did not have as much fight in them – they were an unhealthy bunch of louse-ridden tramps.

MY OTHER HERO IN THE EMERGENCE of medicine from the Dark Ages was French, a man named Claude Bernard. He was an interesting fellow. His father was a wine grower. Claude didn't think much of that as a career, so at the age of nineteen, he became an assistant to a Monsieur Millet, a druggist in Lyon.

But Claude's real ambition was to be a playwright and, after some success with a few pieces for the vaudeville theatres in Lyon, he wrote a play. M Millet was not impressed and dispensed with Claude's services. A critic in Paris agreed with the druggist and, happily for the benefit of mankind, persuaded the young Claude to take up something more reliable like medicine.

Claude Bernard was not a brilliant student until he came under the influence of another great name in French medical science, François Magendie, who was the first to spot a tiny hole in the brain which is now called the Foramen of Magendie. Claude blossomed and shot up the ladder of academic and experimental medicine.

You may not have heard of Claude Bernard and neither had I until I went to University College London in 1952. In our introduction to physiology we were told that, whenever during the course of a lecture the name Claude Bernard was mentioned, we must show homage. We were to stamp our feet, whistle, clap, cheer, whatever. We needed no bidding; enthusiastically we erupted... I would like to think that they still do it at UCL today.

Claude Bernard demonstrated that pancreatic juices and bile were necessary for the absorption of fat from the gut. He also showed that the liver could manufacture glucose from a starchy substance stored in the liver which he called glycogen. He further demonstrated that nerve impulses, in what we now call the sympathetic nervous system, controlled the diameter and hence the pressure inside blood vessels. He also studied carbon monoxide poisoning and the effects of curare.

But it was his concept of the *milieu intérieur* that was to revolutionise the science of medicine. He postulated that an animal's external environment was always changing, but that in order to survive an animal had to maintain a constant internal environment.

A simple concept, but nobody had thought of it.

Thus, for example, the body temperature is regulated to keep it around thirty-seven degrees centigrade. Should we get too hot, various mechanisms come into play; the heart speeds up, the blood vessels in our skin dilate and we lose heat by radiation. We sweat and our skin is cooled when the sweat evaporates.

We have marvellous organs which quietly work away to keep our internal environment steady; liver, lungs, and kidneys are prime workers. So if, for instance, we suspect that a patient has kidney failure, we measure various substances – like the level of urea in the blood or the amount of protein in the urine. If a patient has severe kidney failure, we return his *milieu intérieur* to normal by performing a dialysis to clear his blood of impurities.

If we poison ourselves with too much alcohol, it becomes all too evident that our *milieu intérieur* is up the spout. We get thirsty; alcohol is a diuretic, makes you pee more than you drink. We get a headache from the big veins in the brain being pulled down by dehydration, so we drink more, and the headache gets better. We feel rotten because our liver has exhausted its supply of the enzyme for metabolising alcohol and the metabolism takes alternative, less efficient, pathways producing chemicals which make us feel hung over. In time, when our poor old livers have manufactured more enzymes to get rid of the poisonous by-products and our kidneys, muscles and lungs have played their minor roles, we feel better.

I have it on good authority (and possibly a little personal undergraduate experimentation) that it takes until the next day for the restoration of the *milieu intérieur*.

Claude Bernard's private life was less successful. In 1845, at the age of thirty-three, he married Fanny Martin. She had a nice dowry which would finance his experiments. They had a daughter.

Claude practiced animal experimentation. This disgusted Fanny and their daughter. They left and founded an antivivisection movement.

His greatest written contribution to science was a book entitled *An introduction to experimental medicine*. When he died in 1878, the French government accorded him a state funeral, a first for a scientist. One of his pupils in a memorable eulogy declared, "No one ever made discoveries more simply, more naïvely. He discovered as others breathed."

Whether it be a heart attack, an inflammation of the liver, a sore throat, or indeed any affliction, Mother Nature and doctors work together to restore the internal milieu of Claude Bernard.

WHEN I ARRIVED IN DUBAI IN THE MID-1980s, it was itself emerging from its own Dark Ages. There were tales of doctors, mostly from the subcontinent, who practised there without qualifications but had pleased the ruler and been given licences on that basis. That's not as bizarre as it sounds: the Archbishop of Canterbury was able to grant medical degrees in England until 1840.

The first computerised tomography scanner arrived in Dubai in 1986. It was in the private sector and had been bought by a group of doctors. It was a rebuilt instrument and not very reliable. In the decade to come, scanners in the private sector multiplied in parallel with the burgeoning population. Soon no private hospital could expect to compete with other private hospitals if it didn't have its own scanner. The even more expensive magnetic resonance imaging scanners became commonplace in the private sector. There were no fewer than twelve of these machines when I left Dubai in 2001; perhaps there were no more than that number in the whole of Greater London at that time.

In my experience, care in the public sector in Dubai was a good deal better than that in Saudi Arabia. Still, in the large government hospitals in Dubai, the standard was like a Met Office shipping forecast: variable, good, very good or occasionally bad.

On one occasion, the manager of the Hatta Fort Hotel, Sergio Magnaldi, called me. His wife, Sandra, was in the Rashid Hospital. "She's doing very badly and nothing seems to be happening. Would you go and take a look at her for me?" he asked.

I always felt reluctant to visit patients without being asked to do so by the hospital doctors, but in this case things were indeed going badly, it was a public holiday and nobody was about. I met Sandra's daughter, Nathalie, at the hospital and she took me to the ward.

Sandra was in a lot of pain; her abdomen was distended, generally tender with muscular guarding. I looked at x-rays taken two days before; they showed intestinal obstruction. The junior doctor on the ward told me that more x-rays were planned in a day or two; "perhaps we might think about an operation then."

But to me it was clear that she needed immediate surgery. I arranged for her to be admitted to Al Zahra Hospital, the private hospital in Sharjah where I had first worked in the UAE, and took her there in my car with Nathalie sitting next to her and holding the infusion bottle on high. An operation was carried out within an hour of her admission. She had a loop of small bowel obstructed by an adhesion, gangrenous and verging on perforation. She made an excellent recovery.

IT HAD ALWAYS BEEN IN MY MIND that the opening of a polyclinic in Dubai would be but the first step toward building a hospital. I spent many hours designing a hospital, with the encouragement of our manager, Miro Vladic, and the sheikh, our sponsor. We found land in a prime area in Dubai and enlisted the support of the secretary to the Ruler of Dubai, Nasser Lootah. We were set to go ahead. But whether Miro and the sheikh got cold feet or whether Miro, who clearly disliked the ruler's secretary's major-domo, had upset him once too often, I will never know, but the hospital plans fizzled out.

On reflection, I wasn't too sorry. Not only had the sheikh displayed no genuine interest, Miro was absent from Dubai for long periods and when he was in Dubai, he had many other business interests. He was Yugoslavian, but held a limited UK passport. On one trip to London, he had submitted his passport for renewal but apparently the passport office had lost it and he couldn't get back into Dubai. He claimed that the administrative difficulties in getting a new passport were almost insurmountable and it took more than a year for him to get a new passport. In the meantime, the every-day running of the clinic fell entirely on my shoulders while he half-heartedly managed it from afar.

Another good reason for me not to get involved in building a hospital was that it would have been a project infinitely more complicated and difficult than setting up the clinic. The clinic had been open for nearly fifteen years and I had begun to admit to myself that I had reached an age when my energy was starting to flag.

Moreover, once it was up and running, a hospital would present all sorts of problems, not least for me in handling the medical staff. One thing that is drilled into doctors in training is to 'think for yourself'. Add to that a mixture of the different attitudes of Middle Eastern, Western and Indian doctors and you get a sure recipe for sleepless nights and an early coronary for whoever is in charge.

We had had a few problem doctors in the clinic, mostly paediatricians, some of whom, like their patients, had yet to grow up.

In the clinic's early days, I was approached by an extremely well-qualified paediatrician, Dr Robert Westcott, who had left his consultant post in a Liverpool teaching hospital. "I like to travel and I enjoy the Middle East," he told me. I invited him around for dinner with other doctors from the clinic; together we could size him up.

He put up a serious black mark when he made an obvious pass at Maria while he was alone with her in the kitchen. But I have quite a different image etched on my mind. He was sitting in an armchair, telling us of his great academic achievements, irritatingly drumming his fingers on the arm of the chair. This caught the attention of our pet cat, Jamila – Arabic for princess. Some princess: she was the most bad-tempered feral cat I have ever come across. As Robert continued to drum, Jamila hunkered down. I watched, as fascinated as Jamila. Suddenly with a screech she launched herself, landed on his hand, bit it, scratched it and fled. Robert leapt out of his chair, alarmed, agitated, grasping his hand and uttering highly unprofessional expletives. We dressed his lacerations, calmed him down and reassured him that we thought Jamila was a healthy cat but asked him if his tetanus shots were up to date. To further give reassurance, we told him that the Dubai Health Services held a stock of rabies vaccine.

The paediatrician had given me the names of three referees, two of whom I wasn't able to contact, but I was able to reach the third, the director of a large hospital in Saudi Arabia. I called him, introduced myself and said, "I've got this paediatrician, Robert Westcott, who wants to join my staff. Do you know him? Can you recommend him?"

"Know him?" he replied in a surprised voice. "I'll say I do. So Dubai is where he is now." I waited. "He's on the run you know; had a bust-up with his wife, she divorced him, he was broke after the divorce so he burned down the family house for the insurance money." He paused, "And what's more, we didn't think he was a good paediatrician; in fact we cut his locum short and asked him to leave."

We bade farewell to Dr Westcott. He got a job with another clinic in the Emirates but faded out of sight after a few months.

Twenty Four

A FEW MONTHS AFTER THE CLINIC opened, I received an intriguing proposal from the owner of another clinic, Abdullah Bahraini, a larger-than-life character, constantly smiling and laughing and the sponsor of a large European trading company. He approached me at a reception at the British Embassy. "Bill," he said, "why don't we join forces? We're not in competition. My clinic is as you know surgical, ear, nose and throat. And yours is mostly medical. Think about it." With that he left me and joined another group elsewhere in the embassy garden.

His clinic may have been officially ENT, but I knew his American surgeon-in-charge, Jack McSweeney, was not above a bit of tinkering around outside his speciality, mostly by carrying out expensive investigations he couldn't interpret, taking cardiograms which he couldn't read and treating illnesses well below the neck.

"My dear fellow," said Abdullah half an hour later as he gravitated back to me, placed an affectionate arm around my shoulder and gave a little squeeze (he'd been privately educated in England), "together we can do great things, your clinic and mine. I know all the important people, I have finance and together we can wrap up medical practice in Dubai. What do you think?"

I said I'd consider it and talk to Miro Vladic, our manager. I didn't really see what would be in it for us and suspected that Abdullah was in need of a rescue operation because Jack McSweeney was performing recklessly and beyond his capabilities.

Life became fraught for 'Jack the Knife' after he unwisely removed the tonsils of a young lady under local anaesthesia in his clinic. She nearly bled to death. Her father was a powerful local. Soon the Department of Health was on his case – when suddenly he disappeared. But he wasn't alone. Jack

McSweeney took with him an English lady who had fallen for his charm. She had the added attraction of being the accountant of a very large real estate company. Together they fled with a huge lump of cash, the company's takings for the year.

Within days we learned it wasn't the first time Jack had done a runner. Originally he qualified and practised in California, but moved on from there when he was disbarred for interfering with young boys while they were under anaesthesia. He moved to Bahrain but was soon in the same trouble there, then to South Africa, same story. Where he went after Dubai, nobody knows, but his wandering hands certainly led to a wandering existence.

I HAD A TOTALLY DIFFERENT EXPERIENCE with another American doctor, Barbara Jones. Barbara was an obstetrician and gynaecologist. She was a delightful person, not beautiful but whatever she lacked in appearance she more than made up with her capability, charm and kindness. She applied for a job in the clinic and I hired her.

One morning, about two years after she joined the clinic, Barbara came to see me in my office. It emerged that she had serious problems with her marriage – sadly not uncommon in mixed culture unions. Hesitantly at first, she revealed her harrowing story.

Back in the United States, she had met an Egyptian and fallen for him. They married and had a daughter, now six years old. When the company he worked for posted him back to Egypt, she accompanied him.

The marriage was in tatters; his family treated her abominably. Himself, he was domineering, jealous and violent, especially if she as much as talked to or smiled at another man. She did not have much of a life in Egypt and was relieved when her husband was posted to Dubai.

She went on, "I have to leave him, Dr Larkworthy, for the sake of my sanity and my daughter." I nodded. "I tried once, you know, but we only got as far as the airport. He discovered that I had left with my little girl, we had reached the departures lounge and were about to board our flight. I had enough money, I had our passports and we were nearly free." She choked a little. "He came with a couple of policemen and had me arrested within yards of the boarding gate. The police took me to our flat. They gave me a lecture on the correct way a wife should behave towards her husband in an Islamic marriage and left. Then he beat me, took away our passports and threatened to kill me if I ever attempted again to leave him.

"But Dr Larkworthy, I must tell you now that one day I will not appear for work and for that I apologise. I am making arrangements with my family and a government department in the United States. When it happens I want you to know that I have been very happy working in this fine clinic and I want to thank you for all the kindness you have shown me."

I was touched and told Barbara that I would be very sorry to lose her.

A couple of months later, it happened. Barbara did not turn up one morning. When I finally learned the details, from a source I cannot reveal, it was like a story lifted out of a novel.

Barbara had been told by her husband that at some time in the future, he would be sent by his company to Russia. But he also told her, "Since I don't trust you, you will both come; you will remain in the hotel room for all the time I am there; you will eat in your room; you will go out only when I am with you. I shall inform the hotel of my wishes."

Barbara phoned her family in the States and told them what might happen.

One evening after dinner her husband told her that they would be leaving for Moscow in two days; they would be there for fours days while he attended a conference. And he repeated the restrictions he would impose on her and her daughter.

Luckily Barbara was called to an emergency at the clinic that evening and was able to phone her parents. Her father instantly put into action the arrangements he had made for her escape. It involved a US government department, the Russian mafia and a considerable sum of money.

When they reached Moscow, the Russian mafia soon located them. While her husband was at the conference, she received word to be ready to leave at three the following morning. She and her daughter would be picked up outside the hotel and taken to the airport. The mafia promised they could take care of any problems with her husband but, nonetheless, she had to leave the hotel without being spotted by the staff.

They left without waking her husband, who had enjoyed generous traditional Russian hospitality that evening. Barbara and her little girl crept past the reception desk when the night porter's back was turned. Once outside in the street, the mafia bundled them into a car, handed them special passports which had been supplied by the American Embassy and took them to the airport where they boarded a flight straight to the United States.

In the US, Barbara and her daughter disappeared with new identities. Her family had made the arrangements and supplied the money, but she would not be allowed to contact them for ten years.

What happened in Dubai? Her husband came to see me in my office. He told me he planned to lodge a report with the Dubai police because he knew the clinic was complicit in her escape. I denied any part. I heard no more.

A couple of weeks later, I learned there was a hot rumour circulating in Dubai that the clinic had sacked Barbara and that she had been sent out of the country with no terminal benefits. Dubai is too small a place for that kind of nonsense to be left to fester, so I published a notice in the local press in which I announced that she had left for family reasons, that we were very sorry to lose her and that we wished her well in the future.

ONE MORNING, IN THE MIDDLE OF MY clinic, what I thought was a new patient sat in front of me. "Are you Doctor William Larkworthy?" he asked.

"I am," I replied.

He handed me a large brown envelope. I hesitated; he said, "I don't have to place this in your hand, I can just place it on your desk and it will be properly served. It is a summons concerning a patient whose case you mishandled two years ago." He got up and left.

I sat dumbfounded. I couldn't believe it. I was being sued for malpractice – a physician's biggest nightmare.

The case was that of a young man called Stephen Nelson who had recently undergone a kidney transplant in his home city, Liverpool, and was claiming that if he had been properly treated from the outset, he would not have come to need a transplant. This was the first and only time in my forty-odd years of practice that the suggestion of negligence had been dumped at my door. I was distressed; I was to lose many hours sleep.

I remembered Stephen. He was a young man working as a shipping trader in Dubai. He bought shiploads of anything – garlic, crude oil, timber – and in a few days, when he had found a buyer, sold the cargoes on, usually making a generous profit.

According to Stephen's file, he had first attended the clinic one evening four years earlier with a trivial complaint, an inflammation of the external ear. The doctor who saw him was thorough, not only treated his ear but checked his blood pressure. It was very high; the doctor told him he had a problem and gave him an appointment to see me in a few days. He didn't turn up.

The next time he came to the clinic was a year and a half – eighteen months – later. I saw him then, again about something trivial. I noted the blood pressure level recorded a year and a half before, checked it and found it still disconcertingly high. I told him that because his blood pressure was so high, we would need to carry out a series of tests to determine the cause and to treat it. I arranged for him to return for the tests in a couple of days. He didn't keep the appointment.

I next saw Stephen a year later. By then he was really ill and finally agreed to have investigations. He had kidney failure; it was serious. We discussed the best way to handle his case. I advised him that he should return to his home in Liverpool and be referred urgently by his GP to a kidney specialist at the university hospital there. I gave him a detailed report and copies of the results of our tests.

About six weeks later, I saw him again. He had come back from Liverpool where he had been thoroughly assessed. He had been given treatment and told that he could only return to Dubai on the understanding that he would be under close medical care and would need to return to Liverpool, at intervals, for checks on his progress. His kidney specialist gave me a full report. It wasn't good: Stephen had advanced kidney disease. He was taking medications to control his blood pressure, his blood chemistry was abnormal and he needed close supervision.

But he wouldn't keep appointments. My nurses spoke to Stephen's wife who attended with her children. She understood how important it was for him to be kept under close watch but she could not make him come to the clinic.

The next I heard of him was when the summons appeared. As he was receiving legal aid, he had nothing to lose and a lawyer in Liverpool was happy to string it out as long as possible.

Common sense dictated that he didn't have a leg to stand on: it was his fault if in the first place he didn't turn up for eighteen months and then again not for a year – but was it entirely? Should I have made more strenuous efforts to contact him, efforts beyond phoning him to remind him of appointments? Strange things were happening in those days (and still do); patients were suing doctors for trivial and nonsensical complaints and winning. The driving principle was that if something went wrong somebody must be to blame... and who is the best one to sue? The doctor, of course.

Although my case was watertight, I lost sleep. I was worried that I did not have proper protection. Miro Vladic had arranged cheap insurance locally but the insurer would not take on the case because it had happened long before the current policy had been taken out. Up to then I had been insured by the Medical Protection Society but Miro and our sheikh deemed it to be too expensive to continue. I talked to lawyers in Dubai. They made reassuring noises but said there were 'difficulties' because all my assets in the United Kingdom could be seized if he won the case.

Stephen was not only suing me, he was also suing the clinic, but our Maktoum sheikh sponsor said he wouldn't even bother to communicate with the lawyer because English law has no jurisdiction in Dubai. He was fireproof.

I worried; I was on my own. Then I contacted the Medical Protection Society in England and was given the number of one of their medico-legal experts. I phoned him, introduced myself and his first question was, "Are you Bill Larkworthy?" I said I was; he said, "You may not remember me but I was a doctor in the RAF and based at Akrotiri Hospital in Cyprus when you used to visit. I'm Bill Smith."

I remembered him – and seldom can an old acquaintance have been renewed with such enthusiasm. I was relieved to have an ally. Bill was extremely reassuring when he heard the details. I sent him all the documents; fortunately, as usual, my clinical notes were good. "Leave it with me," he said as he rang off.

Six weeks later, the case was dropped. I knew all along that I was in a strong position, but no matter how strong it appeared to be, I still had doubts and had suffered an enormous amount of anxiety.

IN THE AFTERMATH OF THE CASE, I came to realise how badly I had been shaken by the malpractice threat. The outcome had totally cleared me – it was a ridiculous case from the start – but nonetheless for me it had been touch and go, and apart from the experts of the Medical Protection Society, there was no-one batting for me.

With no hospital on the horizon, I adjusted my mind and got used to the idea that the clinic would be the end of the road as far as my career was concerned. This was as far as we were going to go.

Moreover – and it was a big 'moreover' – Dubai had changed over the years; no longer a land of optimism and opportunity, no longer the continued growth and expansion of the sort envisioned by Sheikh Rashid, it had become like a child with an attention deficit hyperactivity disorder. New projects, crazy projects, attention-seeking projects had mushroomed: an indoor ski slope, a Formula 1 racing track, an elevated railway between Dubai and Abu Dhabi. Artificial lakes and lagoons were contemplated, islands of reclaimed land offshore were planned for the very rich, the roads were choked with traffic, driving courtesy had long since disappeared, the air was polluted, skyscrapers continued to sprout, the tallest building in the world was contemplated – where was it all going to end? Did I want to be there when it did?

Medical practice too was changing. All the trappings of Western society don't come without 'health warnings', and you only needed to look around at the increasing number of seriously obese Emiratis to see the consequences of over-everything.

The idea of retirement suddenly lost its dread; it would not be the end, it could be the beginning of a new life. With a conscious lightening of my spirit, I resolved that while I would continue to practise good medicine, I would enjoy myself. This was as far as I would be going and until I retired, I would enjoy life in Dubai.

To enjoy yourself in Dubai wasn't difficult. Providing you weren't looking for what might be called 'cultural pursuits', there were many diversions. Dubai was fast becoming not only the geographical hub of the Middle East, it was becoming a popular holiday destination and a highly respected financial and business centre. Dubai boasted that it was becoming the Hong Kong of the Middle East.

In the summer in Dubai, not much happened. With temperatures reaching fifty degrees some days and humidity constantly hovering around eighty per cent, life was dominated by the need to keep cool – homes, cars, offices, shops, restaurants all had airconditioning. Electricity bills in the summer were huge.

Despite the conditions, the summers were in a way pleasant because the population dropped dramatically. Families took extended leave in Europe and the local Emiratis, if they could, fled to cooler places. That left the beaches and hotel pools for the mad dogs and Englishmen who had been sold ridiculously cheap package holidays to this exotic location.

The in-between seasons were perfect for exploring closer to home; places like the Musandam Peninsula, a part of the Oman that projects like a finger into the Strait of Hormuz, and its capital, Khasab. It had one hotel when we visited in 2000, a half-star establishment, but it was comfortable and sold cans of beer, albeit at an outrageous price.

The peninsula has so many islands and fiords that it's been dubbed 'The Norway of Arabia.' For centuries the haunt of isolated fishermen and their families, this terrain now provides the perfect cover for a more ambitious and altogether riskier trade, as we discovered when we chugged back into port after a day cruising the area on a *dhow*.

Strange goings-on greeted us in Khasab. The roads leading down to the harbour were full of a bizarre collection of objects, refrigerators, television sets, dismantled cars and stacks of cartons of cigarettes.

"What's this?" I asked our guide.

"Oh, it's for smugglers," he replied. "You need to be here in a couple of hours to see the smugglers leave."

"Where are they going?" I asked.

"Why to Iran, of course."

I was told that wholesale smuggling between the Oman and Iran was a well-established practice and had been going on for generations. Originally there had been a few problems with the authorities, particularly with the Omani Customs, but the Iranian Customs had sent a delegation across to talk to the Omanis. The delegation was well-armed and in no time at all an agreement was reached. The Iranians would 'control' the operations and would exact a fee for their services.

From Iran, the smugglers would bring carpets, goats, sheep and the products of poppy culture; the boats would return laden with electrical goods, cars and most of all millions of cigarettes. The only stipulation made by the Omani authorities was that the smugglers should reach the Oman in daylight and depart before sunset. Seemed reasonable enough…

Our guide advised us to gather at the harbour's edge to watch the smugglers departure that evening – it would be "very, very exciting; very,

very interesting." How many boats? Maybe sixty, all open, about ten metres long with powerful diesel engines. To my eye they were dangerously overloaded: a dismantled car weighs heavy in an open boat; refrigerators and television sets piled high alter the centre of gravity. Only the stacks of Marlboro cigarettes added little ballast to the boats as they sat low, gently rocking in the calm water of the harbour.

I voiced fears that these over-laden craft would never make the twenty mile journey across the Strait of Hormuz. But the guide told me they had been making the journey twice daily for years and knew exactly what they could get away with. He said that the biggest danger to the smugglers was to negotiate the large numbers of giant tankers passing through the strait.

Not long before sunset they all set off together. As one, with roaring diesels, they lifted out of the water and with amazing acceleration they shot seawards. The water boiled and frothed, the boats bounced and were out of sight within five minutes. What a way to make a living.

OUR TIME IN DUBAI WAS DRAWING TO a close. I was now sixty-six and felt it was getting time to retire. But where should we go? We had looked at various parts of Ireland and England. England had changed; it was no longer the England I knew before I began my RAF career more than forty years earlier. Twenty-three years in the sunshine of the Middle East meant that we viewed the English climate with horror.

For a few years we had owned an apartment in Cyprus and another in Spain. The one in Cyprus was in Kato Paphos. It overlooked the harbour and was opposite the old Crusader castle. We had bought off-plan and when we paid the deposit, Paphos was very pleasant, quiet enough, interesting, attractive and the weather was good. But a year or so after we were able to occupy the apartment, there were drastic changes. An airport had been constructed a few kilometres along the coast. Charter aircraft from Manchester and Hamburg flew in and out several times a day, disgorging crowds of pale tourists and refilling with suntanned ones. New hotels had sprung up like mushrooms along the sea front. It had become a package tour operator's paradise.

The sea front of Kato Paphos – and we were right on it – was a noisy nightmare. We put the apartment on the market, anticipating a quick and profitable sale; after all, the Greek Cypriot developer who sold it to us had forecast a vast profit because of its superb location. When we eventually managed to sell it, we made a substantial loss.

The apartment in Spain was on a very pleasant development called an *urbanizacion*, in the hills in the Costa Blanca, not far from Altea, looking down to the sea. We fell out of love with Spain when a friend we had known in Dubai, who had moved to Spain near to us, died. Poor medical care had contributed to his early death.

We had rented the apartment to a German lawyer who needed to live in the area for a couple of years while he dealt with legal issues surrounding the opening of several Mercedes Benz dealerships. That was his story and it seemed plausible, especially when we met his jolly, dumpy wife and their little girl. He gave us passport photocopies and we signed a tenancy agreement.

But he was a crook, a real pro. One morning he left the apartment taking everything with him, down to the last clothes peg; all the furniture, the kitchen appliances, even the light bulbs.

It wasn't just us he'd robbed. A neighbour, a dealer in televisions and videos, had set him up with the best available models. Our tenant paid him with a cheque which – naturally – bounced. He had also put about a rumour that he was an agent who could supply work permits and had sold several forged permits to expatriates hoping to work in Spain.

Our insurance company was not interested in the case. The insurance we carried for the property was nullified because there was no break-in, there was no burglary; he lived in the property, he had a key. The insurance broker told us that we should have taken out special insurance to cover a tenant absconding with all our goods and chattels. His passport photocopy was indeed one of a German lawyer, but it wasn't him; he had inserted his photograph in a passport he had stolen.

The police weren't interested either; they had much bigger fish to fry... rape, murder, arson. So we sold up and, as with the property in Cyprus, we took a loss.

So what to do? Cyprus, Spain, Ireland and England were out. To Maria's amusement, I took a look at a development in Kerala, in southern India, which a Dubai property company had on the drawing boards. But I gave that idea away; much as we loved the idea of a holiday involving curry, sunshine and the sea – for a permanent life – forget it.

A year before we began seriously thinking about retirement, we had been invited by an American friend working in Riyadh to spend a week in a small town in France. He had rented a villa in northern Provence, in the Vaucluse, at the foot of Mont Ventoux.

It was a delightful place; a wine-growing area in the valley of the River Rhône with Châteauneuf du Pape just down the road; long hot summers, invaded by tourists, good restaurants and fascinating Roman history. We hadn't included France in our retirement plans because we had been put off by so many stories of fierce taxes.

However, one evening at the monthly dinner of the Thirteen Club in Dubai, I discovered that no fewer than three fellow members owned properties in France and a couple more were thinking about buying there. They convinced me that, although finances were complicated in France and inheritance was governed by Napoleonic law, it was nonetheless possible to live there providing you were given sound advice and guidance by accountants and lawyers.

When I got home that night, not long after midnight, I got Maria out of bed, sat her in the lounge, placed a glass of chilled white wine in her hand and said, "What do you think of living in France?"

"Good idea," she said, swigged the wine, went back to bed.

First thing next morning, she enrolled us for French courses in the Dubai branch of Alliance Française.

NINE MONTHS LATER WE WENT TO FRANCE and found our house. After looking at various regions, we returned to the very town in northern Provence in which we had spent a week with our American friend. The price was right, the sale was *distressé*, the owners were deeply in hock to more than one bank. It needed major work, the garden was a jungle because, as the owner explained, "I could not clear it because there are little rabbits living there." He also showed us a sapling of an oak tree and some strange flies hovering around its base. "*Voilà!*" he exclaimed, "you will have your own truffles."

Constructed eleven years earlier, but never completed, the house was designed in the style of a *bergerie* – long and on one floor. This style allowed the original *bergers* to keep their sheep and goats in one end in the winter and their family in the other, except when the weather was really nippy

Possibilities: a house designed in the style of a bergerie – long and low.

when herd and herdsmen would mingle to keep warm. Simple, ingenious...
but how about something from this century?

We needed an architect: the estate agent knew just the man. We needed
a builder: the architect knew just the man. We needed a plumber, electrician,
carpenter: the builder had just the men. There seemed to be a good deal of
nepotism in assembling our team.

The architect, Vincent Bouchon, was pompous and forever banging on
about the ethics of his profession, the honesty of French architects, and that
he was paid a honorarium and not a *salaire*. No matter to me, because it
seemed that every time he opened his mouth, I opened my cheque book –
not at all surprising, his precious honorarium was based on the total
building costs and they were only ever going to go in one direction.

Olivier Laroche was our builder. Rock by name, rock by nature: short,
stocky, bow-legged, with skin like a walnut in texture and colour. His jeans
were slung so low a bag hung below his buttocks and when he stooped he
revealed a startling builder's cleavage. He had the fruity cough of a chain
smoker, his face was ruddy, his eyes permanently bloodshot and his nose
streaked with purple veins; in short he was a picture of self-induced ill health.

A year before, he had narrowly escaped the attentions of the grim reaper.
Admitted to the coronary care unit in Avignon with a *crise cardiaque*, he
caused a *crise explosif* among the nursing staff when he was seen to snatch

the oxygen mask off his face to take a puff on a cigarette. A week later, when he was caught ambling down the corridor with an infusion bottle held high in his right hand and a smouldering cigarette cupped in his left, he was – to his relief – chucked out. That meant he no longer needed to swallow the pills they gave him for his high blood pressure and he could return to his *eau de vie, pastis.*

In eighteen months the house was habitable. We left Dubai and moved in. Not long after that, Olivier went bankrupt. He had fallen for the charms of a lady in Vaison. She owned a shoe shop. He rebuilt her façade, maybe using our materials; he was generous to her and she responded in a manner to his liking. He avoided expenditure by not paying his share of his workmen's social security dues and nor did he pay builder's merchants.

How did he do it? How could he survive the booze, the fags, the stress and the women? Looking at him through physician's eyes, I thought he should have croaked long ago... but then all became clear.

A couple had been enjoying a wild party at a night club in Vaison, left in the small hours, drove into a ditch, were picked up by the gendarmes and slung in jail. The couple were Olivier's mother and father. She was ninety-three, he was ninety-four. With those genes, Olivier was well nigh indestructible.

The author and his team of artisans.

Epilogue

THE WORK ON OUR HOUSE WAS completed by another builder and we settled in to a pleasant life in France. Over a couple of years the garden matured. We experienced cold winters with brilliant cloudless blue skies and the world draped in hoar frost when we woke. Summers were long and hot.

We grew to love our little town more and more; it was lively, had industry – a factory which made the paper covers with tiny holes for the filters of cigarettes. Seems the water from Mont Ventoux had special properties ideal for the process. I would amuse myself by thinking that no matter where in the world, Dubai, New York, London or Beijing, whenever somebody lit a fag, they were puffing on a bit of paper from my little town.

We made friends, our French improved and soon we could actually understand what they were saying. I hung out my shingle as a teacher of English, having done the Teaching English for Speakers of Other Languages course in Dubai in the six months before we left, but there was not a lot of interest. My income over a year amounted to two bottles of wine, fifty euros and a stuffed *pintade* (guinea fowl) which was delicious. I was recruited to teach English in the Lien Sociale, an organisation to help children with difficulties in various school subjects. The parents were keen – it was free – but the pupils were unwilling, so I gave it up. It was not only the frustration. I had in my small group a boy who could loudly fart at will. This caused mirth, merriment and collapse of the class. I could not remonstrate because his amazing explosive talent reduced me to helpless tears of laughter every time.

In 2008, we revisited Dubai. In the seven years since we had been gone, a lot of progress had been made but – to those who knew the Dubai of old – it was not upward progress.

When we left in 2001, it had become busy, crowded and polluted but there was simple excitement in making new friends and living and working in the place. Now the excitement, the chatter, centred around the obscene profits made buying and selling local properties; the opening of a new hotel, maybe a bit more luxurious; the rising of the tallest tower in the world; the arrests of expats caught snogging (and worse) on Jumeirah Beach – snigger, snigger. People talked of being housebound in the evenings because the traffic was impossible.

Dubai had lost its soul.

The change was symbolised in a heart-wrenching fashion for me. One morning as Maria and I sat drinking coffee for old times' sake in Magrudy's, one of the first of Dubai's many shopping malls, I recognised an old friend with his wife at a nearby table. Charles had been an important figure in the era of Sheikh Rashid. Naturally he became very rich and had properties in London and the South of France as well as a couple of houses in Dubai.

I went over to him. Charles didn't recognise me.

We chatted and smiled at each other but there was no light in the eyes of my old friend, for Charles, once a brilliant financier, had developed dementia. His wife told me that he preferred living in Dubai, as did she, because they had servants and an easy life and she was better able to care for him.

We parted and as I walked away with a leaden heart, it struck me that Charles symbolised all that had gone wrong with the place. Poor rich Charles could never get back to his *status quo ante* – but Dubai could... by returning to Sheikh Rashid's dream and by stopping behaving like a meretricious, attention-seeking tart.

After Dubai, a few days in Oman and a couple of weeks in South Africa, our town in France with its *micro-climat* – which the mayor says is also a *climat tonique* – looked more appealing than ever.

France has more than 20,000 centenarians; everybody hereabouts says the roots of *la vie prolongée* are the climate and the wine, to which I simply add, "*Tchin-tchin*! *Salut*! Cheers!"

The Larks have landed: the author and Maria at home in Provence.
(Photo: Norbert Stiastny).

Acknowledgements

IT WAS THE CELEBRATED ARABIAN explorer Sir Wilfred Thesiger who, when asked his opinion on the most valuable thing in life, replied simply, "friendship". I endorse this view wholeheartedly. I'm fortunate to have and to have had so many very good friends throughout my life. Friends like Dr Tony Pearson, Squadron Leader Gordon Galletly, the Reverend Derek Crabtree and his wife Christiane who read my first drafts.

I am of course forever indebted to the friends I made in Saudi Arabia, who were courageous in the extreme when I was in serious trouble: doctors John Froude, Michael Kingston and Nicholas Woodhouse. Doctors Don McDonald and David Barkham were also among that cohort but sadly have died in the past year or two.

My thanks go to another good friend from Saudi days, Jean Sasson, now a celebrated author in her own right. She provided vital behind-the-scenes help in those dark days. Jean has displayed enthusiastic interest and given much appreciated support and advice in the genesis of this book.

But my best friend, my wife Maria, I thank for her courage in those evil days, her encouragement in writing the book and not least her computer, photographic and secretarial skills.

My good friends Dr Sean and Dr Ulla Sieck have been helpful and encouraging throughout. Ulla provided many photographs and I still clearly picture in my mind's eye Sean in his straw boater as he drove me in my Santa Claus outfit through the Saudi desert.

Finally I must thank my old friend and colleague Dr Marijcke Jongbloed who introduced me to Chuck Grieve who, as my editor, has guided me through the gestation and parturition of the book.

BL

Lightning Source UK Ltd.
Milton Keynes UK
UKHW010609111119
353305UK00001B/239/P